MW00786257

GLAD & GOLDEN HOURS

GLAD & GOLDEN HOURS
by Lanier Ivester © 2024

Published by:
Rabbit Room Press
3321 Stephens Hill Lane
Nashville, Tennessee 37013

All rights reserved. No part of this book may be reproduced, cooked into a casserole, or transmitted in any form or by any means, electronic, mechanical, or gastrointestinal, including photocopying, or recording, or by any information storage and retrieval system, without permission in fanciful handwriting from the publisher.

ISBN: 9781951872236

Illustrations by Jennifer Trafton © 2024
Cover design by Jennifer Trafton © 2024

GLAD & GOLDEN HOURS

BY LANIER IVESTER

ILLUSTRATIONS BY JENNIFER TRAFTON

For Mama
Claudia Hamrick Adams
1948–2022

I never knew you from the sun.
—Karen Peris

TABLE OF CONTENTS

WEEK TWO

WEEK THREE

WEEK FOUR

In setting out to write a book, it is important to acknowledge who you are writing it for. This book is not for the polished or the elite, the people who have it all or who have it all together. It is not for social media influencers, seeking inspiration to curate little squares of perfection on the internet, or for those seeking to impress other people with their cooking or decorating or craft-making or gift-giving.

It is, however, for the dear souls mentioned in Edmund Hamilton Sears's verse, people crushed by life, toiling along under heavy burdens, desperate for a place of rest. It is for those who long to be re-enchanted by the very old, very true, very beautiful story of Christmas. It is for someone who might never have experienced a truly sacramental holiday in their own homes—and by sacramental I mean quite simply a holiday which articulates unseen realities in practical, tangible ways. It is for the weary, the homesick, the wistful, and the countercultural. It is, above all, for the childlike, for it is only to such hearts that the greatest mysteries are unveiled.

I remember the first time I encountered Sears's lyric. I was playing Christmas carols on the piano in my childhood home when the words fairly leapt off the page. I stopped playing and read them again. Then I typed them up on the computer in a large font, printed them out, and taped them to the refrigerator where everyone in the family could see them every day. I thought the words were beautiful, but something told me that the experience they pointed to was lovelier still. At seventeen years old, I confess that my sensibilities engaged more readily with the promise of those "glad and golden hours" than with any Dantean fellowship of suffering souls in their purgatorial climb. But I loved the idea of Christmas being more than a holiday. It was a *resting place*.

At the same time, I saw so many unhappy attitudes about Christmas in the world around me—from the jaded ennui of my peers to the haggard exhaustion of adults (mostly women), and I longed to remind the whole world that Christmas was still and always would be an absolute miracle. It was worth all the fuss and bother, the messes and the memories; it was, as Washington Irving had said, "king of the year," for the King of creation had dignified the human race with his presence in our midst. No earthly shadow should diminish the glory of what those angels were singing about in the Bethlehem sky, and no amount of effort was too great for so grand a cause.

But I wasn't the one doing all (or even most of) the work to bring this glory down into the practical experience of the people I loved best. That lot fell to my mother, and, as much as she treasured it, sometimes it made her tired. Sometimes it even made her a little exasperated, like on Christmas Eve when my sister and I generated yet another unplanned mess in the kitchen, or an unexpected guest dropped in with an unexpected present, which sent Mama scurrying for the gift stash in the back of her closet for some suitable offering in exchange. There was the year that our pipes froze and then burst on Christmas morning, and the year that the goose she had been basting all day long with brandy and apricot glaze turned out to be full of shot and therefore inedible. There were Christmases spent on the phone with the doctor when my sister was too sick to get out of bed, and there were years in which Mama was stretched so thin with homeschooling three children that the holidays must have felt less like twelve days of merriment and more like the Twelve Labors of Hercules.

Nevertheless, Christmas in our house was a magical respite from the rest of the year; a time in which time itself seemed to bend to the greater laws of divine and familial affection. Looking back, I know it cost my mother considerable effort, enormous intention, and great love. But I hailed those glad and golden hours in my heart because they had always been just that. Mama had seen to it.

I remember standing in the kitchen one Christmas with one of Mama's friends. It was a different year, but still the Sears lyric was taped to the fridge—a bit dog-eared from being removed and replaced over successive holidays. She paused to read it, and then she laughed.

"Wouldn't that be nice," she said with a shake of her head. "But who has time to *rest* this time of year?"

Her words, and the tone in which they were spoken, made me feel self-conscious and green. What did I, an idealistic teenager, know of real weariness, or even of real rest, for that matter? People were tired, and sometimes the holidays were just really hard. Not everyone had grown up in a home where the good times far outweighed the bad times, and some people had reason to distrust some of the sentiment and excesses of Christmas.

Nevertheless, something in me silently pushed back. I knew that Christmas did not have to be a desperate round of commitments and tasks. I knew that even the humblest experiences could be shot through with eternal radiance, and that there had to be some middle ground between "too much" and "not enough," some lovely, overlooked *via media* that could cut through the thickets of overdoing and overwhelm (and overeating and overspending!) with which a modern holiday has come to be associated. There was more going on here than childhood memories and food nostalgia, more even than the simple acknowledgement of Christ's birth. In celebrating Christmas, we were not just remembering, we were *reliving* the fact that God had become one of us.

Later, as I started to tease out some of these intimations in my own home, I began to understand just how tricky it could be to create a meaningful holiday without losing sight of what it was all about. Christmas was a resting place, but it was one that must be cared for and cultivated. Preparations were important, particularly if I wanted to give my people a thoughtful taste of a coming kingdom that is already in our midst, but those preparations would always have to give way to the people themselves, not the other way around. Furthermore, even the most sacramentally intentional Christmas could be a lot of work, a sort of practical liturgy of generosity, hospitality, attention, and love, and sometimes I would get tired. Sometimes I would lose my bearings, or my way, or my temper, or my peace, and need to be shepherded back to my soul's rest. And always I would need the sweet simplicity of Christ.

For over two decades I have grappled joyously with these tensions because I believe that there is gold at their heart. I believe that it is not only possible, but crucial, to steward these set-apart days in a way that makes space for mystery and wonder amid the rituals and traditions of our lives. And I believe that ritual and tradition are always the servants of relationship, with God and with other people. Without relationship, even the most exquisite holiday is about as lovely as a child banging a pot with a stick.

And so, if you are tired, or disillusioned, or curious about shaping a holiday season that makes present the astonishing fact of God-with-us, then I would like you to consider this book my gift to you. It's not a manual or a how-to, or a glorified to-do list, but a companion, in the neighborliest sense of the word. Whether you choose to read this book, this story, simply to enter into its twists and turns, its hopes and sorrows, its people and its places, or whether you elect to participate in it yourself via its many recipes, crafts, and holiday suggestions, my prayer is that you will find a friend in these pages, and that the ideas and activities with which these reflections are threaded will be like small domestic liturgies, tangible acts that integrate what we believe with what we do. You might try only a single recipe or craft each week, or even each year; you are welcome to pick and choose, selecting only that which suits your needs and desires. For the meals and menus and ideas in these pages, even the suggestions themselves, are merely that: suggestions to help you contemplate your own holiday with creativity and significance.

It is, above all, an invitation, regardless of your age, marital status, or living situation, to experience Christmas as a place of rest—not in spite of, but in the very midst of the merriment of these glad and golden hours. His glory is already breaking over the rim of the world, my friends. Let us turn eastward—with the devotion of our hearts and the work of our hands—and watch for the steady rise of our great Daystar.

Lanier A. Ivester
Ruff House
October 2023

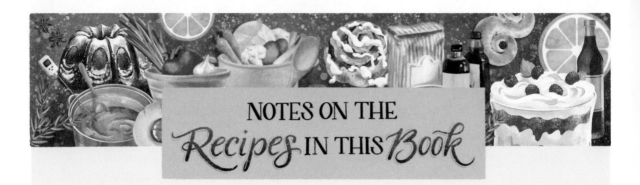

NOTES ON THE
Recipes IN THIS Book

KOSHER SALT: Unless otherwise noted, I recommend the use of kosher salt. Not only does it taste better, but its large flake makes it difficult to oversalt your food, particularly when the recipe instructs you to "salt to taste." Additionally, kosher salt rarely contains additives, which I try to steer clear of. Years ago my sister-in-law, Edie, put me on to Redmond's Real Salt on account of its purity and trace minerals and I have never looked back.

REAL VANILLA: I make a case for real vanilla (see page 14), and Nielsen-Massey is the brand I like best. It feels like a little gift to myself in the kitchen, and I hardly ever open the bottle without taking an appreciative sniff.

UNSALTED BUTTER: If at all possible, stick to unsalted butter. This will allow you to replicate the salt recommendations in these recipes and avoid over-salting. The way I see it, the salt in a recipe should come from a cook's own hand, not as part of another ingredient.

BEST QUALITY CHOCOLATE: At the risk of sounding pretentious, many of these recipes call for "good quality chocolate," which simply means chocolate produced without fillers and additives, which can alter the outcome of your recipe. There are a few cases where it doesn't matter as much, but I have noted, where necessary, when to spring for the good stuff. Lindt is a good brand, as is Guittard.

ROOM TEMPERATURE EGGS: I've kept chickens for over 20 years, and early on I realized that a farm-fresh egg rarely needs to be refrigerated unless it has been washed. Since we use our eggs up pretty quickly I leave them in a basket and wash them just before use—which means that pretty much every egg I cook with is at room temperature. This makes them much easier to combine with other ingredients, not to mention causing cakes to rise more consistently. Grocery store eggs will, of course, need to remain in the refrigerator, but you can take them out a couple of hours prior to use and let them come to room temperature.

WHOLE MILK: Is there any other kind? In all seriousness, the fat content is important, especially in baked goods. It also adds a richness you just can't get from the low-fat options. I am an advocate for full-fat dairy as it's healthier overall. If you do need to make a substitution, however, stick with 2% milk. But avoid low-fat milk in casseroles and egg dishes, as it can cause them to become watery.

Also note that some of these recipes contain specialty ingredients that are only in season for a short time or that may not be available in your area. In each case I have provided substitutions that will produce similar results.

FINALLY, be sure to read through a recipe thoroughly before undertaking to make it, as some of the instructions require resting times or overnight stints in the refrigerator. Above all, have fun! *None* of the recipes in this book are meant to impress or intimidate, but merely to inspire a few holiday treats and traditions of your own.

BEFORE
IT BEGINS

Otium Sanctum

It had been a morning of misadventure and I was growing desperate. My guests, the girls of Ms. Cain's Domestic Science class, clustered around my kitchen table, observing the proceedings with wide, attentive eyes, and I began to sense that prickle at the back of my neck and that pounding of my heart which inevitably accompanies plans gone awry. Already we had attempted Victorian-style paper cones crammed with candy and nuts. But one of the girls had a nut allergy, and all of the cones fell apart owing to the fact that they were fashioned with vintage wallpaper so yellowed and impliable it cracked when rolled into a conical shape. I had been sensible enough to move on, however, and now the components of a gingerbread house were spread before me on the table, accompanied by a mixing bowl filled with what ought to have been a thick, stiff, glossy decorator icing but which was, in fact, a thin, insipid mess.

I seized a slab of gingerbread, piping the edges liberally with ill-fated frosting, and jammed it alongside an adjoining wall, praying, against all the laws of chemistry, that the stupid thing would stick. It did not. It stood there for a breathless second or two, as if debating its options, and then fell, face-down, taking out the opposite wall in its course.

I sighed and dredged up a smile.

"Looks like we need just a little more powdered sugar," I said with far more optimism than I felt. It would take a lot more than powdered sugar to get me out of this mess. It would take a miracle.

And how, you ask, did I find myself in this predicament? I asked myself the same thing as I dumped sugar into the bowl without bothering to measure it out. I had, I knew, overmixed the icing to begin with. And it was a wet day, which never did icing any favors, and I had been racing around, doing too many things at once. That was it, of course: the very thing Mama was always warning me against; the very thing my friend Lauren and I were always resolving *not* to do.

Whisking determinedly, I reflected upon the events of the previous Christmas: the visit of Lauren and her crew from Oxmoor House Publishing, the excitement and happy upheaval of a photoshoot, the lush garland and boxwood wreaths strewn about by the stylist with dizzying abandon. Lauren was the editor of *Christmas with Southern Living*, an annual hardcover crammed with world-famous recipes and photographs of immaculate homes decked to perfection. For a girl growing up in the South, *Southern Living* was the epitome of taste, culinary and otherwise, and I was astonished when Lauren had floated her idea: "What about a shoot at the Ruff House?"

I had known all along that the draw was not me so much as my home—I had, after all, only been married a little over a year and my domestic prowess was largely untested. The Ruff House, on the other hand, named for its mid-nineteenth century builder, is an increasing rarity in our part of the world: a sensible white-clapboard farmhouse settled in a scrap of undeveloped farmland. First-time visitors are often amazed to find it tucked away amid its suburban setting—I know I was. Even more amazing is the way this old house wraps its welcome around you the moment you step inside, as if it were glad to see you and eager to provide shelter. Independent of anything I have ever done to put my stamp on its big, high-ceilinged rooms, it seems to have gathered up the warmth and light and life of all the times it has ever known—even the hard times—so that its substance is like a living presence. For the Ruff House isn't just a house. It is one of the principal characters in my story, and, as you will see in the pages to come, its fortunes are tied with mine in a way that I believe transcends this life.

In advance of the team from Oxmoor House, our friends had come alongside to help us get ready. Jenijoy spent an afternoon with me making garland for the staircase out of Fraser fir trimmings I'd collected from tree lots all over town, and Taylor offered his collection of silverplate ornaments to adorn our tree. My mother provided armloads of magnolia from the stately specimens in her yard and an ample serving of unsolicited advice.

"Don't get carried away," she told me. "And, whatever you do, don't compare yourself. This is not a competition."

Cheerfully ignoring her on both counts, I proceeded to wear myself out cleaning and polishing, saturating the woodwork with Scott's Liquid Gold and dusting our meager furniture until I threatened to rub off the veneer. The photoshoot was a resounding success, thanks to Lauren's laidback sincerity and her stylist's tasteful eye, and when the book came out the following October, Mama bought multiple copies. Philip's mother, Janice, bought multiple copies, as well, and was instrumental in my being asked to speak at that month's event hosted by the women's ministry of the church. Lauren was asked, too, and together with another capable young *Southern Living* editor, we gave an hour-long presentation on preparing for the holidays and being present to its joys. In my enthusiasm I may have overstepped my time allotment, reducing Lauren's floral demonstration to a rushed, five-minute affair. But the crowded room had seemed so receptive to my untried opinions and naïve assertions that I just couldn't reign myself in. I was, it seemed, a Christmas Professional, and the thrill of the thing went to my head like wine.

After the program, a woman introduced herself. She was the teacher of a fledgling home arts class based upon the ideals in Edith Schaeffer's book *The Hidden Art of Homemaking*, and during my presentation it had occurred to her that perhaps I'd be open to a visit from her high school-aged girls later that year. She didn't have to ask me twice, and before parting we had agreed upon a date in early December upon which she would bring her students to the Ruff House for a morning of domestic instruction and inspiration.

In retrospect, it is easy to see how my idealism and inexperience combined to produce the disastrous results on display in my kitchen that day. Scarcely a decade older than the fresh-faced girls around my table, I had yet to face off perfectionism for the foe that it was, and I still believed that every line in my planner was meant to be filled by some task or idea with which I was meant to exhaust myself. I was old enough to be influenced by the domestic tastemakers of the day, and young enough to think I could do it all. Accordingly, I had stacked that morning with expectations and the days leading up to it with feverish preparation, not only for this gathering, but for Christmas itself.

But the icing just wasn't cooperating. *If only one thing would go right today!* I was just lowering the gingerbread roof onto the irresolute little structure when the phone rang. These were the days of answering machines blaring messages to whomever happened to be within earshot, and this message was from my mother.

"Oh, Lanier," she gasped, electrifying the whole room with her panic. "Pray for Belle! She just ate rat poison and we're racing to Dr. Wolf!"

There was silence—tense, questioning, somewhat appalled. I blushed to the roots of my hair.

"Belle is my mother's dog," I hastened to explain. "And Dr. Wolf is a very good vet. He will know what to do. I'm sure she'll be fine."

Another uncomfortable moment, then one of the girls spoke up. She had a porcelain complexion and a wide, red mouth that looked like it had never known anything but smiles.

"Should we—pray? For Belle?"

We did, and then I resumed my demonstration. But the last remnants of proficiency had drained out of me. I attached the chimney, then watched in quiet resignation as the structure buckled in upon itself and slithered to the table in a heap of frosting-smeared gingerbread. I looked up and regarded the bright, albeit bewildered, faces.

"And the lesson here, ladies," I said, mopping my hands on a dishcloth, "is that sometimes things just don't work out."

It was a lesson I was loath to embrace at the time. I still believed that with proper planning and a goodly amount of discipline I could "get it all done" and still have margin in my life for the things that made life meaningful. By "all," I meant, of course, a perfectly clean house, an orderly and productive garden, a routine that ran like clockwork, and a weekly menu of delicious and nutritious meals. Oh, and a personal fitness regimen, a daily quiet time, a yards-long reading list, a writing rhythm, church membership, and a social life. Nothing unreasonable.

Life would, in time, batter down the obstinacy with which my standards were enshrined. Mama, on the other hand, urged me to hold those standards loosely, never confusing them with holy ideals of homemaking, hospitality, and beauty. She sometimes took the direct approach: the talking-to when it appeared I was getting tangled up in perfectionism, or the extended exhortation when she discerned I was running myself ragged over other people's expectations. But often it was the gentle route, the email or handwritten note containing a quotation or two from the endless collection she kept of helpful and beautiful words. Once she quoted St. Paul from I Thessalonians 4: "Let it be a point of honor with you to remain calm." Another time it was St. Theresa of Ávila (emphasis Mama's):

> Remember that you have only one soul; that you have only one death to
> die; *that you have only one life, which is short* and has to be lived by you
> alone; and there is only one Glory, which is eternal. If you do this, there
> will be many things about which you care nothing.

There were, indeed, many things about which my mother cared nothing, like perfectly clean houses and what anyone else thought of her. I have never known anyone more willing to laugh at herself, or more indifferent to keeping up appearances. And yet, her whole life was an embodiment of hospitality. She was an excellent (largely self-taught) cook, a cheerfully dismal gardener, and she had a lively, highly literate mind. Our modest home was tasteful and inviting, and Mama was never happier than when it was filled to bursting with people she loved. The things she didn't care about made abundant room for the things she did.

One night when I was about nineteen years old, I was standing beside her in a receiving line at the front of a small Baptist church my family had just joined. Mama was, by this time, a seasoned Christian and a passionate encourager of other women, particularly young mothers. But she rarely missed an opportunity to shoot from the hip. A woman came down the line, carrying a baby, with two or three small children clinging to or attempting to climb her person. She looked weary and bedraggled, and there was a gleam of desperation in her eyes.

"I'm *so* glad you're here," she panted when she reached my mother. "It's a *lot* of work."

"Not me, sister," Mama rejoined without missing a beat. "I did all my Christian work before I got saved."

It was true. Before giving her life to Christ, Mama had done all the things. She had taught Sunday school out of a vague sense of Christian duty and attended committee meetings uncountable, all while serving on the right boards in the community, maintaining an active membership in the Junior League, and raising three small children. I know her heart went out to that woman because she had once been her—exhausted, encumbered, desperate. In Jesus, however, Mama had discovered a new freedom, not merely to do the right things—the things to which she personally had been called—but to release the rest with light-hearted abandon. She had learned, in short, to serve from the resting place of God's unconditional love. This is not to say that she never got tired or overwhelmed. But when she did, she always found her way back to that refuge.

One of the things Lauren and I loved to talk about was how to enflesh our callings—particularly in the domestic sphere—without allowing our ideals to obscure the realities to which they point. Home, hospitality, beauty, were not merely ends in themselves, but contexts within which time-bound souls experienced their belovedness as children of God. A few years after the photoshoot Lauren shared an ancient Latin phrase she had discovered: *otium sanctum*, or "holy leisure." The church fathers used it to describe a posture of heart that promoted awareness of the presence of God in the details of life and the particular freedom that accompanied it. Holy leisure didn't mean that we did not work, but that we did it, with faith and fidelity, from a place of peace. It also cleared the ground for the right things to grow, namely, relationships, with God and with one another. All of our work should ultimately serve this end, we agreed, or we ought to be questioning whether we should do it at all.

Mama's exhortations and Lauren's *otium sanctum* eventually began to breathe a new expansiveness into my overdriven existence, allowing me to embrace my limitations, not as hindrances, but as guardrails to guide me along the path to abundant life. But as I stood there in my kitchen with Ms. Cain's class that day, my limitations on full display, all I could see was a mess of my own making. The morning had been a complete disaster and I had nothing but my own embarrassment to show for it.

This is not to rank the ruin of a gingerbread house among the real disasters of life, of which I've seen a few. But it underscores my tendency, especially in the early days, to elevate preparations over the thing prepared for—in this case, an opportunity to demonstrate to these younger women not only that beauty and hospitality mattered, but *why*.

Two decades later I was kneeling on the hearth in that same kitchen, stoking up the fire to a merry blaze. From all around came the music of talking and laughter, fellowship and the sounds of feasting. It was Christmas Eve and my rooms were full, likewise my heart. I looked up to see my friend Louise's teenaged daughter Evelyn smiling down at me. I had known Evie since she was a baby; Philip's and Louise's parents had been friends before either of them were born.

"Mrs. Lanier, you won't believe it," she gushed, "but a lady I babysit for says she knows you. She said she came here once, back in high school!"

I felt the color rise to my cheeks. *Surely not . . .*

"She told me you had her class out to talk about homemaking and Christmas and all that, and she said she's never forgotten it—she said it gave her this whole vision of what she wanted her life to look like, you know, making things beautiful and not worrying about it being perfect."

I laughed outright, not in derision, but from pure joy. I had gotten my miracle after all, it seemed, for only God could take such a series of mishaps and shape them into something transcendent. And it was always his way, transfiguring broken things with beauty. I'd had plenty of cause to bear witness to this over the intervening years, as well as to the inherent holiness brimming beneath the material substance of life. Nothing was beyond his use or his reach—even a collapsed gingerbread house.

These days my preparations for Christmas are no less enthusiastic—I would even say idealistic—than they were when as a young wife I sought to embody my joy at Christ's coming with every means at my disposal. But I have learned, by the grace of God, to work from a place of rest, fueled by my acceptance in the beloved to undertake only that which contributes to my peace and to that of my household. I don't have to do it all. What's more, I don't want to. Like my mother before me, I want to cultivate a playful unconcern over the things which lie beyond the pale of my priorities, bringing my best to the things that actually matter. I want the freedom to take traditions up as well as to let them go. I want, above all, to have a heart that's made room for Love himself.

It takes work to maintain a home, care for relationships, and, yes, prepare for Christmas, even a simple one. But we have a resting place, my friends, within which quandaries are quieted, messes are redeemed, and all the cares of life fall away before the consuming fire of a perfect love.

Preparing Heart and Home

As late as the 13th century, nearly all the sacred music associated with Advent and Christmas was still being written in ecclesiastical Latin—intended for choirs but unintelligible to ordinary men and women. It wasn't until the Franciscan poet and friar Jacopone da Todi began to pen his laudes in the vernacular that the songs of the church started to seep into the practical experience of the congregation. History may remember him as the writer of the "Stabat Mater," one of the most famous hymns of all time. But we also have him to thank for one of our earliest Christmas carols, written, for the first time, in the language of the people:

Give now your thought and care,
Prepare, prepare . . .
Sweep hearth and floor,
Be all your vessel's store
Shining and clean.
Then bring the little guest
And give Him of your best

Of meat and drink. Yet more
Ye owe than meat.
One gift at your King's feet
Lay now, I mean
A heart full to the brim
Of love, and all for Him
And from all envy clean.

I love the way this carol brings the reality of the Incarnation down into the tangible matters of our lives, seamlessly merging personal devotion with practical love. We are to prepare, Fra Jacopone urges, not only our hearts, but our homes, offering clean rooms and a stocked larder alongside a newly swept conscience and gleaming motives. This is no time to compare our "best" with someone else's, or to start making frantic lists; this is the time to pause and reflect upon how we might actually welcome Jesus into our lives and our celebrations, and how we can welcome others in his name. What activities or rhythms will best serve the members of our household or our immediate circle? Which traditions are worth fighting for, and which ones might need to be laid gently to rest? What can we actually afford, in terms of time, money, and effort? Above all, how are we going to protect that "better part" (Luke 10:42) of an attentive, listening heart in the midst of our planning and preparations?

Seeing as morning prayer is central to a Christ-centered holiday for me, mid-November is the time I like to start thinking about which Advent devotional I'd like to use that year. It is also when I begin to make space in my calendar for a few simple household tasks which will facilitate easy hospitality in the weeks to come, like cleaning out the back hall coat closet and taking stock of my candle supply. I always organize and scrub the larder shelves before Thanksgiving, in advance of all the extra ingredients and once-a-year treats with which they will soon be crowded, and I regard the deep freeze in the basement with a ruthless eye, tossing old ham bones and frost-burned vegetables to clear the way for cookies and cakes, casseroles, bags of pecans, and pans of cinnamon rolls. I also make sure I have batteries for my candle lamps, stamps for my invitations, and plenty of 22-gauge paddle wire for garlands and greenery.

One of my favorite pre-holiday tasks is polishing the silver punch bowl and coffee service that my parents gave us as wedding gifts and the silver candelabras, which belonged to my grandmother. Silver has rather slipped out of fashion these days, particularly pieces as big as these, but I cherish the sparkle it lends to a room or a festive table. I use my silver because I think it is beautiful and because it lends an effortless touch of contrast between the everyday and the exceptional—I've been known to lug that coffee service into the middle of a field for more than one picnic over the years—but I also use it because I don't believe in having things that are never pressed into active duty in the name of love. Each year I polish up this little "vessel's store" not to impress or to distract, but to *serve*.

Another thing I try to do ahead of time is to stock the freezer with cookie dough. I love having lots of homemade cookies on hand throughout the holiday season to give as gifts or to share with guests. But I enjoy it so much more when my freezer is already well-supplied with dough just waiting to be rolled out, decorated, and baked at my whimsey or leisure. Making up the dough in November grants me a little more margin in December when kitchen time is at a premium—and when one less mess to clean up feels like nothing short of a heavenly blessing.

I usually set aside an afternoon around the middle of the month and make a real spree of it: sugar cookie dough, gingerbread dough, jam thumbprints and snowball cookies, teacakes and the makings of mince tartlets. At the end of the day, I have flour on my nose (and likely in my hair), a sink piled with every mixing accouterment I own, and a molasses-and-milk-spattered countertop. But I also have an array of tidy packets ranged in the freezer downstairs, wrapped and labeled, each one a little gift of time to myself that will become a gift of love to someone else.

None of this matters in the least, however, if my heart is cluttered with misplaced priorities or anxious care. These must be cleaned out, as well, and my soul given a thorough airing before I can begin to approach this holiday season with any sort of holy intent. Historically, Advent has been a time of self-examination and penitence; an opportunity to trim the wicks of our lamps, as it were, and to invite the Holy Spirit to point out areas in our lives that need his light. No amount of advance preparation can produce in me the kind of heart I want to pour out in love for God and others—only Jesus himself can do that. But it is a process I can and must cooperate with, inviting him into the details of my days and offering my frailty and my hope— and this story is rife with both—as evidence of my need for him.

THINGS TO HAVE ON HAND BEFORE ADVENT BEGINS:

Smokeless, dripless tapers, assorted heights
Votive candles
Stick-Um candle adhesive
22-gauge paddle wire
Cardstock for invitations, place cards, and gift tags
Wrapping paper, ribbon, and tape
Batteries for candle lamps
Flower bulbs (narcissus and amaryllis)
Candy boxes
Aluminum pans
Prepared mincemeat

TIP: My friend Jenijoy showed me a way to remove tarnish that involves more magic than elbow grease: simply line the bottom of your sink with heavy duty aluminum foil, sprinkle it liberally with baking soda, and heat a large kettle or pot to the boil. Place your silver in the sink, making contact with the foil, and pour in the boiling water until the silver is completely submerged. Then stand back and marvel as the chemical reaction safely dissolves the oxidization.

NOTES ON THESE RECIPES: Each of the following recipes can be made with a cup-for-cup gluten-free flour if need be, but steer clear of nut-based flours as these will alter the taste and texture of your cookies. And please, if at all possible, avoid imitation vanilla—there's a reason it's so much cheaper than the real thing, and it's not a good one. I realize that one more splurge this time of year might be prohibitive, but if you can manage it, Madagascar bourbon vanilla extract is everything the mind can conceive and the heart could wish of vanilla, not only because it doesn't "bake out" and leave a metallic taste behind, but because the flavor is so ambrosian you might be tempted to wonder if God himself did not use it to make manna.

Also, each of the following recipes can be frozen in the following manner: divide the dough into two balls and wrap tightly in plastic wrap. Place the balls in a labeled freezer bag and freeze for up to six weeks. When ready to bake, defrost the dough in the refrigerator overnight, then let it stand at room temperature for 1 hour.

For baking instructions, refer to the
"Cookies in Company" recipes in Week Two (page 111).

RECIPE: Sugar Cookie Dough

1 pound unsalted butter, softened
2 cups sugar
2 eggs
1 Tbsp. Madagascar bourbon vanilla

5 cups flour
1/4 tsp. salt
2 Tbsp. milk
1 tsp. baking soda

In the bowl of a stand mixer (or in a large bowl with a hand-held mixer) cream the butter, then add the sugar, eggs, and vanilla, beating at medium speed to incorporate. Sift the flour and salt together in a large bowl, then add to the butter mixture, one cup at a time, mixing thoroughly after each addition.

In a small bowl, whisk the milk and baking soda together. Then add to the large mixing bowl. Beat on medium-high speed until the dough is smooth and does not stick to your finger when lightly touched.

Divide and freeze as directed.

YIELD: 3 DOZEN

RECIPE: *Christmas Nut Cookie Dough*

Sugar Cookie dough (see previous recipe)   3 cups pecans
A pinch of kosher salt   or walnuts

Preheat the oven to 375° and line a large, rimmed baking sheet with parchment paper. Using a blender or a food processor, chop the nuts to the consistency of coarse meal. Toss the nuts on the baking sheet with a pinch of kosher salt, then toast them for 5-7 minutes, or until fragrant. Using an electric stand mixer or hand mixer, thoroughly incorporate into the Sugar Cookie dough.

Divide and freeze as directed.   YIELD: 6 DOZEN

RECIPE: *Gingerbread Cookie Dough*

5 cups sifted flour   ½ tsp. nutmeg   2 tsp. ginger
1½ tsp. salt   1 tsp. baking soda   ¼ tsp. allspice
1 cup unsalted butter, softened   1 cup sugar
1 cup unsulfured molasses   ½ cup water

Whisk dry ingredients in a large bowl until thoroughly combined. In the bowl of a stand mixer (or in another large bowl with a hand-held mixer) cream the butter and sugar. Stir in the molasses and water, then add the dry ingredients and mix well. Divide and freeze as directed.

YIELD: 3 DOZEN

RECIPE: Snowball Cookie Dough

1 cup pecans, finely chopped
1 1/2 cup unsalted butter, softened
1/4 cup vegetable shortening
3/4 cup sugar

2 Tbsp. Madagascar
    bourbon vanilla extract
4 cups flour
1/2 tsp. salt

Place chopped pecans in a cast-iron skillet and toast gently over medium-high heat until lightly browned and fragrant (about 5 minutes), stirring constantly. Remove from heat immediately.

Cream the butter and shortening, then add sugar, toasted pecans, vanilla, flour, and salt. Mix well, making sure to incorporate all the ingredients thoroughly. Divide and freeze as directed.

YIELD: 8 DOZEN

Waiting Days

"I t was a labor of love," she said. She smiled and handed me a tissue-wrapped package at the front door on a late November day.

As I slipped it from its folds and turned the package over in my hands, there was no doubt of either the labor or the love. A host of paper leaves, hand-tinted in varying hues, encircled a month's worth of tiny paper doors, each one numbered in fine black ink. Rachel had invested countless hours of careful work, and the joy Philip and I had in it that December was measureless. We took turns each day folding back the stiff flaps to reveal a quarter-inch scrap of enchantment within: dancing couples and sledding children, glitter-dusted angels and cross-shaped stars.

It was the first Advent calendar I'd had since I was a child. But even decades later, I still remembered the tingle of excitement when it was my day to turn back a well-creased paper door or window and peek in at the angel or shepherd or star within. The waiting for those small moments of revelation seemed endless back then; the long December days stretched out into impossibility and Christmas Eve was a miracle itself, emerging radiant and triumphant from a month of anticipation.

Christmas comes around more quickly than I'd like to admit now. But the sweet expectation lingers—is sweeter than ever, perhaps, for I know now what it really means

to wait. The expectancy of Advent throws a reflected light over the waiting days of our lives. *All my desire is before thee*, we whisper. And ranged in the shadows of time that surround us on all sides, a multitude without number sends up an echo that has not been silenced since God's promise first taught man to hope in his coming–his coming to the human race, and his coming to each of us in the intimacy of our need.

The centuries of yearning behind the fulfillment of our Lord's appearance have myriad small incarnations in the hearts of his people. We're all waiting on something. Waiting for God to fix a problem. Waiting for him to give us the desire of our hearts. Waiting to see him face to face. It's tempting to let the season underscore what we still don't have, even though another year has rolled around. But how much richer it is, I am learning, to embrace the stark solemnity of the great universal waiting for the Messiah and to find a parable of it in my own desires.

God doesn't give us the big picture all at once. He opens one window at a time, giving us glimpses of the glories undergirding the everyday.

HOW TO MAKE AN
Advent Calendar

1. Trace the oval template* on two pieces of paper and cut to create two ovals of the same size. One oval will be the back, and one will be the front.

MATERIALS:
Pencil
Scissors
Oval Advent Wreath template
2 sheets 8½ × 11-inch white or ivory cardstock
Small clipart
(2 cm square)
Craft knife fitted with fine point blade
Watercolor paper
(or green cardstock)
Watercolor brushes
(#8 round, #1 fine)
Watercolor paints
Glue
Glitter
Ribbon

2. Trace light squares on both ovals. On the back, these will be used to place the clip-art in the correct location. On the front oval, trace the squares on three sides leaving off the left side of the line. Place this oval on a cutting mat and with the knife razor cut the three sides of the lines on each square to create an opening (the uncut left side is the hinge). Once the openings are cut, you can turn the front oval over so that the pencils markings don't show on the front side.

3. Using the back template with lightly-traced squares, cut small pictures of clipart to place on each of the 25 squares (visit GladandGolden.com to download art ideas or use your own). Secure with glue. Glitter clipart as desired using fine dots of glue. Let dry.

4. Once the back is dry, place the front template over the back template and secure together with glue applied on the edge of the back oval.

20

5. Trace leaf shapes and watercolor them with pale green over the whole leaf, adding brown stems and veins for texture. Bend each leaf slightly down the middle and begin gluing along the edge of the calendar. Make as many leaves as needed to completely cover the outside of the calendar. Overlap the leaves as desired. (Shortcut: You can also use green cardstock if painting each leaf is too time consuming.)

6. On the front of the Advent calendar, pencil the days of December beginning with "1" at the top and ending with "25" at the end. Carefully trace over the penciled numbers with a fine tipped pen. Attach a ribbon to the back to create a hanger for the back of the calendar.

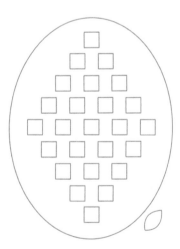

Templates for this and other craft ideas are available at WWW.GLADANDGOLDEN.COM.

2 1

ADVENT
WEEK ONE

PEOPLE, LOOK EAST. The time is near of the crowning of the year.

Make your HOUSE fair as you are able, Trim the HEARTH and set the TABLE.

PEOPLE, LOOK EAST and Sing today.

Love

the
GUEST,

is on the way.

Eleanor Farjeon, "Carol of the Advent"

What Sweeter Music

I knelt to place the last of the Thanksgiving dishes back in the old sideboard, lingering a moment before the lower cupboard to breathe in the scent. It was one of my favorite smells, though infamously difficult to describe–sort of an incense of old china and chipped porcelain, starched linen and tarnished silver. There were top notes of lemon oil and sugar cube mingling over a fragrant base of musky walnut, like a priceless oud extracted from the resin of memory.

It did smell, in fact, like memory itself, overlapping the present moment in a surge that engulfed me with a strange, rather desperate consolation. That these dishes, and the sideboard that housed them, should be in my possession was still a source of bewilderment—they ought to be over at Mama's house, pressed into service with habitual use on both high days and ordinary ones. But Mama had been dead these seven months, and the house I grew up in on Chestnut Drive had been sold. I ran my hand over the polished surface, feeling for the cracks that were as familiar as wrinkles on the face of a beloved friend, reassured by its sturdy substantiality. My mother-in-law, Janice, was gone, too, within mere weeks of my mother, and this would be our first Christmas without either one of them. It was hard to believe that an entire generation had passed and that their mantle now rested on my entirely inadequate shoulders.

I was not alone, of course. I had Laura and Rachel to keep me honest in the pursuit of my ideals, Katie to pray me through quandaries great and small, my sister, my sisters-in-law, my husband. I had the Ruff House, its familiar rooms and simple comforts a refuge in a troubling world, and its imperfections a foil to my perfectionism. I had my mother's example of sacrificial homemaking and open-handed entertaining. And I had her things, material objects she had offered in the service of love, over and over again.

"Love people. Use things," Philip and I used to quip in the early days of our marriage, when our ideals of hospitality were so young and untested. Well, they had certainly been tested over the past two decades, I thought now, gazing around the room, and us along with them. Even the Ruff House had been tested, and the years had stripped away so many things that didn't matter. But the adage held, for what *did* matter was more precious than ever, and the fact that physical objects could communicate affection, warmth, welcome, to immortal souls was an ever-increasing wonder. I wanted my mother's things because they made me feel close to her, but also because I wanted to use them in the same spirit of love.

I knew I was unequal to hers or Janice's role in our family; I was, at best, a happenstance matriarch, struggling to orient myself here at the tail end of my 40s. But I had a new clarity, which is the gift of the grieving, and it steeled my resolve: relationships were priority—with God and with people—for they were the only things that endured. I thought back to the faces that had so recently encircled this table, the "family" with which we had celebrated Thanksgiving, some of whom we were actually related to and others we had only lately met. I smiled. Almost nothing in my life looked like I thought it would. And yet it was all I had ever wanted: a warm and loving home full of life and people I loved. Strange how loss, grief, even the death of dreams, could yield such a harvest.

And now Advent was upon us once more, with Christmas gleaming at its extremity like a house of mirth, and I yearned toward it with a new keenness. I had always loved the season; as a girl I would flit through the house tying red ribbons on everything that stood still—and some things, like the dog, that didn't. In late October I would begin accumulating my stash of supplies for gifts and crafts: fabric for handmade dolls and pillows, aida cloth and embroidery floss for cross-stitched samplers, a skein of wool for an awkwardly knitted scarf. I scraped together babysitting money for glitter and felt, hot glue and fiberfill, and plotted little surprises with my sister for everyone from our widowed neighbor to the postman. I decorated my dollhouse with bits of juniper snipped from the bush outside my window, and, as I got older—and bolder—I slipped surreptitiously up to the far back corner of our suburban lot where, shadowed by magnolia and leafless dogwood trees, I would clip feathery boughs of hemlock, drooping irresistibly over our fence from the yard next door. These I draped over our pictures and wreathed around the chandeliers, hoping, rather ruefully, that Mr. Owen wouldn't recognize them when he brought over a loaf of his wife's banana bread as a Christmas gift.

When I came to the Ruff House as a bride, Christmas unfurled like a canvas, stretched with limitless possibility. The archway in the hall and the low banister railing were just asking for garland and red ribbons, and the property surrounding the house was populated with holly trees, glossy box, and ancient cedars more lovely and plumose than even my neighbor's coveted hemlock had been. I dried oranges to string with cranberry and bay above the kitchen hearth. I made gingerbread ornaments for the tree, and royal icing snowflakes, and a three-dimensional tinsel star which, against all odds, has survived twenty-plus years and counting. I even wrapped our gifts 1850s-style in colored tissue paper fastened with gold sealing wax stamped with the initial "I."

But I had begun to intuit something in the intervening years, pressing as firmly upon my ideals as that little brass stamp into warm, pliable wax: namely, that all of it actually mattered. That, somehow, my deep love of Christmas and all its comforts and beauties was intrinsically bound to my greater love for God and the people he had placed in my life. That, in a way I could scarcely articulate, he might receive all these

Devotional
RECOMMENDATIONS

BRIGHT EVENING STAR
Madeleine L'Engle

WAITING ON THE WORD
Malcolm Guite

WATCH FOR THE LIGHT
Plough Publishing House

HAPHAZARD BY STARLIGHT
Janet Morley

ADVENT WITH
EVELYN UNDERHILL
edited by Christopher L. Webber

WINTER FIRE: CHRISTMAS
WITH G.K. CHESTERTON
Ryan Whitaker Smith

THE ADVENT OF THE
LAMB OF GOD
Russ Ramsey

lesser loves as offerings of touchable, tastable devotion. I had found both articulation and affirmation of this hope couched among the lines of the Elizabethan poet Robert Herrick in his courtly carol "What Sweeter Music Can We Bring:"

The darling of the world is come,
And fit it is, we find a room
To welcome Him. The nobler part
Of all the house here, is the heart,

Which we will give Him; and bequeath
This holly, and this ivy wreath,
To do Him honor; who's our King,
And Lord of all this reveling.

These lines assured me that all things were material for devotion and that it truly was possible to enflesh my joy at Christ's coming as a lesser incarnation alongside his far greater one. For the Incarnation had changed everything, mending the division between the spiritual and the concrete, restoring the seamlessness of creation with myriad invisible threads. In Herrick's holly and ivy I saw my own oblations of ribbon and tinsel, cedar and box, lifted likewise to a worthy King. And I realized, with a shock of delight, that he actually prized them as such. It was the very thing I had always been reaching for in my decorating and celebrating, in the traditions dear to me since childhood and the ones my new husband and I were so sweetly establishing in our own home. The hope, hovering just this side of the unseen, that all of it actually mattered, and that, offered with loving intention, the everyday substance of life becomes the material of everyday sacrament, breaking down any supposed borders between the sacred and the secular and making vividly present something true about God and his love for us.

This was still my hope, after all these years, and now more than ever. I wanted to translate, in sugar and spice, holly, ivy, feasting and song, Christ's particular affection and God's great, house-filling mirth. I wanted to set a table right in the face of death, and to celebrate redemption with the artlessness of a child. Above all, I wanted to meet Jesus in the midst of it, bringing my battle-scarred soul into the rest of his presence, merging what I believed in my heart and what I made with my hands into a holy and undivided whole.

I opened one of the deep drawers of the sideboard, moving so easily on its well-made slides, and laid Mama's silver scallop-shell butter dish inside. Soon enough I'd be getting it out again, for the Notions Club, Christmas Eve brunch, Christmas Dinner. What a dance these days would be, between being and doing, preparation and contemplation. And all of it mattered. Every bit.

What SWEETER MUSIC can we bring
Than a carol, for to sing
The birth of this our heavenly KING?
Awake the voice! Awake the string!

Dark and dull night, fly hence away,
And give the honor to this day,
That sees DECEMBER turned to MAY.

Why does the chilling winter's morn
Smile, like a field beset with corn?
Or smell like a meadow newly-shorn,
Thus, on the sudden? COME and SEE
The cause, why things thus fragrant be:

TIS HE IS BORN, whose quickening birth
Gives life and luster, public mirth
To heaven, and the under-earth.

We see him come, and know him ours,
Who, with his sunshine and his showers,
Turns all the patient ground to flowers.

The DARLING of the WORLD is come
And fit it is, we find a room
To welcome him. The nobler part
Of all the HOME here, is the HEART.

Which we will give him; and bequeath
This holly, and this ivy wreath,
To do him honour, who's our King,
And LORD of all this revelling.

What SWEETER MUSIC can we bring
Than a carol, for to sing
The birth of this our heavenly KING?

ROBERT HERRICK

Discovering Advent

Our den was a picture of contentment. A fire crackled in the woodburning stove and cats and dogs were strewn about in varying states of repose. Across the room a stately Christmas tree presided between the big, double-hung windows, and on the coffee table the flames of fat pillar candles wavered and danced above a half-finished jigsaw puzzle. I took a sip of Russian Tea from the mug cradled in my hands and frowned.

"What's wrong?" Philip asked from the depths of his armchair. He had been puttering about the farm all day, making improvements in the barn and scheming projects for the coming year, and now, as afternoon began to bow towards evening, he sat with his feet up on the coffee table, reading the book my sister had given him for Christmas.

"It's been such a wonderful holiday," I said petulantly.

"And you're sad about that?"

I was. I was sad that Philip was going back to the office the next day and that our magical week of post-Christmas quiet was at an end.

"It's not over yet," he reminded me, reading my thoughts.

It may as well have been. No matter what we did with the remaining hours of our holiday, I could not unknow that we had only that—hours. And it *had* been so lovely. I felt just like I did when, as a little girl, I couldn't help crying on Christmas night because all of the anticipation and magic had come to an end. Mama used to beat a path between my room and Zach's, consoling us as best she could. Only Liz, it seemed, was made of more philosophical stuff. She was probably just happy with her new doll and the fact that she was not spending Christmas in the emergency room with one of her asthma attacks.

I heaved a theatrical sigh. Philip's native optimism made me mopier than ever. Like my book friend Anne Shirley, away at college for the first time and pining for Green Gables, I just wanted to be miserable. But Philip wasn't having it.

"Why don't you write about it?" he asked. "Writing always makes you feel better. I could set you up with a laptop—I think I've got an extra one lying around."

(This was, dear reader, back in the prehistoric days of early 2004 when I did all of my writing exclusively on college-ruled paper with #2 pencils. Also, software engineers always have laptops "lying around." They're like phone chargers or extra pairs of readers for the rest of us.)

My interest was piqued. I liked the thought of drowning my sorrows in a tumble of black characters on a computer screen. Never mind that I was an abysmal typist. It could be fun to hang out with Christmas a little while longer, even if the rest of the world had moved on. It might even, you know, lead to something. At the very least it could provide an outlet for this bright burden of holiday sentiment I carried around with me from year to year.

At first I wasn't sure what to write about, allowing my words to meander among various memories and loved traditions. Soon, however, an idea began to emerge, solidifying into a fully-formed intention, so that by the time Philip came home from the office on his second day back at work, I was bubbling over.

"A Christmas devotional?" He nodded thoughtfully. "That's right up your alley!"

The details of the project fell into place rapidly after that. It was not a book for publication; it was a book for my friends, those dear sisters and kindreds who shared my love of Christmas and sought for something more beyond the outward trappings of the season. I set up a card table in the corner of the den with my watercolor supplies where, when I wasn't writing, I could use my creative time to paint swags of holly, tiny Christmas trees, platters of roasted turkey, renderings of favorite ornaments, and ribbon-clad wreaths to adorn the pages and serve as headers. I sourced old carols and poems to accompany the daily readings and arranged Scripture verses to serve as prompts. And I wrote joyously and unselfconsciously, immersing myself in work so meaningful it felt like its own reward.

It was a sweet time, and I couldn't wait to get to my card-table desk each day. But as the little book grew under my hands, a new awareness was gathering in my mind. I had intended to craft a reading for each day, from December 1st to the 25th. As I searched the internet for historical context and the origins of some of our customs, however, I began to realize that in many traditions—even contemporary ones—Christmas was cele-brated as a twelve-day feast and Advent was a season of its own. I was astonished. Like many brought up in the evangelical tradition, Christmas commenced for me as soon as the turkey sandwiches were polished off on Thanksgiving night and ended, with heart-rending abruptness, on the 26th of December. It was a few, flurried weeks into which must needs be crammed every tradition, carol, recipe, party, movie, book, gift, visit, and card—not to mention the infrastructure of preparation undergirding it all. I had no idea that for centuries the Church had set apart the weeks leading up to Christmas for making ready, and the twelve days after Christmas for actually celebrating.

I began to realize that Advent was an invitation to carve out space to contemplate what the Incarnation actually meant, teaching us to look for Christ's coming on a personal level. The whole thing was so rich and expansive in contrast with the modern tendency to leap from one holiday to the next, and this new knowledge was so exciting that I extended my book to January 6 to include the Feast of the Epiphany. Checking a liturgical calendar online, I made note of when Advent actually began that year so that my friends would have their copies in plenty of time. I even changed the title from *Christmas Devotions* to *Advent Meditations* to reflect the shift in my understanding.

I sensed that the observance of Advent would become one of the most cherished rhythms of my year, allowing me to bring my sorrows and my questions into the radiant circle of the season's joys. For we weave our longings into the narrative each time we retrace the old story of our redemption; we recognize our own desperation in the anguish of all those lost generations walking in a darkness so great only Almighty Love could vanquish it. Every time we touch a match to a candle on our Advent wreath, we confess our need for light. Every time we acknowledge Christ's coming—in reading or reflection or simple, heartfelt prayer—we give root-room to the promise that he is coming again. The hope of Advent, after all, is an unfinished one. Just because we know how the story will end doesn't mean that it's over.

As the autumn days slipped by, my book took physical shape. Philip and I made a late-night foray in late October to a 24-hour print shop to run the color copies and have them cut to size, and he set up his drill press in the basement to punch holes in the text blocks. My sister, who'd had a book-arts class as part of her BFA, taught me how to wrap the boards and sew them together in the traditional stab binding method, and with covers of Japanese paper in every color of the rainbow, coordinating vellum endpapers, and thin, silk velvet side-stitching, they looked like a flower garden of books spread out on the kitchen table.

The fun I had distributing them was immeasurable. No one but Liz and Philip had known what I was up to, but now the sweet secret was out. I gave one to Laura and one to Rachel, my compatriots in Christmas-love, and one each to Louise and Lori, the lifelong friends I had inherited upon marrying Philip. I mailed one to Lauren in Birmingham and delivered one to Mama, Janice, and my sisters-in-law. I gave one to Liz, even though it was no surprise. And I kept one for myself, in token of the year I had learned to write through my sadness into a spacious place of sacred discovery.

That book, however, was not this book. But certainly it was a seed—the beginning of a new understanding and a new appreciation for the audacity of hope for which Advent makes space. I like to think that perhaps that seed is giving forth now its fruit.

HOW TO MAKE AN
Advent Wreath

Advent begins on the Sunday that falls on or closest to November 30th. And one of the first things I do, on this very first Sunday of the season, is to make my Advent wreath.

There is no one right way to make an Advent wreath. It can be as simple as a circle of candlesticks on the kitchen table or as elaborate as a ring of fresh greens, studded with dried fruits and berries. And while liturgical traditions specify certain colors of candles for the weeks leading up to Christmas, there are as many interpretations for the home Advent wreath as there are people to fashion them. Most years I use solid ivory tapers, switching over to deep crimson during Christmastide. The most important thing is that your wreath be centrally located, so that you can enjoy its flicker and glow during your Advent readings and meditations or simply as a twinkling companion throughout your December evenings.

I take my inspiration from the Scandinavian tradition of a hanging wreath, and to this end I use a sturdy wire form fitted with four tulip-shaped candle holders. Eastern red cedar is my live material of choice, but any readily available greens—such as fir, hemlock, juniper, or short-needled pine—will work. I also discovered years ago that an initial layer of artificial boxwood greens creates a solid base for a wonderfully lush wreath. (Another benefit of artificial greens is that you can leave them attached to the form at the end of the season—when you assemble your Advent wreath the following year, you're more than halfway there!)

We hang ours in the den, before one of the wide, double-hung windows, and when the candles are lit they throw back their twinkling doubles in the old wavy glass. Apart from the Christmas tree, the Advent wreath is my very favorite decoration and the first signal to my home that the longed-for season has arrived. I miss it so much after Christmas is over that a lovely red glass lantern swings in its place all the rest of the year, like a hint and a promise of the good that is always coming.

1. Measure the distance from the ceiling to where you want your wreath to hang–far enough below the ceiling not to be a fire hazard–and place your hook accordingly, using a drill fitted with a bit smaller than the threads of the hook. Do not screw directly into drywall—you will need to find a stud to anchor your hook in order to support the weight of the wreath.

2. Leaving a 4-inch tail, tie the end of one of the ribbons to one of the cross-pieces on the wreath form, directly between two of the candleholders. Attach the other end of the ribbon to the

corresponding cross-piece directly opposite, again, leaving a 4-inch tail. Repeat with the other ribbon, spaced evenly between the remaining candleholders.

3.   Wrap the outer ring of the wreath form with 22-gauge wire, leaving the end of the wire attached to the paddle. Space two of the boxwood sprigs evenly over one section of the wreath and wrap with wire several times to secure them. Repeat with the remaining boxwood over the remaining three sections of the wreath, leaving the paddle wire attached.

4.   Clip the live greens into 5-inch bunches. Gathering 3-4 bunches at a time, wrap the wire around the cut ends and secure to the wreath. Continue around the frame, working in the same direction and overlapping each bunch of greens.

5.   Slip the ribbons over the prepared hook and position the wreath; you may need to adjust the ribbons to ensure that it hangs evenly. Clip several more sprigs of greenery and tuck them in around the top, sides, and bottom of the wreath until it reaches the desired fullness.

6.   Using a knife or your fingers, attach a pea-sized amount of Sticky Wax to the bottom of each taper and secure into the candleholders, making sure to support the wreath from the bottom so that it continues to hang evenly.

MATERIALS:

Drill
1 one-inch heavy duty screw-hook
1 two-wire Advent wreath form
    fitted with candle holders
1 spool of 22-gauge green
    paddle wire
2 satin ribbons, double the length
    from the desired placement of
    your wreath to the ceiling, plus
    an additional 8 inches
8 sprigs of artificial boxwood
Fresh greenery of your choice
Wire cutters
Clippers
4 twelve-inch dripless tapers
"Sticky Wax" candle adhesive

NOTES: Advent wreath-forms can be inexpensively sourced from Amazon, church supply stores, or from your local wholesale florist.

Live greenery is highly flammable. Never leave your wreath unattended when lit, and always be sure to replace the candles if they begin to burn too low. You can also use battery-operated candles to avoid this risk altogether.

Other natural materials, like wild rosehips, holly, or even dried flowers, can enhance the beauty of your wreath. Be as creative as you like!

I THINK *when it's done* PROPERLY, *you only light one candle the first week, and two the second, and so on. It was so beautiful* I JUST LIT THEM ALL AT ONCE *and have done so ever since! One should always feel* FREE *to* ALTER TRADITIONS *as one sees fit.*
~TASHA TUDOR

Bringing in the Greens

Few rituals in the year are equal to that of the first morning, early in December, when I slip out of the house, clippers in hand and a gathering basket slung over my arm, to begin the process of bringing in the greens. I say process, because decorating the Ruff House is a slow affair, starting simply in early Advent and mounting toward a glorious, bowery culmination at Christmas itself.

There is a countercultural joy in this practice for me, a pushing-back against the strange pressure we feel in our modern world to have our houses decked to perfection before the Thanksgiving turkey has cooled—or, in some cases, has even been cooked. In early December, a few sprigs of fir on the mantle or a small vase of holly in the larder suffice to tell us that Christmas is still *coming*—we are not "behind" or "ahead" of things, we are right where we are meant to be, anchored in the present moment by tangible witnesses of good things to come.

Years ago, Philip and I attended a candlelight Christmas tour at a nineteenth-century farm. Outside, a beloved local storyteller held an audience spellbound with African folk tales. His hands and expressions leapt in concert with sparks from the campfire, while, across the yard, a cloaked docent holding a lantern described the relative privations of an 1840s holiday. As this was roughly the era of our own farmhouse, I couldn't

Boxwood

Ivy

Cedar

Holly

Christmas greenery

Pine

Magnolia

Winterberry

Eucalyptus

Fir

wait to see what the decorations looked like inside, but as we passed through the low doorway and into the warm, candlelit space, I stopped myself short. The honest beauty of it all was disarming: the table set with fine, serviceable, old willow ware glinting companionably in the firelight; a jug of pine on the mantle and an earthenware bowl full of clove-studded oranges; the scent of gingerbread and a rosy glow wavering over whitewashed ceiling and walls. Most touching of all were the small sprigs of holly crowning each windowsill, modest and unpretentious, yet lending an air of such wholesome festivity as to make the room sparkle with mirth. It was tasteful, possessing even a rustic elegance, but it was evident that these decorations had been the work of minutes, not hours. I thanked the curators in my heart for resisting the temptation to overdo, knowing how easy it might have been to try and impress their paying guests with elaborate adornments, rather than give them an authentic taste of a simpler time. To be fair, the oranges might have been a stretch for a family of this status. But that holly couldn't be argued with. It had been clipped from the farmhouse yard, planted, perhaps, for that very purpose.

Men and women have brought greenery and natural materials into their homes since pagan times, but it was the early church fathers who decreed that such ancient practices might be appropriated to serve a sacred office. Thereby, the evergreen, long-associated with immortality, became a Christian figure for eternal life, and the ring-like wreath bore witness to God's unbroken love and faithfulness. Holly, ivy, and mistletoe were revered for the seeming miracle of their winter-borne fruit, and while mistletoe's "golden bough"—once thought the cure of all illnesses—was translated into an image of Christ's healing power, it was the holly which, as the old Cornish carol would have it, "bore the crown." For from holly, the legend goes, the crown of thorns was made. And it never bore its scarlet fruit until the blood flowed from the Savior's brow.

Like all good things in this goodly creation, the greens and berries of winter bear witness in their very being—in what G. M. Hopkins might call their "thisness"—to a loving Creator. In December, the old cedars around our place greet the dawn dew-span-gled, like Christmas trees showered in diamonds, and gathering the westerly gold of the dying day into their dark, feathery boughs. The hollies shelter birds' and squirrels' nests innumerable and are the special province of the cedar waxwings who visit us each January and gorge themselves for days on the ruby fruit. The boxwoods, relieved of their summer struggle against drought and heat, turn glossy and pert, and the ivy in my special, secret clipping place far in the woods tumbles in long, green ribbons from the bare trees. I watch my little world eagerly for such harbingers; farther afield, I notice that my mother's white sasanqua is covered in tight buds, swelling to burst into frothy bloom, and that even the privet along the roadside is weighted with dusky blue berries, a feast for the wild things in leaner months.

And these things are a feast for me, as well, a generous banquet from which I might select my own small symbols of life and peace and the goodness of God-with-us. I saunter forth, fists plunged in the pockets of my dad's old hunting jacket, my breath a white vapor in the chilly air. I visit cedar, boxwood, and ivy in turn; I am selective over the holly, thinking at once of the birds and of future decorating in that far-off fourth week of Advent. But there is plenty to spare. Nature, after all, is never spent. Not really.

Back in the warmth of the house I spread the bright harvest on the kitchen table. The boxwood will become wreaths for the two windows over the sink, a sight to gladden my heart every morning from now until Epiphany. The other materials I finger and sort, dividing them among small silver trumpet vases and colored glass jars. The finest pieces are reserved, perhaps, for the tarnished pedestal bowl on the mantle; arranged in well-soaked floral foam and watered with care, they will keep fresh until Christmas.

A single sprig of holly remains. I place it, with a smile, along the windowsill.

HOW TO MAKE A
Boxwood Wreath

Decorating with live greenery might seem daunting if you have never done it before, or if you don't have a holly tree growing right outside your kitchen door. But nature abounds with materials to adorn our homes and awaken our senses to the unique joys of the season—nuts, seeds, berries, fruit, flowering shrubs, and silvery bare branches. Watch the world around you for evergreen trees and shrubs; note the fruiting plants in your area and ask to clip from a neighbor's yard, if necessary. One year a friend brought me a large floral box filled with lacy ground ferns which she had cut before the first frost and soaked in glycerin to preserve their freshness. I twined the delicate strands around the chandelier in the dining room and trailed them along the mantle, where they remained pliable and green until well after the New Year. They were still so pretty, in fact, as they mellowed into a pale honey-gold, that I left them in place until Easter!

Often Christmas tree lots provide a free trimmings bin—be sure to ask first, however, as many small businesses make their wreaths from their own clippings. And if you have room, you may want to consider planting an evergreen, a holly, or even a boxwood hedge in your own yard.

Making a boxwood wreath could not be simpler, particularly if you start with an inexpensive grapevine form (available at most craft stores or see GladandGolden.com for suggestions) for a base. Using this method,

MATERIALS:
Grapevine wreath form
Clippings of fresh boxwood or
   other greenery of your choice
Paddle wire (if necessary)
Satin ribbon for bows/hanging

I find that even paddle wire is often unnecessary, as small bunches of boxwood can be wedged between the rings of the existing wreath until the desired fullness is reached. Be sure to keep your clippings roughly the same size, especially if you are making multiple wreaths. Boxwood is a traditional and forgiving material, but any sturdy evergreen, such as cedar, fir, balsam, or short-needled pine, will do.

ALL THINGS THEREFORE
ARE CHARGED WITH
LOVE, ARE CHARGED
WITH GOD, AND IF WE
KNOW HOW TO TOUCH
THEM GIVE OFF SPARKS
AND TAKE FIRE,
YIELD DROPS AND FLOW,
RING AND TELL OF HIM.

GERARD MANLEY HOPKINS

Getting OUT THE Decorations

My "permanent" decorations are few—each year I strive against my tendency to accumulate in order to keep it that way—but they are precious to me: the pale blue mid-century bowl, once my mother's, and her mother's before her, beflecked with glitter and boasting a froth of plastic fir and tarnished glass balls (both of which bear evidence of having once been dusted with a light snowfall of white paint); the homely, moss-lined crèche, purchased from a discount store early in our marriage; a small flock of artificial redbreasts and nuthatches for the little tree in our bedroom; and the mantle garland fashioned from vintage ornaments strung along a length of real German tinsel. These emerge from the attic in late November and are unearthed from swaddlings of tissue paper and scattered about the house in their time-honored locations. The little feather tree always goes on great-grandmother Gann's marble-topped table at the head of the stairs. The wooden nutcrackers Mama and Daddy gave me a decade apart—one as a teenager having just danced my first (and only) "Waltz of the Flowers" with our regional ballet company, the other as a young wife celebrating my first Christmas in my new home—always preside from the plate rail in the den. There is the small, plaster angel, with her reverent face and folded hands, parted long ago from her nativity set, kneeling on the kitchen windowsill to remind me to hold space for the holy in all the happy bustle, and a cluster of colored candleholders and bottlebrush trees on the table, gifts from friends in Christmases past.

And I still tie red ribbons on everything—the sconces, the candlesticks, the banister, the dogs. A lustrous bundle of hand-dyed silk in varying lengths is one of the treasures of our household. Transmuting in hue from crimson to violet to amber and back to crimson again, they were the incidental gift of that long-ago *Southern Living* photo shoot. I still remember the prodigality with which the stylist cut and looped them amid the garland framing our front door; it made my head swim, knowing full well what that ribbon must cost by the yard. But how I rejoiced when she left them behind! Every year since, I have ironed them carefully and knotted them on the chandelier in the front hall in big, drooping bows, announcing to the Ruff House that the festal season is upon us. Every year, that is, except for that terrible one when there was no chandelier to hang them on and no Ruff House to decorate.

For the rest of my life I will bless the fact that we were home when the fire broke out. Had we been away, the Ruff House would have burned to the ground, with our cats and dogs inside. As it was, one of our Pyrenees bolted in terror and was struck on the four-lane back of our property; she would have to be euthanized. And Philip would be hospitalized briefly for the burns to his face and arm sustained while battling the blaze with the garden hose as we waited for the firetrucks to arrive. ("I heard about Philip's water-hose action," our friend Fr. Thomas McKenzie wrote shortly thereafter. "I hope you are mending from that. Please never do that again. Hearing about it scared the hell out of me.")

It was a night of horrors, flames leaping out of my pretty yellow kitchen, sirens and the doomful thrum of diesel engines. I remember racing to the end of the driveway to open the gate for the emergency crews, the gravel cutting into my bare feet, and stumbling around like a deranged woman in the dark after they arrived. I repeated to anyone who would listen that there were still four cats unaccounted for. Even after our cats were rescued, there were further losses to fear, and we confronted them the next day, stepping into the dark, reeking spaces of our home.

The damage from smoke and water rivaled even that of the fire, seeping into every crack and crevice, staining each ceiling and wall with a horrible fretwork of "smoke-webbing." Even the contents of my desk drawers—behind a closed door, upstairs, on the opposite end of the house—were covered in a sickening, grey film. And when it came to my bins of Christmas decorations, located in a closet directly above where the fire broke out, my heart sank. I could hardly bear to crack them open; when I did, the diabolical stench rushed out like a genie. Everything we owned would have to be taken out of the house for cleaning and storage. And, it being summer, with no electricity to fend off our Southern humidity, it would have to be done fast.

"We don't clean Christmas decorations," Marissa from the contents company explained.

Her eyes were kind, but her mouth was no-nonsense. She had been packing out my house for a week-and-a-half, and she and her team were tired.

I was tired, too, reeling from trauma and desperately, deeply homesick. Philip and I had been told to prepare for at least a year-long exile from the Ruff House, and as I stood there, clutching a box of ornaments and vintage balls, each one swathed and wrapped with loving care just a few months earlier, I felt that one more bit of bad news would pull me under.

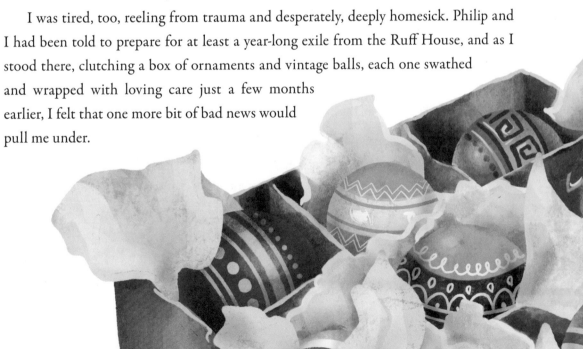

"Please," I whispered, clutching the box.

Her eyes softened, and the no-nonsense mouth lifted into a half-smile.

"All right," she said and held out her hands.

Eighteen months after the fire, I pulled my Christmas bins from my newly constructed attic and knelt before them with a quaking heart. Everything inside had been unwrapped, cleaned, ozoned, and re-wrapped by strangers' hands. Of all the irreverences and indecencies a disaster of this nature can expose one to, I had found the scattering and sorting and processing of our most precious things perhaps the most disorienting. I wept in relief when my piano was returned unscathed; I wept with frustration when much of our artwork came back amateurishly repaired beyond repair.

And what, what of my blue bowl, my nutcrackers, my bottlebrush trees? Were they, as so many well-meaning souls had assured me after the fire, "just things," expendable trifles of a temporal existence? Did it even matter how they had fared, or whether they survived at all? Or was there, as I had always suspected in the nearly nonverbal reaches of my mind, something meaningful—dare I say sacred—clinging to the quotidian objects that form the mise-en-scène of an immortal soul? Not sacred in and of themselves, any more than an ordinary chalice is sacred apart from its consecrated use. But set apart, somehow, assigned to furnish material consolation, to make the meaning of home for the natively homesick. This was the reason I was so thankful to have my favorite Brown Betty teapot with me during our exile from the Ruff House, and why the loss of my cookbooks felt like a sacrilege.

I opened the first box, marked "Nativity & Nutcrackers," and stared. If Philip and I had not gone, quite literally, through fire and water in the past year-and-a-half, I would have found it hard to believe that the contents had been disturbed since I had last put them away. The tissue paper was new, of course, but everything had been wrapped and returned just exactly as I had left it. I flung open the next box, and the next, disbelieving the evidence of my own eyes. Marissa and her team had not only cleaned my Christmas decorations, they had treated them with a kindness akin to reverence. I fumbled anxiously for the little packet of red silk ribbons and buried my nose in their luminous folds. Not a hint of smoke. Only God himself could know what it all meant to me.

I used to wonder, in my trepidatious way, what would happen between putting the decorations away at the end of the season and getting them out again the following year. What tidings would we receive, and what losses were in store? What clouds of disappointment or grief might be gathering on our horizon?

Now, when I tie those ribbons on the branched arms of the chandelier, I think, as I always have done, of Christmases past, and all the memories with which they are inextricably twined. But I also think of the unseen mercies coming our way, the goodness of God winging toward us through all the stretches of the unknown year. Even in our hardest places, that goodness is coming—is, in fact, already present, though we humans can rarely see it but in retrospect. Marissa's kindness began long months before I saw its fruit, but it typifies for me the affection of God revealed in the extravagance of red silk, in the very matter of life and shaping all things for our good and his glory.

Decorating the Barn

The first Christmas our barn was populated with goats and sheep, I swung a paper chain along the center beam of the hallway, and to the posts I tacked little red wire cones filled with silvery tufts of long-leaf pine. Philip watched me with a bemused smile; it was the very spirit, he knew, which had induced me to plant shrub roses all along the western fence the previous spring, insisting that *my* goats would never dream of touching them, what with such abundant pasturage and woodland forage at their disposal. I had underestimated the caprice of the goat, however, and the imperviousness of their stately heads and long necks to the flimsy suggestion of a hog-wire fence. Within days, fourteen rose bushes had gone the way of Puck and Pansy's elaborate stomachs, leaving only the fresh eggs I had planted underneath as fertilizer–and these were thanklessly picked off by the racoons.

Having decorated, I wasn't in the barn that afternoon when Puck and Co. came running in for their mid-afternoon siesta, but Philip was, and he nearly doubled over with laughter at the sight. Puck took in the delectable treat of pine boughs dangling overhead in one glance, and in a moment more the decorations were gone. He did share a bit with his sister, Pansy, and Sebastian the sheep managed a nibble or two while Ophelia and Benedick pranced around the barnyard with bits of bedraggled paper chain trailing from their mouths.

I couldn't fault them, of course. In their minds, Christmas had already come, with ovine and caprine sugar plums sprouting magically from the ceiling. Besides, the sheep would likely have left them alone altogether without their goat ringleaders to show them how to be naughty. The next year, however, I exercised prudence. The paper chain, much repaired, was relegated to the feed room, while the wire cones remained empty until Christmas Eve. A friend, updating her own decorations, had given me a couple of old lengths of artificial garland, and these I looped—with many a stout nail for good measure—down the rafters of the hallway, topping things off with a silk fir wreath at the eastern opening.

I watched carefully as we opened the stalls the next morning. Puck was out in a bound, dancing on his hind legs under the garland, and nibbling away with evident zest. Pansy, always the lady, stepped lightly onto the long bench in the hallway and, with one hoof poised upon a support post and her pendulous ears falling back from her upturned head, ventured a taste. Sneezing in disgust, she stepped down again and sauntered over to see if someone happened to have left the feed room door unlocked. Puck came to his senses, dropped to all fours, shook his head as he passed the wreath at the end of the barn, and gave it a sidelong sniff and a shudder. The sheep, ever willing to profit by others' experience, never so much as looked at it.

And thus, my barn decorations remain safe to this day, though other goats have succeeded the fabled Puck and Pansy, and though I've tentatively extended my reach to include a sprig of plastic mistletoe over the feed room door and a large wreath hung from the banister rail of the loft—just where Panav the peacock likes to perch.

Adorning the barn is a matter of minutes, especially if Philip is on hand to help me hang the garland (and to keep me from obsessing over the position of the paper chain). Once the bin of decorations is extracted from its shadowy corner of the loft, it only remains to fluff things up a bit; tie a ribbon on the egg basket, perhaps, or put out a festive hand towel in the feed room. But everything, howsoever simple, has meaning to me. The paper chain is from our first Christmas tree; the wreaths over the sink are accented with little silver bells saved from a friend's wedding sendoff. Swinging in the window opening into the hallway is a funny little wooden "Santa's clothesline," which my parents painted fancifully their first Christmas when they were too poor to buy any other decorations. On the Hoosier cabinet I place a popsicle stick Nativity, made for me by a child I've had the privilege to see grow into a young woman.

None of it is fancy, or even photo-worthy. I doubt that the animals even notice, apart from their first, cursory acknowledgement when I let them out of their stalls the morning after I've decorated—although I can't help but wonder if their stomachs begin to rumble a bit for the coming Christmas Eve treats and greens they know it all signifies. But I do it every year because it gives us joy whenever we set foot in our barn. It makes me, quite simply, happy, in a way that's the closest to childlikeness of anything I've known in adult life.

And I do it because it seems meet and proper to honor this rustic space, even before turning my hand to the house itself. For generations, the life of the Ruff House depended upon the life in this barn; for centuries Christians have celebrated the fact that our Savior was essentially born in a stable, "between the ox and the grey donkey"[1]—a fact which has often been sentimentalized to the point of unrecognizability. I once read a rather saccharine story about a little lamb which gave up sleeping *in its manger* for the sake of the Baby Jesus (as if any self-respecting sheep would sleep in its

For unto us a Child is Born

[1] "Entre le bœuf et l'âne gris," French traditional carol

feeding trough!); as far back as the Victorian author of that story, it seemed, we had already forgotten that the word "manger" derives from the French *manger*, to eat.

Indeed, we forgot much earlier than that. It was the beloved Francis, thirteen-century friar of Assisi and patron saint of the natural world, who, taking issue with the elaborate and utterly unrealistic representations of the Nativity popular in the Roman church at that time, decided to create his own version in the Italian village of Greccio. On Christmas Eve 1223 he conducted mass in a natural cave, illumined by torchlight and adorned with a hay-filled manger. In a final touch of loving simplicity, an ox and a donkey were led in beside it, prompting Thomas of Celano to declare that, "of Greccio there was made, as it were, a new Bethlehem."

We have Francis to thank for our own little living room Nativity sets, thatched with straw or lined with moss, peopled with figures familiar as the faces of our own kindred: the rapt little Mary in her gown of blue; tender Joseph brooding over Mother and Son; the dumbfounded but devout shepherds. And the animals—always the animals.

I love the mangers Philip built for our goats and sheep, sturdy affairs of rough-sawn cedar, with deep troughs and stout legs resting upon wide and well-built bases. They are impossible for a rowdy dinnertime crew to overturn—but not, I am afraid, any sort of foil to the goat who prefers not only to sleep in his dinner plate, but to stand in it, as well. Often in the winter evenings, after Philip and I have put everyone down for the night, we sit in the hallway together, listening to the contented munchings on the other side of the tarpaulined stall doors. Occasionally, a goat whimpers low over the toothsomeness of timothy hay, or a hen ruffles her feathers in the henhouse at the end of the barn. The air is sweet with the fragrance of masticated grass, like summer condensed and distilled into the chilly night. Though the stalls are warm and snug, we can see our breath out in the hall. A barred owl back in the woods wants to know who's cooking for us that night. "I am," I always want to say.

Our barn is a pleasant place, full of loved and cared-for creatures. But it is also

Music
RECOMMENDATIONS

A JOLLY CHRISTMAS
Frank Sinatra

TO DRIVE THE COLD
WINTER AWAY
Loreena McKennitt

ADVENT AT EPHESUS
Benedictines of Mary
Queen of the Apostles

SONGS FOR CHRISTMAS
Sufjan Stevens

A RENAISSANCE
CHRISTMAS CELEBRATION
The Waverly Consort

BEHOLD THE LAMB OF GOD
Andrew Peterson

CHRISTMAS
Jill Phillips & Andy Gullahorn

a place of dirt. It is a place of waste—waste hay the animals have dropped and soiled; waste they have created themselves which must needs be mucked on a regular basis. In winter, the barnyard is a place of mud, particularly at the openings where the animals like to congregate. In summer we sprinkle diatomaceous earth in the stalls to deter parasites and put out a sulfur lick to keep flies off the sheep. I cannot help but think, particularly in December, how pleased I am to offer my beasts a manger-full of soft, fragrant Bermuda–but how little I'd rejoice to lay a newborn baby there. Clean as I strive to keep my barn, I doubt many women would regard it as an enviable place to give birth.

"I would fain," Saint Francis said of his live Nativity, "make a memorial of that Child that was born in Bethlehem and in some sort behold with bodily eyes His infant hardships."

Hardship is not a word I would typically associate with my barn, or the lives of the animals who live in it. But somehow, between the tatty garland and the popsicle-stick nativity, the overflowing mangers and the mended and re-mended paper chain, I catch a glimpse of that love which was too great not to stoop to the lowliest place.

The Tree

O n the day after Thanksgiving, we load the dogs into the car and set off in quest of the Perfect Tree. Fortunately, we don't have far to go; the local stand from which we've purchased our trees many years running is scarcely three miles down the road. But the familiar lot feels like an enchanted forest, couched between the four-lane to our left and the discount store across the parking lot; somewhere, in all this fragrant maze, stands a stout-hearted fir aspiring to be transformed into the tinseled and spangled glory of a Ruff House Christmas tree, and like the seeker in a fairy tale, I know I will recognize true worth when I see it. I thread the aisles with sharp eyes, grasping the branch of a potential candidate and running my fingers over its length, crushing a needle between my fingers to release the scent. Philip knows it won't take long; in another five minutes a little cry of conquest will go up from the other side of a thick hedge of trees, and once he finally manages to locate me, we confer. It is tall and thin; the needles are of a dark, blue-frosted green, not a one of which came off in my hand when I ran the branch test. There is enough shelving to support some of our heavier ornaments and to reveal glimpses of smooth, silvery trunk. *Yes, it's perfect.*

The perfect tree, like everything else in this lovely old post-Edenic world, is a myth. But, like all myths, it is an ideal with a grain of truth at its heart, for, once we have settled on our tree, it *becomes* the perfect tree—not because it is flawless, but because it is *ours*. I track down an attendant to wrap it for the short journey home, and Philip haggles good-naturedly with the owner of the lot, adding a tree for my mother to our tab for good measure. The owner, who does not deliver trees, very kindly agrees to personally convey and install my mother's, and knocks twenty-five dollars off the price of our fir in memory of the dozen duck eggs I gave him last spring.

Once the tree has been netted and paid for, Philip takes over. He politely declines the attendant's offer to take a slice off the bottom of the trunk with a chainsaw, believing it best to cut the tree at home, immediately before placing it in water to ensure the sap doesn't harden again and clog the capillaries that will enable it to drink for weeks on end. He also believes that tying it to the top of the car exposes it unnecessarily to drying drafts, and, since this tree must stay fresh right through to the final hours of Twelfth Night, I agree that we cannot take chances. Into the back of the Explorer it goes, perforce, bottom end foremost, and seeing as this will likely be a nine-or-ten foot tree, Philip begs a little of the attendant's unused twine to gently tie the back hatch down above the protruding tip. Our Australian shepherd will be obliged to ride home in my lap, while our Great Pyrenees crouches in the back with her head wedged against the ceiling, eyeing the strange, prickly entity with a suspicious gaze.

At home, we extricate ourselves, our dogs, and our tree from the car, and while Philip goes to get the saw, I track down the stand. Often, I stir up a dubious concoction at this point; Philip has dubbed it "Tree Brew": a blend of molasses and hot water, seasoned with bleach, Epsom salts, and liquid iron, which promises to keep the tree hydrated and fragrant all season long. After years of experimentation, I have come to the conclusion that the best merits of Tree Brew likely rest in making me feel that I am Doing Something for my tree; indeed, while Tree Brew certainly won't hurt, and may indeed help, the best insurance is to purchase a tree which passes the branch test (little to no needles should fall) and to top it off with clean, hot water, every single day,

RECIPE: *Tree Brew*

1 pint (2 cups) corn syrup

1/4 cup bleach   1 tsp. chelated iron

1/2 tsp. Borax   (such as Ferti-lome)

1/8 tsp. Epsom salts

Fill a large bucket with 2 gallons of very hot water and add all ingredients, stirring to dissolve.

After making a fresh cut off the bottom of your tree, plunge the trunk into the bucket and let stand for 24 hours. When you're ready to bring the tree in the house, place it in a stand with a deep well, and as soon as it is in place, fill the well with the solution. Keep the rest of the brew nearby to top off the well every day, making up more as needed. I usually go through at least 3 buckets a season.

(If you have dogs, or curious cats, you may want to cover the well of your tree stand with a screen of hardware cloth or 1/2" wire mesh, to keep them from sampling the brew. Ours have never tried it, but I can't think it would be good for them if they did.)

without fail. Another thing that helps is to run a humidifier in the room with your Christmas tree; not only will this offset the drying effects of your fireplace or furnace, it will make your houseplants think they've achieved a second youth.

We've mastered the furniture-moving game by now, but once the tree is in place and the house is set to rights, we give it (and ourselves) a rest. It's best to let the branches settle a bit and allow the tree to take on some water before winding it with hundreds of lights. We usually wait a couple of days—it is, after all, still November. This gives me time to pull the bins of ornaments out of the attic, to make sure last year's lights are in working order, and to bake my traditional Christmas-tree gingerbread.

This is not a cookie for eating; its purpose is purely decorative—sturdily, reliably, odoriferously so. But ever since the alchemy of gingerbread and fir imprinted itself upon my memory that first Christmas at the Ruff House, it is a sensory aid I simply cannot do without—one whiff and every Christmas is before me in an instant, indeed, it is the very essence and innocence of Christmas itself. The same must be true for my dogs, who make a careful inventory of the location and relative accessibility of each and every gingerbread man on the tree. To their credit, they know those cookies are off limits,

RECIPE: *Merry Maker*

3 oz. London dry gin
6 oz. orange juice

Ground cinnamon
Soft peppermint sticks
(optional)

Divide the gin equally between two lowball glasses and top with ice. Pour the orange juice evenly over the gin and top with a dash of ground cinnamon and a peppermint swizzle stick, if you like.

SERVES 2

but that doesn't keep Bonnie from sniffing the air longingly and lovingly, or Luna from gobbling the occasional "drops" which tumble from the branches when our Southern humidity soars. I have learned over the years to bake them a little longer to combat that humidity, and to make slightly larger holes than seems necessary in the cutouts for the ribbon hangers *before* placing them in the oven. I have also learned that an easily store-bought can of piped frosting works just as well for decorating as does a labor-intensive homemade batch of Royal icing. Just be sure to give yourself time to let the decorated cookies harden a bit in a cool (dog-safe) place before hanging them on your tree.

We have many rituals surrounding the decorating of the tree, one of which is the first appearance of a favorite holiday cocktail. We call it the Merry Maker, a spin on the old Waldorf-Astoria Orange Blossom. Splitting the gin and orange juice into equal parts and dispensing with the vermouth (what gin drinker, after all, isn't eager to dispense with the vermouth?), we serve it on the rocks with a dash of cinnamon and maybe a peppermint "swizzle stick." Just keep in mind that this is no time for one of those fancy floral gins—a nice London dry will do quite well. The point here is the simple conviviality of juniper and citrus, time-honored since British doctors discovered that a little sugar and lime made the quinine go down.

Holiday music has its own order of ceremonies in our house, and while *A Charlie Brown Christmas* will inevitably accompany the tree-fetching operation, the first honor of tree-decorating night always goes to Frank Sinatra. This would be my dad's doing, as it was the very record he spun when my family decorated our Christmas tree growing up, and few things can connect me to the shivery anticipation of my childhood like that first jingling of bells at the beginning of Side A. But Frank can only take us so far—it is, after all, a nine-foot tree—so as soon as the needle arm returns to its cradle we turn things over to Sufjan Stevens. His whimsical, oft-times tender, occasionally ridiculous collection of Christmas EPs will carry us right through to the star on top. And if we happen to find ourselves flagging at 11:45 over the prospect of

200 tin icicles as a finishing touch, we agree that it's a very good time to "Boogey to the Elf Dance."

At last, we are done, and turning out the other lights in the room I collapse beside Philip on the couch. The dogs, Bonnie and Luna, are asleep; Oliver the cat has made his yearly nest in a pile of tissue paper. Before my tired eyes the multitudinous lights elongate and glitter—my tree is dowered with diamonds, nay, stars! The tree's limbs are blossoming in baubles and colored glass, flowering with the beloved trinkets of a shared life, and, suddenly, the wonderful strangeness of it all gathers every Christmas I have known into a lovely whole. A tatty little cornhusk doll from my childhood rubs shoulders with the porcelain angels that belonged to my grandmother; a kindergarten-era ornament made from the cap off a can of crescent-roll dough swings alongside the exquisite etched-glass balls Philip gave me years ago. There are gilded walnuts and glittered plastic snowflakes, a hand-painted bluebird with a real feather tail and a cherubic snowman who has had his head glued back on multiple times. Only on a Christmas tree can such harmony exist, our past and our present jostled together in happy confusion, our story told back to us in tinsel and gilt like the tiers of an old-fashioned candle carousel.

I think my favorite ornament might be the tarnished blue ball, its original hanger replaced with a tattered loop of ancient yellow curling ribbon—a repair effected in my father's childhood by *his* father. A bit of Scotch-Irish frugality at the time, perhaps, but every year Daddy would lift it out of its box with a reverence which sent a cascade of happiness shimmering through my small frame.

"Ah, here's the *real* gem," he would say, slipping it over a branch near the top.

It felt like a hint and whisper of impossible things, a laughing little nudge at the limitations of the seen world. That shabby ornament was the real gem because Daddy had shown us its inherent beauty as a witness to the worth of things which love alone has made lovely.

Every Christmas tree, I think now, *every* real *Christmas tree, is an enchanted thing.*

Such a tree is a Cinderella story of coinherence, familiar yet utterly fantastical, transfigured by light and long affection into a radiance that makes the very shadows flee.

TREE-DECORATING TIPS: Philip recommends cutting at least an inch off of the bottom of the tree in addition to making vertical cuts with a saw before placing it in the stand. Also, if you don't want to make up a batch of Tree Brew, you can always pour hot water into the basin of your stand once you have the tree in place. This will prevent the sap from congealing and keep the capillaries open.

To achieve an enchantingly starry look, grasp each sizable branch as close to the trunk as possible and wrap it loosely with lights, continuing around the tree from bottom to top. Just remember not to connect more than three strands together at a time as it could be an electrical hazard.

ESPECIALLY BLESSED AND happy is he WHO FINDS A Bird's Nest IN HIS Christmas TREE

Swedish proverb

RECIPE: Gingerbread Ornaments

1 cup unsalted butter, softened
1 cup dark brown sugar
3 eggs, beaten
1½ cups molasses
6 cups flour

2 Tbsp. ground ginger
2½ tsp. salt
1½ tsp. baking soda
2 tsp. cinnamon

Thin ribbon, yarn, or embroidery floss for hangers
One 8.4-oz. can cupcake icing with decorating tips

Sift together flour, salt, soda, & spices, and set aside. In a large mixing bowl, beat the butter until light and fluffy. Add the sugar, eggs, and molasses and mix well. Add the dry ingredients to the butter mixture, mixing in 1 cup at a time until flour is thoroughly incorporated. Divide dough into two equal-sized portions and chill for at least two hours or overnight.

Preheat oven to 350° and line two baking sheets with parchment paper. Roll out dough on a floured surface to a ¼-inch thickness and cut into desired shapes. Place on prepared baking sheets, and, using the cap of a pen or an unsharpened pencil, make a hole in each cookie at least ¾" from the top.

Bake for 20-25 minutes, or until very hard and nicely browned, being careful not to overcook. Once the cookies are cool, thread a length of ribbon, yarn, or floss through each hole and knot securely. Decorate with piped icing and leave them to harden overnight before hanging on the tree.

YIELD: Makes approximately 2 dozen 6-inch ornaments. You can make the cookies larger or smaller, but the cooking time may need to be adjusted accordingly.

HOW TO POT
Paperwhites

Long-regarded as a symbol of rebirth and renewal, a pot of fragrant paperwhite narcissi is a lovely grace this time of year, and, since they require no pre-chilling, can easily be "forced" to bloom at Christmas (roughly 4-6 weeks, from planting to flowering). Order your bulbs in early autumn from a reputable supplier (see www.GladandGolden.com) and store in a dark spot with plenty of air circulation until ready to pot.

Paperwhites are so good-natured they thrive equally in gravel, sand, or soil; I prefer pea gravel so that you can easily keep an eye on the water level in the pot. To plant paperwhites, select a vessel at least 4 inches deep and wide enough to accommodate as many bulbs as you desire—paperwhites really shine en masse! Fill the vessel a little over halfway with gravel, then nestle in the bulbs, root end down. Add more gravel, just enough to cover 2/3 of each bulb, and water to the base of the bulbs. Check the water level each day, but do not allow it above the base or the bulbs will rot.

To keep your paperwhites from growing too leggy and falling over, when the shoots are 2 inches tall you can switch out plain water for a mixture of water and alcohol: 7 parts water to 1 part 80-proof whiskey or vodka. Water your paperwhites exclusively with this solution until the blooms appear. Alternatively, you can tie the leaves and stems loosely together with a length of pretty ribbon to keep your paperwhites upright.

Advent Tea

It's more of a brunch, really, though we've called it "tea" from the beginning. For one thing, we start with coffee, or perhaps steaming mugs of cardamom-laced cocoa, rich with bittersweet chocolate and heavy cream. If the Advent wreath and all its attendant solemnity the Sunday before was the threshold of the season, then this moment, standing in Laura's or Rachel's kitchen, sipping hot beverages while Loreena McKennitt wavers out the haunting strains of "The Wexford Carol" in the background, is the vestibule: a sweetly fleeting space from which the anticipation of Advent and the abundance of Christmas open before us like a house of many rooms. And though we always close such festivities with a proper round of the Blessed Stimulant, it is only after a full and hearty meal of breakfast fare has been consumed and we have retired to the fireside, where we are treated to a selection of green and black teas—or, perhaps a rooibos, if our hostess has been fortunate enough to secure a packet of "Sweet Lemon Cream." Nevertheless, though even the most informal associations could scarcely refer to an event beginning at half-past ten in the morning as a "tea"—Laura's British grandmother and my Southern one would doubtless shake their heads over such casual usage—for nearly two decades running we have been doing just that. Advent Tea it was, when, as young wives we were inspired to gather in the newborn days of the season to affirm our intentions and celebrate our shared excitement. And Advent Tea it will remain, until the last trumpet sounds or we all go to glory, world without end, Amen.

In the early years we used to talk about which crafts we were limiting ourselves to; what worked and didn't work from last year's "For Next Year" list; how to keep things simple and Christ-centered. Rachel had the details on the best price for double-faced satin ribbon and where to find "luster dust" for fruit centerpieces. I weighed in on the virtues and drawbacks of American versus English holly, while Laura revealed her secret source for vintage giftwrap (Etsy) and made sure we had our calendars synced for the Lessons and Carols service at the cathedral downtown. More than once I subjected a pile of velvet and antique lace to my friends' trusted opinions, being afflicted each November with a seasonal madness prompting me, amidst everything else, to sew a new Christmas dress. We vowed not to hurry through December; we articulated the difference between happy bustle and "huffing about." We prayed for each other and promised to hold one another accountable to our highest ideals.

Somewhere along the way, however, the light changed; the axis of the world shifted. Life made great demands of us each in turn, and sorrow began to erode some of the fixtures we all thought permanent. One morning I made the hour-long drive to Laura's while wrestling back tears that would surely ruin my makeup. Yet another negative pregnancy test had confirmed my darkest fears; infertility, it appeared, would be not just a season for me, but a way of life. My heart was so heavy when I walked in the door that I was shocked to find the whole house didn't groan under the weight of it. But I summoned up a smile and accepted my mug of cocoa, assuming an air of festivity that was nothing short of theatrical. Some wounds were too private for even the kindest of eyes.

I kept up my pretense all throughout the meal, laughing and bantering as though my only cares were those of finishing up my Christmas shopping and securing "Madonna and Child" postage stamps before they were all sold out. It was over our tea, however, with the fire hissing on Laura's hearth and the pretty paper "Twelve Ladies Dancing" garland lifting and swaying with the heat, that my resistance finally broke.

"So, what are y'all struggling with this year?" Rachel wanted to know.

It was an open question, as much of a tradition as mimosas with our meal and a pip of chocolate with our tea.

I swallowed hard, willing down the words. Yet under Rachel's friendly smile, they tumbled out.

"I'm struggling with how quiet the house is," I said softly. "Christmas always makes it harder—"

I didn't trust myself to say more. But I didn't have to—Laura gasped, and Rachel's eyes filled with tears. They understood, imaginatively if not experientially, and in an instant they entered into my pain, stepping alongside me with an empathy that seemed almost palpable. I felt my burden shift slightly, as though lifted from either side; sensed the awful isolation of sorrow collapse before such a relentless fellowship. They, too, were acquainted with grief; they knew the meaning of bad news and hopes deferred. And they loved me. In that moment, my pain was their own.

"Of course it does," Laura said gently.

"I'm so sorry," Rachel added. "I'm just so sorry."

They did not try to rationalize, mitigate, or solve my problem. They did not offer solutions (if there is one thing a woman who is struggling with infertility does not want to hear it is, "Have you considered adoption?" *Wow, thank you! Why didn't I think of that?*) They simply grieved with me. And I came away from Advent Tea that day companioned by the compassion of my friends, strengthened for the next leg of my wilderness journey, and ready to open both heart and hands to the thorny beauties of that particular holiday season. The great, two-faced lie of pain, of course, is that it is meaningless and that it is solitary. But Laura and Rachel had refuted such falsehoods with a single stroke of friendship. It was why we started meeting together in the first place, though we scarcely understood it at the time. Advent Tea is not just a tradition or a shared anticipation. It is a sacred space where we have learned to invite one another into the hope and meaning of Advent itself.

We still love all the trimmings and to-dos of the season; there is still room at our gatherings for music recommendations and movie reviews, teacher-gift quandaries and recipe tips. We still dress up, and set the table with china and damask, because in a world increasingly characterized by a lack of ceremony and the worship of convenience, we find it all the more important to honor each other and the season we love with a little extra care. This is not to say that Advent Tea is burdensome to the hostess, or that she spends her time toiling over table decorations or food; we've learned by now to keep our menus simple enough to make in our sleep—or, at the very least, mid-current in conversation. An easy-but-special main dish is usually in order, like *oeufs en cocotte* (baked eggs), redolent with garlic and herbs, accompanied by a last-minute sauté of greens brightened at the end with a burst of Meyer lemon juice. And anyone, we agree, who insists on frying bacon on top of the stove when a wire cooling rack set on a baking pan in the oven accomplishes the job virtually mess-free, is either a martyr or a lunatic. (This is not even to mention the fact that oven-cooked bacon turns out crisp and well-drained every time and you don't have to go around with your hair smelling like grease all day.) You will always find Rachel's lace cookies or Laura's grandmother's gingersnaps on our tea tray, and our playlist will always be dominated by King's College, The Waverly Consort, and John Rutter.

But every year there's a little less talk of sparkle and crafts, and a little more acknowledgement of what Christ's coming among us really means. We confess our hurts and our hopes to one another, embracing what the Orthodox Church has so aptly termed the "bright sadness" of our holy seasons. Advent, we have discovered, is precisely the place for the wounded, the weary, the question-askers, and the waiting; it is where the Now and the Not-Yet have met together and mourning and celebration have kissed one another. It is the steady advance of God's light upon our darkness, bright like a fire on the hearth, keen as kindness in the eyes of a friend.

A MENU FOR ADVENT TEA

MIMOSAS
CARDAMOM HOT CHOCOLATE
OEUFS EN COCOTTE
SAUTÉED KALE *with* MEYER LEMON
SUGAR-*and*-SPICE BACON

TEA (BLACK, GREEN,
WHITE, *or* RED)

NANNY'S GINGERSNAPS

MIMOSAS
SERVES 4

8 ounces freshly squeezed orange juice

750 ml Prosecco or dry champagne

Divide the orange juice evenly between four chilled champagne flutes. Top with Prosecco and serve immediately.

CARDAMOM HOT CHOCOLATE
SERVES 6

Cardamom pods can be found at Indian grocery stores or purchased online from bulk spice dealers. If you can't find the dried pods you can substitute up to 1 teaspoon of ground cardamom, whisking it well into the milk as it simmers. This chocolate is very rich, which is why I serve it in small "demitasse" (literally, "half cup") teacups.

12 dried cardamom pods

4 cups whole milk

5 ounces bittersweet chocolate, chopped

4 ounces semisweet chocolate, chopped

1 cup heavy cream

2 tablespoons packed brown sugar, plus more to taste

2 teaspoons Madagascar bourbon vanilla extract

Crush the cardamom pods with the butt of a knife and combine with the milk in a medium-sized saucepan. Heat cardamom and milk over low heat and simmer, without boiling, for 10 minutes. Add chocolate, heavy cream, and brown sugar, whisking until the chocolate has completely melted and the mixture is hot. Remove from heat and lift out cardamom pods with a slotted spoon. Add more sugar to taste, if needed, and stir in vanilla. Serve immediately.

OEUFS EN COCOTTE
SERVES 4

This is a simple recipe for an elegant breakfast. To prepare ahead of time, combine the herbs and cheese in a small bowl and crack the eggs into the buttered ramekins. Twenty minutes before you plan to serve them, preheat the oven and put the kettle on to boil, then bake as directed.

½ teaspoon minced fresh garlic

½ teaspoon minced fresh thyme leaves

½ teaspoon minced fresh rosemary leaves

½ teaspoon minced fresh parsley

2 tablespoons freshly grated Parmesan cheese

8 large eggs

2 tablespoons unsalted butter, at room temperature

¼ cup crème fraîche

Kosher salt

Freshly ground black pepper

Baguette or brioche for serving, sliced thin and toasted with butter

Preheat the oven to 350 degrees and place a kettle of water on to boil. Combine the garlic, thyme, rosemary, parsley, and Parmesan cheese in a small bowl and set aside.

Brush the insides of 4 6-ounce ramekins with the softened butter and carefully crack 2 eggs into each one, without breaking the yolks. Season with salt and pepper.

When the water has boiled, place the ramekins in a baking dish and transfer to the oven. Carefully pour enough boiling water into the pan to come ¾ of the way up the sides of the ramekins. Bake until whites are barely opaque, but still jiggle, 10 to 12 minutes. Carefully remove from the oven, transfer the ramekins to a baking sheet, and preheat the broiler.

Spoon 2 teaspoons crème fraîche atop each ramekin and sprinkle evenly with the garlic and herb mixture. Place under the broiler for 3 to 5 minutes, until the whites are almost cooked, rotating the pan once to ensure even cooking (keep in mind that the eggs will continue to cook after they are removed from the oven).

Allow the eggs to set for 1 minute, then serve hot with buttered toast.

SAUTÉED KALE WITH MEYER LEMON
SERVES 4

Meyer lemons are a seasonal treat available from late autumn to early spring—they are, in fact, not lemons at all, but a cross between an Asian citron and a mandarin. Characterized by smooth skin and an ambrosial flavor, they really add a bright note to any dish. If you can't find Meyer lemons you can substitute with the zest of one regular lemon, 1 teaspoon lemon juice, and 1 teaspoon orange juice.

1½ pounds fresh Tuscan kale (2–3 bunches)
2 tablespoons olive oil
2 garlic cloves, minced
Kosher salt and freshly ground black pepper
Zest and juice of 1 Meyer lemon

Wash kale well then trim by folding at the stem and cutting the leaves lengthwise. Discard stems and tear leaves into 2-inch pieces.

Bring a large pot of salted water to the boil and cook kale until just tender, 3 to 4 minutes. Drain well.

Heat the oil in a large skillet over medium-high heat and add garlic. Cook until fragrant but not brown, about 1 minute. Add the kale and lemon zest and season generously with salt and pepper. Sauté until wilted, stirring frequently, for 5 minutes. Sprinkle with lemon juice and toss to incorporate. Serve immediately.

SUGAR & SPICE BACON
SERVES 4

The bacon may take more or less than 20 minutes to crisp up, depending on your oven, but flipping each strip halfway through the cooking time will allow both sides to brown without burning the spices. Keep in mind that it will continue to harden slightly after removing from the oven, so be careful not to overcook.

4 tablespoons brown sugar

1 teaspoon chili powder

½ teaspoon ground cinnamon

8 slices thick-cut bacon (about 8 ounces)

In a small bowl, combine sugar and spices. Set aside.

Line a large, rimmed baking sheet with aluminum foil and set a wire rack on top. Arrange the bacon in a single layer on the rack and sprinkle evenly with half of the sugar and spice mixture.

Place baking sheet in a cold oven and turn up the heat to 400 degrees. Bake, rotating halfway through, for 10 minutes, then remove and flip each piece, sprinkling with the remaining sugar and spice. Bake 10 minutes more, or until bacon is brown and crisp. Remove from the oven and cool on the rack for 5 minutes, loosening with a spatula or fork. Serve warm.

NANNY'S GINGERSNAPS
YIELD: 3 DOZEN

Laura's grandmother's recipe is perfection in cookie form, with a chewy center and a crisp, sugar-dusted crust. Pairs beautifully with a cup of tea.

2 cups flour

2 teaspoons baking soda

¼ teaspoon salt

1 teaspoon ginger

1 teaspoon cinnamon

⅛ teaspoon cloves

10 tablespoons unsalted butter, softened

1 cup sugar, plus ¼ cup sugar for dipping

1 egg

⅓ cup dark molasses

Sift together flour, soda, salt, and spices in a bowl. In a separate bowl, cream butter; add 1 cup sugar and cream until fluffy. Add egg and molasses. Stir in dry ingredients. Chill 30 minutes.

Take 1 tablespoon or so of batter at a time and mold with hands into balls. Roll balls in ¼ cup sugar. Place at least 2 inches apart on an ungreased cookie sheet. Bake in preheated 350-degree oven for 13–15 minutes.

St. Nicholas Day

December 6th marks the feast day of St. Nicholas, 4th-century Bishop of Myra, famous, among other things, for his secret acts of generosity. Over three dark nights, the legend goes, Nicholas tossed a bag of gold coins through the bedroom window of the three daughters of an impoverished nobleman, ensuring the dowries that would enable them to make respectable marriages. It was only on the third night that the father of the girls caught him at his work, upon which the nobleman fell on his knees, thanking the good bishop for saving his daughters from a life of poverty and ill-repute. Though Nicholas insisted that the gifts remain anonymous, the nobleman evidently couldn't keep a secret, for the tale worked its way over continents and spun itself down through centuries, materializing, at length, into our own very modern, very American version of Santa Claus. Although parents might cherish understandable reservations about Santa, and the massive cult of materialism with which he has come to be associated, the real, historical figure of St. Nicholas gives us a refreshing counter-point to the frenzied getting and spending of the Christmas shopping scene.

So great was Nicholas's influence that medieval nuns secretly distributed baskets of food to the poor on the night of his feast, and in many European cultures legendary figures arose, typifying the saint's benevolence toward children in particular—Holland's

Sinterklaas, Austria's *der Heilige Nikolaus*, and *Saint-Nicolas* of France. In some countries, children still leave out carrots for the donkey reputed to accompany St. Nicholas on his yearly visit and place their shoes by the door to be filled with little toys and candies and homemade treats. Even our own Christmas stockings bear witness to Nicholas's gifts with pouches of foil-covered chocolate coins and crosier-shaped candy canes.

Whether or not you grew up in the tradition of St. Nicholas Day and its attendant rites and festivities, this might be a good time to sit down and contemplate the means and the method of your own gift-giving. With the ubiquitous "gift guides" of internet influencers thronging our feeds this time of year, it can be difficult to distinguish between gifts given to check someone off of your list and gifts people will actually need, use, or love (or, happily, a combination of all three). But with a little forethought, and a lot of intention, we can give without letting gifts obliterate the meaning behind it all.

To begin with, make your list carefully. This might seem obvious, but it's tempting to purchase gifts out of habit or obligation. Just because someone gave you an unexpected present last year, or because you've always bought a trinket for your first-grade best friend's second cousin doesn't mean you have to do that this year. Be honest about who is actually in your life and what you mean to each other. The names on your Christmas list are a sacred fellowship, gathered there by love and providence into a society unique to your experience. Sincerity, in gift-giving as in all things relational, is the First Rule.

Secondly, set a budget. Thirdly, stick to it. No one will benefit in any lasting way by things you will still be paying off next Christmas. Trust me on this. Give generously; give sacrificially—but don't give what you don't have. Laura Ingalls Wilder was right: it truly is the "sweet, simple things of life which are the real ones after all," and this goes for the most genuine giving as well. I refer you to the First Rule.

Finally, and perhaps most crucially of all, pray over your list. Hold each name and the face associated with it before God; see them, not only with your mind's eye, but with the eyes of your heart. What are their interests, tastes, passions, or dreams? Have they had a life-change in the past year, or a setback, or a longed-for fulfillment? I remember the year that Philip and I bought our vintage travel trailer, my mother gave us an assortment of second-hand accouterments—a Melmac cream and sugar, a colorful bridge cloth, a butter dish. I can still hear her delighted declarations of, "Airstream!" each time we opened one of the packages. Her participation in our joy was as much a gift as the presents themselves.

St. Nicholas Day can also be an opportunity to think about anonymous giving—not just to an organization (which can be great), but perhaps to someone nearer at hand: the lonely widow down the street; a family in need identified by your church; a stranger in the grocery store. I was once the recipient of a free meal in a drive-through, compliments of the person in front of me in line, and the simple kindness of the thing stayed with me for days. Following Nicholas's lead, conspire to show a little secret generosity to someone. Believe me, they won't be the only ones who are blessed.

Another way to remember St. Nicholas on his feast day is to prepare an unassuming meal in his honor—a plain, monastery-style soup, perhaps, made only slightly less ascetic by the substitution of broth for the customary water. Croutons, while certainly not essential, add layers of flavor and texture, not to mention a hint of virtuous thrift, seeing as they are traditionally made with day-old bread. Even as early in the season as December 6th, many of us might already feel bombarded by complicated recipes and rich fare, but soup is an easy way to commemorate the unpretentious generosity of this patron saint of children and fishermen, pharmacists and pawnbrokers, repentant thieves, the falsely accused, and university students—not to mention a means of getting your vegetables this time of year.

RECIPE: St. Nicholas Soup

This recipe makes a big pot of soup—I often end up freezing a jar or two to enjoy later. It can also be easily cut in half to serve a smaller number of people.

6 Tbsp. unsalted butter
3 cloves garlic, minced
2 leeks, white and light green parts only
4 good-sized carrots
6 Yukon Gold potatoes

1 pound cauliflower florets
1 small head white cabbage
2 tsp. Kosher salt
4 quarts vegetable or chicken broth
1/2 cup flat-leaf parsley, chopped

Wash, peel, and chop the vegetables. Melt the butter in a large stock pot, then add garlic, vegetables, and salt. Toss with a wooden spoon until fragrant, turn off heat, and allow to rest, covered, for 30 minutes.

Add the stock and bring to a boil. Reduce heat to medium-low and simmer, covered, for 40 minutes, stirring occasionally.

At this point all or most of the soup may be blended with either a canister or an immersion blender for a creamy texture. Season to taste with more salt, if necessary, and freshly ground black pepper. Serve hot, garnished with croutons and chopped fresh parsley.

SERVES: 6-8

RECIPE: Croutons

½ pound crusty, country-style bread,
torn into bite-sized pieces
2 garlic cloves, minced
¼ cup olive oil
Kosher salt and freshly-ground black pepper

Preheat oven to 400° and line a rimmed baking sheet with parchment paper. In a large bowl, toss together the bread, garlic, and olive oil. Season to taste with salt and pepper.

Bake, stirring occasionally, for 8-10 minutes. The croutons should be crisp on the outside and chewy in the center.

Let cool. When ready to use, they may be rewarmed in a 250° oven for 5 minutes.

SERVES: 6

ADVENT
WEEK TWO

Birds,

though you long have ceased to build,
GUARD the NEST that must be filled.
Even the hour when WINGS are frozen
GOD for fledgling time has chosen.

PEOPLE, LOOK EAST
and SING Today:

LOVE, THE bird, IS ON THE WAY.

Eleanor Farjeon, "Carol of the Advent"

Advent Rhythms

It happens every year.

During the first week of Advent, I leap joyously into a round of preparations so familiar they have become traditions in themselves. In a burst of pent-up joy I bedeck and be-ribbon, swapping out lamps and picture frames for tabletop trees and bowls of fresh greenery. The red glass lantern which hangs all the rest of the year in one of the west-facing windows has been bundled into the attic to make way for the Advent wreath, and all the Christmas mugs and bits of holiday china, brought out of hibernation from the upper kitchen cupboards, now repose, washed and ready for service, in the glass-fronted cabinets below. There is a wreath on the door and garland on the gate, and a magnificent tree sparkles from the back windows, suffusing the early winter dusk with the promise of peace within.

Alas, the appearance of peace is no guarantee of peace itself. Far too often, particularly in the early years, I have found myself careening rather breathlessly into the second week of Advent.

What? my heart cries. *The second Sunday already? How can this be? It's all going by too fast!*

One gentle check upon said heart, however, will remind me that Advent—or even time itself—is not to blame. I am the one moving too fast, gathering momentum with each loved task until I fairly topple over myself with precipitousness. I've found this muddle at play my whole life; as a small child, I used to get up in the middle of the night to dress for school, going back to bed in my clothes so that I would be ahead of the game the next morning. When Philip and I were planning our wedding at the Ruff House, I worked myself into a tearful tizzy one day over an escalating series of projects and ideas and non-optional deadlines. Seizing my "To Do" list, he edited it with loving—albeit bemused—ruthlessness.

"Slip-cover the sofa?" he asked incredulously. "What on earth does that have to do with putting on a wedding?"

Nothing, I grudgingly allowed. I simply thought it would look pretty in the otherwise bare bedroom.

"I just want to get it all done so that I can *enjoy*!"

Philip laughed outright.

"Are you enjoying this?"

I had to admit that, amidst all my enthusiasm and romantic ideals, I'd let the details siphon some of the delight out of the happiest event of my life. I was breathless, exhausted, and ready to elope. To be sure, we wanted all the details of our wedding to point, howsoever subtly, to the larger beauties of God's faithfulness and love. But it was such a relief to relinquish some of those particulars before the greater goodness of the whole; to remember that we weren't just throwing a party, we were sealing a covenant.

Just so with Christmas, and her lady-in-waiting days of Advent: even with the best intentions it's easy to misalign ourselves with the meaning amid all this much-ado. Besides, there are lists to make and presents to buy and people to feed. We feel the pull, perhaps, of multitudinous projects and invitations and possibilities; we glimpse the festive cover of a magazine in the checkout line and wonder if we oughtn't peruse its "101 Ideas for a Stress-Free Holiday," although the very thought makes our breath come a little faster. We scroll the social media feeds of friends and strangers alike with a prick of our own inadequacy: if only we had the time or the resources or the talents to make our holiday as meaningful, or as delicious, or as photogenic as theirs. And we are strained by the irony that Advent is supposed to be a reflective time; a chance to reorient ourselves and our household toward that Light whose coming has changed everything. We would love to ponder the mysteries of the Incarnation for a moment—if only we had a few more moments in the day.

"Christmas is not an emergency," my friend Laura once said with her typical sagacity.

I agree—but I'm also guilty. Much as I love all the trappings and trim, dearly as I long to lift it all in adoration and joy, I'm tempted to get so revved up with the doing that I forget how to *be*. There is a very slim margin, I realize, between happy bustle and huffing about; I need a governor on my heart to limit its speed, a wisdom not my own to sort through the onslaught of possibilities the season affords. I need, in the lovely old Quaker sense, to "center down": to silence the clamor of my own heart in order to attend to what Thomas Kelly calls the Holy Within.

It is one of the many paradoxes of the season that the very thing I often feel I don't have time for is the thing I need most of all. But, as Kelly reminds us in his kindly, yet no-nonsense essay, "The Simplification of Life," it doesn't take much time to love God. "One can have a very busy day, outwardly speaking," he writes, "and yet be steadily in the holy Presence." With a simple turning of the heart, a whispered prayer, an acknowledgement of our weakness, foolishness, and need, the riches of his guidance are at our disposal. For if there is one thing that the Incarnation affirms to me, again and again, it is that God has entered into the minutia of our lives: fully human, Jesus knows what it means to feel tired, or hungry, or pressed with endless demands; fully God, he delights to bring his wisdom and peace down into our ordinary quandaries and cares.

By the second week of Advent, I'm often in need of a gentle recalibration of my inner compass. Between the first sweet flurry of preparation and all the expected guests and festivities to come, now is the perfect time to pause and put a finger on the pulse of my attitudes. How is it with my soul? What hopes am I holding before the Lord for this particular holiday season? How can I love my loved ones in the ways that will mean the most to them?

One of the sturdiest helps I have found to keep my heart and mind tethered to essential things is the practice of set prayer. Praying the hours—far from a rote exercise or, worse yet, a stand-in for real intimacy with God—holds me in a habit of prayer whether I happen to "feel" like praying or not. The Benedictine model calls for seven separate hours of prayer throughout the day and night, but for years I have been following a significantly more approachable lay version, compiled by Phyllis Tickle in *The Divine Hours*. Broken into Morning and Midday Prayer, Vespers, and Compline, these manuals companion me throughout the year, providing daily liturgies which are closely aligned with that of *The Book of Common Prayer*. But during Advent this ritual becomes doubly precious. It only takes five minutes to read through each allotment, but it is a habit that unfailingly catches me when I might otherwise feel too distracted or busy (or sleepy!) to pray. And while I am not typically among the earliest birds of the morning, during Advent I spring out of bed while it is yet dark in order to see the dawn emerge from the oaks and beeches of our wooded valley, drawing rainbow-tinted mists from the damp earth and spilling over the treetops like a blessing tipped from a golden bowl. With a candle or two on the low table beside my favorite chair, and my fingers wrapped around a mug of cinnamon-laced coffee, I watch for that light, flowering out beyond my shining Christmas tree. It is a moment that feels like prayer itself, mantling the world with the mercies of God.

In the late afternoons, I watch the light go with banners of glory over the western ridge. Often I will light the tapers on the Advent wreath for this golden hour, especially during the second week when pausing is such an essential pattern to establish for the busier days ahead. A cup of tea is most welcome now; perhaps a small sampling of Christmas cookies, gleaned from the day's industry in the kitchen. Sometimes I might read a poem, or glance dreamily through an old and much-loved *Victoria* magazine. But always there is my prayer book at hand. I may skip Vespers more often than I like to admit all the rest of the year, but I never miss it during Advent. This is my version of that "good portion" (Luke 10:42) that Jesus pointed out to Mary and Martha, my own sacred core of being amidst all the happy doing.

A small rhythm, weaving my days into a larger order of quiet hope and confident expectation.

A Pleasing Aroma

The year I was eight my father was a candidate in a special election. Voting day was scheduled—rather Scrooge-ishly, in my opinion—just a few days before Christmas, and instead of making cookies and wrapping presents, my mother spent her waking hours campaigning with Daddy. It was a demanding time, and she was glad, I know, to be at her husband's side, even in what proved to be a losing battle. But it was hard to be so estranged from the sweet work of shaping a memorable holiday for her young family. My parents were not professing Christians at the time; the unexpected loss of this election, would, in fact, be the blow which dismantled their self-reliance and revealed their desperate need for God's grace. Even then, however, Mama and Daddy both knew there was far more to Christmas than a date on the calendar or an ocean of wrapping paper on the living room floor. They longed to make it meaningful for us. But that year there just wasn't time.

After the campaign commenced, Mama hired a babysitter for my siblings and me. Judy was a retiree who picked us up from school, prepped dinner, and had us ready for bed by the time our parents got home at the end of each long day. As a child, I knew little to nothing about where Judy came from, or what factors and forces went into the shaping of her story. I only knew that she was a kind and calming presence in an otherwise disorienting season. Judy made little Christmas cakes for our dolls and helped us add festive touches of greenery around the house. Most memorably, she always had an aromatic boil going on the back burner of the stove: a simple concoction of water, spices, and fruit that filled our home with the heart-achingly familiar scents of Christmas. It only took a moment to slice an orange or two, toss in a cinnamon stick and a pinch of cloves. But in that simple act, Judy gathered this holiday into happier ones, both past and future. I still remember the bright alchemy of citrus and spice mingling amid the steam and stabbing my young heart with inarticulable delight. Nothing else in my life was the same that year, but Judy's little bubbling pot told me that Christmas was coming anyway. It could not be forestalled by circumstances or confined to appearances—Christmas simply was. And sometimes the simpler the better.

I can only imagine what it meant to my mother to walk into a house redolent with holiday warmth when she was too weary and burdened to make it so herself. But I know what it meant to me: scarcely a day goes by now, from Advent Sunday to Epiphany, that I don't have one of Judy's ambrosial concoctions simmering away on the back burner of my stove, suffusing my home with the memory-laden now of Christmas.

HOW TO MAKE A
Christmas Simmer Pot

To make a fragrant simmer pot, fill a saucepan about ⅔ full of water and add a couple of sliced oranges, or a combination of oranges and lemons. With regard to spice, allow both affection and personal preference to lead the way. To the conventional cinnamon sticks (2–3) and whole cloves (6–7), try adding a dozen or so cardamom pods, crushed with the butt of a knife, or half a dozen star anise. Bay leaves will lend a piquant touch, as will a small handful of pink peppercorn berries. And for a different take altogether, combine a tablespoon of vanilla extract with sliced grapefruit, oranges, and a couple of fresh rosemary sprigs. Bring it to a boil, then reduce to the lowest possible simmer, keeping a close watch on the water level in the pot and topping it off as necessary. Less expensive—and far-less allergy-inducing—than a candle, a fragrant boil will keep for several days in a covered saucepan and can be uncovered and reheated at will.

POSSIBLE INGREDIENTS:
Oranges
Lemons
Cinnamon sticks
Whole cloves
Cardamom pods
Star anise
Bay leaves
Pink peppercorn berries
Vanilla extract
Grapefruit
Rosemary sprigs

LORD JESUS, MASTER OF BOTH THE LIGHT AND THE DARKNESS, send your HOLY SPIRIT upon our PREPARATIONS FOR Christmas. WE WHO HAVE SO MUCH TO DO seek QUIET places to hear your voice each day. We who are anxious about many things look forward to your COMING among us. We who are blessed in so many ways long for the complete JOY of your KINGDOM. We whose hearts are heavy seek the joy of your Presence.

WE ARE YOUR PEOPLE, WALKING IN DARKNESS, YET SEEKING THE LIGHT.

TO YOU we say, "COME LORD JESUS!"

HENRI NOUWEN

St. Lucy's Day

Everything was going according to plan.

At fourteen years old, I felt quite the mistress of the occasion. My family was waiting obediently in the living room and the tea tray before me was laid with Christmas mugs, festive napkins, and a plate of warm cinnamon rolls. As if on cue, the kettle on the stove gave a sputter then broke into a happy wail. I portioned the water carefully among the waiting mugs, whisked in the Swiss Miss, and whipped it to a chocolatey froth. Then I considered the marshmallows. They weren't quite authentic, of course, but neither were the canned rolls I had turned to in my ignorance of yeast dough and its mysterious ways. Besides, my siblings would demand marshmallows, which would send me back to the kitchen in a huff and ruin the effect of my resplendent entrance.

Earlier that week my younger sister had given us a demure presentation on Christmas traditions in Germany—a topic upon which we all felt her more than qualified to speak, owing to the fact of her best friend's grandmother being of almost direct German descent. Liz explained the history of the Christmas tree and treated us to *pfeffernüsse*, compliments of the German grandmother. A few days later, under cover of an early winter nightfall, my eight-year-old brother led the entire family across the yard and up the slope at the back of our house to a cramped little dogwood tree fighting for life under a canopy of magnolias.

"My country is England," he announced, lifting the lantern he bore so that its light flickered puckishly over his face. "And they do this thing where they go around in the dark singing about a bowl of cider. And then they say a prayer for the apple trees and dump the cider on the ground."

A rather imaginative conflation of pagan and pious ceremony to be sure but closer, perhaps, to the actual Anglo-Saxon mélange of pre- and post-Christian custom than any of us may have imagined. Mama glanced down at the steaming pot of apple cider she had been instructed to provide for the occasion.

"We don't have any apple trees," Zach went on, gazing up into the twisted boughs, "but this kinda looks like one."

In the end, Liz and I led the family in a rousing rendition of "Here We Come A-Wassailing," and we all had a mug of hot cider, Mama having convinced Zach that a small cup would suffice for the tree. At Zach's request, Daddy said the prayer.

"Dear God," Daddy began, with unflinching solemnity, "we ask your blessing upon this here tree, and pray that it might bear, if not apples, then a veritable fecundity of dogwood berries."

The presentations had been my idea. We had just started homeschooling that fall, and while my exhausted mother had been trying to figure out how to manage Christmas on top of teaching three grades at once, I had been busy contemplating just how I might contrive to be a Lucia Queen—with the most possible validity, of course, and the least possible resistance from my family. I had read about the custom of Saint Lucia in Jennie Lindquist's enchanting book *The Little Silver House* wherein Swedish families were roused before dawn on the morning of December 13th by a version of Lucia herself bearing a tray of coffee and sweet saffron buns. Lucy always wore white to symbolize her purity and a red sash to commemorate her martyrdom. Most arresting, however, was her crown of evergreens adorned with real lighted candles. I had a weakness for candles, not to mention botanical headpieces of any description. And while in Lindquist's version it was the woman of the home who performed the charming rite, I knew from intimate acquaintance with the American Girls Collection (my sister being the proud owner of a Kirsten doll) that custom typically bestowed such a coveted role upon the eldest daughter.

As you can probably imagine by now, I was never content merely to read of something that captivated my fancy; my instinct was to give it form and substance amid the more prosaic realities of my late-20th century suburban life. Accordingly, I championed the Christmas projects, in which my siblings and I would each choose a country and invite the rest of the family into the tastes and traditions of faraway places. The scheme suited everyone: Mama was relieved of a bit of lesson planning; Liz, though miffed I had beaten her to Sweden (she was, after all, the one with the Kirsten doll), started dreaming of German peasant dress; Zach was game. And I? I was a Lucia Queen in the making.

The details of our individual presentations were desperately secret. Mama, I knew, had pretended not to notice when I slipped her ivory satin, flannel-lined nightgown from the wash, but the ruffled lace neckline was just too fetching not to hazard the attempt. Of the carefully wrought crown, however, no one

had the least idea. I had fashioned it with care, seizing upon a shower of catbrier vines tumbling from the mulberry tree outside my bedroom window and trimming it out with ribbon, greens, and the requisite tapers wedged firmly amid the tendrils and thorns.

And now, at last, its moment had come. I touched a match to each of the four candles and lifted it carefully onto my head, settling it firmly so that the stiff briers caught the fine strands of my hair. The candles themselves were scarcely more than nubs—we kept a drawer in the sideboard devoted to those too short for extended use and too long for the trashcan, for no wax light in our house ever departed this life as anything less than a puddle of paraffin and an exhausted wick. They were slightly less than queenly but a necessary compromise. I had sailed, perhaps, too close to the wind by absconding with that nightgown. There was no way Mama would have failed to miss four of her prized 12-inch tapers.

Straightening my red satin sash, I picked up my tray and started for the living room. The Lucia Queen, as I knew, was wont to herald her coming with a song, illumining the darkness with music as well as light. I didn't know the tune of the standard Swedish carol, so I selected one of my favorites and started to sing.

Oh little town of Bethlehem, how still we see thee lie!

I processed slowly, as much to keep the candles from guttering as for solemnity's sake. Nevertheless, just as I stepped into the living room a trickle of hot wax seared my scalp. An unlooked-for development but a surmountable one. Surely, I was not the first Lucia Queen to meet such a challenge, and I doubted I would be the last. Smiling upon my astonished family, I continued to sing, distributing my treats and wincing as another drip landed above my left temple.

The effect was gratifying to say the least: Liz's eyes were round, and Zach's mouth hung open. Mama, on the other hand, was stupefied.

"Um, sweet girl—," she managed to say.

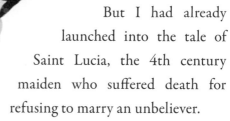

But I had already launched into the tale of Saint Lucia, the 4th century maiden who suffered death for refusing to marry an unbeliever.

"Her name means 'light,'" I told them, "and—*ouch*!" A cavalcade of drops spattered the back of my head. This pain did not subside as the others had done, for one of the little thorns was pressing firmly into my skin.

"Why don't we go ahead and blow out the candles," Mama said with a pained smile. "Then you can tell us all about Saint Lucia."

I winced again. One quick glance in the big pier mirror hanging over the couch told me that the candles had all but burned down to nothing, and I consented to their extinguishing. It was an inglorious end to my short-lived Lucian career. As I reached to lift off the crown, however, the situation deteriorated: it was stuck fast, pinned to my head with thorns and melted wax.

Mama was at my side in an instant, prying gently to the tune of my anguished yelps. The dog barked, and Liz hovered, biting her lip in consternation. Only Zach was unperturbed; with a staccato burst of laughter he helped himself to another cinnamon roll and leaned back to enjoy the show.

The crown would have to be cut to pieces. And I would spend the rest of the morning leaning over the kitchen sink under a faucet of hot water, picking wax from my hair and reflecting on the fact that life was generally more prose than poetry. But the poetry—ah, that made it all worthwhile.

The original Lucia, of course, was saintlier than my imperfect rendering of her. Legend purports that during the Diocletian Persecution she visited the Christians hiding in the catacombs of Rome, wearing a candlelit wreath which left her hands free to bear food on a tray. After suffering martyrdom at the hands of the governor of Syracuse, the Church venerated her as a "bringer of light," instituting her feast day to coincide with the pre-Gregorian Winter Solstice of December 13th. In Scandinavian countries, especially, with their long winters and seemingly endless dark, Lucy is celebrated as a promise, not only of returning light, but of the true Light that, St. John tells us, "gives light to everyone."

Even if you don't live in a place that observes it as a holiday, Lucy's Saint Day can be a simple and cheerful affair. Put out a few extra candles; surprise someone you love with coffee or hot chocolate in bed; think of ways you might bring a little light and beauty into the life of a neighbor or a friend. A warm plate of Lucia buns, endearingly S-shaped and studded with currants or raisins, is a welcome treat on this day. Soft, plump, delicately spiced and slightly sweet, they are the bun version of a grandmotherly hug—the kind you melt into and feel suddenly as safe and as happy as a little child. They are also a forgiving introduction to yeast breads if you've never tried your hand at one. Whether borne on a tray, served over tea, or carried next door with a packet of cocoa, they are unpretentiously special and unapologetically homey–not to mention safer than a headfull of lighted candles.

RECIPE: *Lucia Buns*

These buns are flavorful without being overly sweet. If you can't find dried currants, you can substitute raisins.

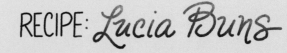

1½ Tbsp. active dry yeast
1 tsp. fine sea salt
1 tsp. ground cardamom
⅓ cup granulated sugar
4-4½ cups sifted all-purpose flour
1¼ cup whole milk
8 Tbsp. unsalted butter, softened

1 egg
Cooking spray
Dried currants

1 egg white, slightly beaten
Coarse white sugar crystals for dusting

In the bowl of a stand mixer fitted with a paddle attachment (or in a large mixing bowl), combine the yeast, salt, cardamom, granulated sugar, and 1½ cups flour. Whisk well and set aside.

In a medium saucepan over low heat, gently warm milk and butter until the butter is melted and mixture begins to steam – 120 degrees. Be careful not to let the milk and butter get too hot, or this will kill the yeast.

With stand mixer (or handheld mixer) at low speed, slowly beat milk mixture into flour mixture until fully blended. Increase to medium and beat for 2 minutes. Add egg and 1 cup flour and beat for 2 minutes more.

Stir in remaining flour, ½ cup at a time, until dough is soft and only slightly sticky. Turn out the dough onto a lightly floured board and knead until smooth and elastic, no more than 5 minutes.

Coat a large bowl with cooking spray and place dough in the bowl, turning it over so that it is greased on all sides. Cover with a clean tea towel and place in a warm spot, away from all drafts, until doubled in size, 45 minutes to an hour. When dough has risen, punch it down and divide in half. Cover with the tea towel and let it rest for 10 minutes.

Preheat oven to 400°. Divide each half of dough into 16 equally sized pieces, 32 pieces in all. On a lightly floured board, roll each piece into a 10-inch rope. To form the rolls, hold 2 ropes together and coil the ends back to form an "S" shape. Pinch ends slightly to seal and repeat with remaining ropes, placing them 2 inches apart on a parchment-lined baking sheet. Press a dried currant into the center of each coil and cover with a tea towel. Let buns rise in a warm place until doubled, about 40-45 minutes.

Before baking, gently brush each bun with egg white and sprinkle with coarse sugar. Bake 10-12 minutes, or until buns are golden brown and have a hollow sound when lightly tapped. Remove from baking sheets and allow to cool on wire racks.

MAKES 16 BUNS

Cookies in Company

The dough was stiff and cold as marble as I thumped it out on the counter. *Just like me*, I thought, breaking the lump in two and rolling one of the halves back into a round. Outwardly I was serene. The kitchen around me was quiet and neat, fragrant with the golden aromas of vanilla and nutmeg, and the long dining table in the next room boasted an array of cookies, many and varied enough to warm the most seasoned homemaker's heart. Inwardly, however, I was frozen, ice-bound in longing and worn-out hopes. I did not want quiet and neat. I wanted fuss and bother and mess; I wanted sticky fingers and freckled, flour-dusted noses and small hands patting out the dough into imperfect shapes. I wanted to tie an old hostess apron about a tiny form and pull a kitchen stool up to the counter beside me as my mother had once done with me. I wanted, in other words, to know the blessed inefficiency and unholy mess that is cooking with little children. *My* children.

I floured the surface and applied Philip's grandmother's rolling pin to the dough with a firm hand. For six Christmases I had stood in this same kitchen, rolling out these same cookies with the same daydream haunting my heart and mind. In the early days it had felt sweet and faintly near at hand, for it is always safe to dream of things over which no shadow of forestallment has fallen. As the years gathered, however, the desire began to constrict somewhat, to solidify into desperation and tighten its hold. This morning it was choking me.

I thought of the long-ago fun my siblings and I had known, making cookies together in Mama's avocado green and mustard yellow kitchen. I thought of my friends who had little ones underfoot in kitchens of their own, and my heart lurched with envy and wild yearning, like a frenzied bird trapped in a windowless room. I knew that motherhood would effectively abolish the quiet I generally loved about the Ruff House. Her tidy rooms would see smashed china and runny noses and unsanctioned wall art; her peace would be broken by cries of anguish or excitement or fear, and her long wooden hallways would rumble with the thunder of small feet. And the Ruff House, I sensed, wanted it all as badly as I did.

Maybe next year.

It was the refrain my tired heart had learned to incant. Maybe next year this ache would be healed and this void filled; maybe new life would swell within me like the promise of spring. Perhaps—I blushed a bit at the audacity of the thing—a little one might sleep in a bassinet near at hand while I worked. My eyes darted instinctively toward the corner of the room where such a mirage might materialize, and the image suddenly blurred and slipped away. I wiped my eyes, took a deep breath, and returned to my dough. Sugar cookies were the hardest of all because they were my favorite, and because they were so inextricably linked with memories of childhood—memories I longed to share. I pressed an aluminum reindeer into the cool surface and gently tapped it out onto a parchment-lined baking sheet with a surge of self-pity. Maybe God would answer my prayers. Maybe this time next year the Ruff House wouldn't be so empty.

One year later both scene and circumstance were much the same, but the house was far from empty. My friend Jenijoy had filled it with her bright, endearing brand of chitchat from the moment she walked in the door. JJ possessed a wealth of knowledge and an exquisite vocabulary, and her conversation both delighted and enthralled me.

Already we had covered the topics of natural skincare, homeopathic remedies for dogs, removing stains from linen, principles of Japanese flower arranging, and proper protein intake, all while rolling, baking, cooling, and packing dozens of homemade cookies. Earlier that week she had offered to come and help me bake, and while—daydreams notwithstanding—my general rule in the kitchen is "she travels fastest who travels alone," I had accepted her offer with a slight inward tint of benevolence. JJ's kitchen was under construction that year and holiday baking was out of the question. Besides, she was always game to come and help me prepare for the holidays, be it weaving garland for the stairs from tree-lot clippings or staying late to help wash up after our Christmas party. Sacrificing a little solitude was the least I could do for so steadfast a friend.

It did not take long, however, to realize that Jenijoy had brought all the benevolence. Her cheerful presence banished the gloom which was becoming dangerously associated with my most sacred holiday traditions. Without even trying she made me forget myself, which is, after all, the most reliable tenet of true happiness. At the end of the day, we had piles of cookies safely stashed in plastic bags and ready for the freezer. And I had a much merrier state of mind. With joy I mounded a plate of gingerbread, snowball, sugar, and mince pie cookies for Jenijoy to take home—it was, after all, the least I could do.

The following year I was more proactive: I invited not only Jenijoy but my sister-in-law, Edie, and my as-good-as-a-little-sister, Griffin. Once more my kitchen was a scene of happy industry, but the cheer was trebled by Griffin's humor and Edie's gentle smile. Again and again the kettle sang as cup after cup of strong, black tea—"chatterbroth," JJ called it—was poured out into waiting Blue Willow cups. We bustled about, cutting and decorating, dividing our spoils among the wall oven, the range, and the warming drawer on its highest setting. Edie pressed candied cherries into hazelnut-studded rounds while Griffin adorned fluted circles of dough with teaspoons of mincemeat. Jenijoy, having removed the last pan of snowball cookies and set them in the dining room to cool, betook herself to rolling peanut butter balls for chocolate-dipped buckeyes. I unwrapped a packet of sugar-cookie dough and set it gently on the table before me.

The kitchen was an absolute mess. My checkerboard floor was gritty with sugar and cookie crumbs, and the oak tabletop was a jumble of canisters, cutters, rolling pins and raisins. The sink brimmed with baking sheets and mixing bowls, wooden spoons and spatulas, and the countertops bore a light dusting of flour. My friends were all chatting companionably and Bing Crosby crooned "I'll be Home for Christmas" in the background. I smiled. The bright sadness was always there, haunting the shadows of life, permeating our darkness with inextinguishable light. But moments like this made it so real. Every woman in that room was waiting for something, some holy desire which enlivened her at times and likely stabbed at others. It would be impossible, I thought, to assemble a roomful of people of which it could be said otherwise, for while some longings have a season, the nature of longing itself is universal. God has written everlastingness into our DNA; these time-bound hearts of ours were made to live forever, and when we cease to yearn and dream and ache and aspire, we cease to catch that soft, sweet song haunting the borders of life, subtly, persistently, ardently calling us home.

These friends of mine had borne more than cheer that day; in their presence and their mien they brought me word of the goodness of God. We had tasted it together in cookies and tea and laughter and Christmas music; each of them would carry plates and baskets of it that night to roommates, parents, husbands—with good measure, pressed down and shaken and running over to share. The dry cleaner would savor a hint of that sweetness, the neighbors, the vet, the loved one longing for a memory in the shape of a prancing reindeer or a tiny mince pie. The ridiculous plentitude of the thing bordered on hilarity. But to imagine that substances so humble as candied cherries and colored sugar were incapable of bearing such grace would be to stop one's ears and cover one's eyes to the rampant mercies with which our lives thronged.

WEEK TWO

I had wanted my kitchen to be full. I wanted to be defined by love, not lack. But I thought I knew what that looked like. How easy it is to feel lonely in our longings, to live toward the imagined space of how we want things to be, rather than find our place in the sacredness of how they are. It is easy to isolate, nursing our need and throwing up private defenses against the vulnerabilities which might shatter us at any moment. It is easy to put off giving until we ourselves are filled.

Easier still, I've found, is to let people into the life we already have, into our messy kitchens and our bruised hearts and our outlandish hope that it all really matters. All God asks of us is the loaves and fishes of our ordinary days, the tea and the cookies and the kinship upon which both we and our guests might feast and be satisfied. The love that "came down at Christmas," in Christina Rossetti's phrase, is no cool, detached condescension or untouchable aura, but a strong, lively, practical affection which incarnates itself among us in the most quotidian—and sometimes, the tastiest—ways.

A MENU FOR

Cookies
—IN—
Company

CHRISTMAS NUT COOKIES
with CANDIED CHERRIES
MINCE PIE COOKIES
SUGAR COOKIES
GINGERBREAD COOKIES
SNOWBALL COOKIES
GRIFFIN'S MACAROONS
RUBY THUMBPRINTS

CHRISTMAS NUT COOKIES
Makes 6 dozen

I love the way the toasted nuts elevate the taste and texture of this recipe. You can dispense with the candied cherries if you're not a fan, but I think they add a festive note of Christmas color, not to mention a pop of sweetness.

> Christmas Nut Cookie dough (see page 16)
> Unbleached parchment paper
> All-purpose flour for dusting
> 2-inch round biscuit or cookie cutter
> Candied cherries (see below)
> Granulated sugar

Preheat the oven to 350 degrees. Cut the parchment to fit two large baking sheets and set aside.

On a lightly floured board, roll the dough to ¼ inch thick. Cut and place the cookies on the parchment-lined sheets and top each with half a candied cherry. Dust with sugar and bake for 10–12 minutes, until lightly browned. Cool on wire racks.

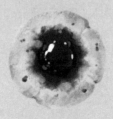

CANDIED CHERRIES

MAKES ABOUT ¾ CUP

A candy thermometer is a must for this recipe, as is the cooking time. Depending upon your cooktop (gas, electric, induction) you may need to nudge the heat up and down a bit to keep the temperature rising steadily but not too fast. These also make a fun garnish for holiday cocktails!

1 10-ounce jar maraschino cherries, de-stemmed
¾ cup sugar
Candy thermometer
Unbleached parchment paper

Spread a baking sheet with parchment paper and set aside.

Drain the cherries in a colander, reserving ¼ cup of the juice. Combine the reserved juice and the sugar in a medium saucepan and cook slowly over medium-low heat until sugar is almost completely dissolved, about 2–3 minutes.

Add the cherries and bring to a boil, then cover and reduce heat to the lowest simmer. Cook on low, stirring gently every 10 minutes until the mixture reaches 235 degrees and the cherries are firm when touched with a spoon, about 45–55 minutes. Remove from heat; uncover the pan and allow the cherries to cool to room temperature.

When cool, lift the cherries from the pot with a slotted spoon and transfer to the parchment-lined baking sheet. At this point the cherries can be used immediately, or they can be stored in an airtight container in the refrigerator for up to 6 months.

WEEK TWO

MINCE PIE COOKIES

Makes 3 dozen

Tasha Tudor has had a profound influence upon my sensibilities. I love her integration of art and life, her cheerful determination to live in the era of her choice (the 1830s), her passion for Christmas. I also love a lot of her recipes, including this one, which has been adapted from her original "receipt" of the same name. According to Tasha, these cookies are "a great favorite with the gentlemen." I have found, however, that they are also a great favorite with anyone who tastes them, even those who insist they don't like mincemeat! Prepared mincemeat is increasingly difficult to find on this side of the Pond, so be sure to order in advance from Amazon or another online source.

Sugar Cookie dough (see page 15)
Unbleached parchment paper
All-purpose flour for dusting
2-inch round biscuit or cookie cutter
1 27-ounce jar prepared mincemeat
Granulated sugar
Ground nutmeg

Preheat the oven to 350 degrees. Cut the parchment to fit 2 large baking sheets and set aside.

Roll out the dough on a lightly floured surface to ⅛ inch thick and cut two rounds for each cookie. Place one layer of rounds on the baking sheets, 2 inches apart, and spoon a scant teaspoon of mincemeat into the center of each. Top each cookie with the remaining rounds and crimp the edges to seal with the tines of a fork that has been dipped in flour. Prick the tops with the fork and dust lightly with sugar and nutmeg.

Bake for 12–15 minutes, until the edges are golden brown, and cool on wire racks. Be sure to store them in a tin of their own, as the mincemeat will make other cookies soft.

SUGAR COOKIES
MAKES 6 DOZEN

Of all the treats I bake at Christmas, these simple sugar cookies are my favorite. When I lost my collection of cookie cutters in the house fire, my friend April sent me a lovely batch of new ones, which speaks to how well she knows me and how much the material objects of our lives bear witness to intangible substance. Now April's cookie cutters mingle with the ones I used as a child in a little personal tribute to my story, which has been threaded with mercies great and small.

Sugar Cookie dough (see page 15)
Unbleached parchment paper
All-purpose flour for dusting
Colored sugar for decorating (see next page)

Preheat the oven to 350 degrees and line 2 baking sheets with parchment paper. Roll out dough on a lightly floured board to ¼ inch thickness and cut into desired shapes. Sprinkle prodigiously with colored sugar, then bake for 10–12 minutes until lightly browned.

COLORED SUGAR

MAKES ½ CUP

½ cup sugar
7–8 drops plant-based food coloring

Place the sugar in a small jar with a tight-fitting lid and add the food coloring, one drop at a time. Cover and shake vigorously. Adjust coloring as desired and store, tightly closed, for up to 3 months.

GINGERBREAD COOKIES

MAKES 3 DOZEN

About as old-fashioned as it gets, I make gingerbread men for the children, and I make hearts, stars, and diamonds to go with my afternoon tea.

Gingerbread Cookie dough (see page 16)
Unbleached parchment paper
All-purpose flour for dusting
Raisins or sweetened, dried cranberries (or a combination of both)

Preheat the oven to 375 degrees and line 2 baking sheets with parchment paper. Roll out dough on a lightly floured board to ¼ inch thickness and cut into desired shapes. Decorate before baking with raisins or sweetened, dried cranberries pressed firmly into the dough. Bake 1 inch apart for 10–12 minutes and cool on wire racks.

SNOWBALL COOKIES

MAKES 8 DOZEN

I like to store these with a little extra powdered sugar in the tin so that I can give them another quick toss before setting them out on a tray or packaging them up to give as gifts.

Snowball Cookie dough (see page 17)
Unbleached parchment paper
1 pound powdered sugar

Preheat the oven to 300 degrees and line a baking sheet with parchment paper. Roll the dough into 1 ½-inch balls and bake 1 inch apart for 25–30 minutes until the bottoms are just beginning to brown. Cool for 10 minutes before rolling in powdered sugar.

GRIFFIN'S MACAROONS

MAKES 3 DOZEN

My friend Griffin is a marvelous cook and these quick, candy-like cookies are a favorite of hers. Sometimes she dips them in chocolate for an extra bit of decadence. They also lend themselves to a cup-for-cup gluten-free flour, if need be. Store in the refrigerator for up to two weeks.

1 14-ounce package sweetened shredded coconut
⅔ cup sugar
6 tablespoons flour
¼ teaspoon salt

4 egg whites, lightly beaten
1 teaspoon almond extract
½ teaspoon Madagascar bourbon vanilla extract
12 ounces semi-sweet chocolate chips (optional)

Preheat the oven to 325 degrees. Grease and lightly flour two large baking sheets.

In a large bowl combine coconut, sugar, flour, and salt; mix well. Add the egg whites, almond extract, and vanilla and stir until well-blended.

Drop cookies by the tablespoonful onto the prepared sheets in small mounds, 2 inches apart, and bake for 20–25 minutes, or until the edges are golden brown. Remove from the baking sheets and place on wire racks to cool.

If you plan to dip them in chocolate, allow the macaroons to cool completely, then melt the chocolate slowly in a microwave-safe bowl, pausing to stir every 30-40 seconds. Dip half of each macaroon into the chocolate, then set on a sheet of waxed paper to harden. These cookies freeze well, but if you decide to do so it needs to be before the chocolate step.

RUBY THUMBPRINTS
MAKES 6 DOZEN

These cookies will seem soft when you take them out of the oven, but they will firm up as they cool. Depending upon the size of your thumb and the depth of your impressions you may want to experiment a bit with the amount of jelly you use to make sure it doesn't spill over the sides of your cookies as they bake.

Unbleached parchment paper

1 pound (4 sticks) unsalted butter, softened

1 cup sugar

½ teaspoon salt

4 egg yolks, beaten

4 cups flour, sifted

1 teaspoon almond extract

1 10-ounce jar red currant jelly

Preheat the oven to 350 degrees. Line two baking sheets with parchment paper and set aside.

In a large mixing bowl (or a stand mixer fitted with the paddle attachment), combine the butter, sugar, salt, egg yolks, flour, and almond extract.

Roll the dough into 1-inch balls and place 2 inches apart on the parchment-lined baking sheets. Make a deep impression in each ball with your thumb and fill with ¼–½ teaspoon of red currant jelly.

Bake for 10–15 minutes, until lightly browned. Remove from pan and cool on wire racks.

NOTE: *All of these recipes can be frozen after baking as well. Simply arrange them in a single layer (or slightly overlapping) in gallon-sized, labeled freezer bags and freeze for up to 8 weeks.*

WEEK TWO

THE TIME OF **BUSINESS** *does not with me differ from* THE TIME OF **PRAYER** AND IN THE *NOISE* AND *CLATTER* of my KITCHEN, *while* SEVERAL PERSONS *are at the* SAME TIME *calling for* DIFFERENT THINGS, I POSSESS GOD *in as* great TRANQUILITY *as if I were* UPON MY KNEES AT THE *blessed* SACRAMENT

BROTHER LAWRENCE

Candy-Making

If a day's cookie-making among friends is a happy melee of rolling, sprinkling, baking, and cooling—not to mention unflagging conversation and laughter—I would like you to imagine the almost ecclesial quiet of another morning. It is the same week, the same kitchen. The same sink full of dishes and the same oaken table cluttered with notebooks, cookery books, and the accouterments of tea. A fire capers on the hearth now, and a cat has rolled itself into a tight ball of contentment on a chair drawn close to the warmth. There may be a touch of frost rounding the corners of the windows; there will most certainly be a glimpse of clear blue sky springing serenely over the tree-line to the west.

Earlier that morning I will have called my friend Rachel with a yearly, if seemingly arbitrary question: *How is your hair today?* But there is nothing arbitrary about her reply. If she answers, as she has done on this day, that her soft brown tresses are rather static-y and flyaway, I will be found, as I am now, standing at the stove, presiding over a pot of bubbling sweetness like a domestic priestess of butter and sugar and cream. If, on the other hand, her elegant bob is more manageable and will hold a curl, then the gingercake caramels will just have to wait for another—and drier—day.

In much the way our foremothers read the natural world for tidings of frost or fine weather, I have learned to trust the barometer of Rachel's hair more than the forecast or even the relative humidity—always a force to be calculated upon in the Deep South. Our humidity down here, as another friend is wont to say, makes our skin soft and our hair curl. But it is no friend to homemade candy. Cookies can be made any day of the week; most recipes—with a very few notable exceptions, of course, like tuiles or meringues—care not for what's happening in the world beyond their oven. They only want a warm place to crisp up and a safe place to cool off.

Candy, on the other hand, is more sophisticated. It is mystical, enigmatic, deceptively complicated and surprisingly simple. The flexibility required, the moment's-notice nature of its prime conditions, the attention it demands, only add to its charms in my estimation. As such, any day I deem worthy of the effort receives half-holiday treatment at the least. This is both extravagant and indulgent and entirely appropriate to the magnificent homeliness of homemade candy.

Candy-making is, for me at least, a sweetly solitary affair. It is an event to which I am keenly present, wherein hand, eye, and heart are linked in a fellowship of loving concern. I do not multitask when making candy; there is no aggregate clamoring for my attention, no disgruntled voice whispering in my ear that I ought to be more efficient, more productive, more *more*. Reducing myself to a single thing has enlarged me to stand up to the bullies. Let the to-do list queue up outside the door of my mind, I declare, with a swirl of a wooden spoon, and let the ought-tos wait for another day. Somehow, the act of giving myself singly to a single act has restored time itself to its timely right. I clip a candy thermometer to the side of the pot and wait.

Time, of course, is not the only thing. Any seasoned home confectioner will tell you that it really doesn't take much time to whip up a batch of fudge or bring a pot of butter and sugar to the hard crack stage of English toffee. The real commitment, in most cases, lies in the not-so-patient wait for the candy to solidify to its final state—anywhere from a few hours to overnight. But neither is time an opponent to be raced against. In my kitchen this morning, time is gift, grace, a still point claimed from a world whirling with haste and inattention. As I stand at my stove, watching the mercury grapple its way up the thin glass tube, I find myself rooted in the goodness of this given moment, breathing deep into the burnt-sugar substance of *this* holiday, not because it is perfect or because things are going according to plan, but simply because it is here and I am here in the midst of it. I have made caramel under all kinds of inner weather over the years, for if external conditions are *sine qua non*, the internal ones are anything goes. I have seen Christmases gloomed with grief and holidays fairly bursting with mirth. I have watched this pot in plenty and in want, at least in an emotional sense, and by habit and long affection I am now caught and held amidst the verities of Christmas itself. This is why the act of candy-making feels like such a sacrament, and why I prefer to do it alone.

One of the virtues of homemade sweets lies in their unseen largesse. In a world where few people make candy anymore, much less suspect the generosity inherent in its cooking, cutting, wrapping, and boxing, there is a secret side to its goodness, a hidden-ness which, when tied with a ribbon and given as a gift, contains a drop of true humility. It is but a drop among all the other ingredients but it seasons things straight through. This is true of candy that "turns out" and candy that is less than ideal. I have given away some terrible caramel over the years, particularly when I was learning how to make it, but this is not the point. All mastery is built upon failure; learning to do anything is a risk, howsoever small. You may be out a few pints of heavy cream and a pound or two of good butter at the start, but to the cheerful giver this matters not at all. According to Saint Paul you are loved by God for even the attempt. Better a pan of hard caramels where love is than a houseful of exquisite confections with strife.

Rachel used to try to persuade me to take a year off from caramels from time to time. Not that she misprized the results—Rachel is the most disciplined person I know but even her willpower topples before my gingercake caramels. She just thought it might make things simpler for me in such a full season. I tried to explain to her that candy-making, fraught as it is, is one of the few things this time of year that feels inherently simple in itself.

What do I mean by that? I ask myself now, stirring down a sudden upsurge of bubbles and adjusting the flame under the pot. I say I want simplicity but I often act in complexity. Candy-making, however, keeps me honest. *I mean that it is old-fashioned*, I mentally reply. It's a link to the past, conjuring images of snowbound cottages and children playing pick-up sticks on the kitchen floor and mothers clad in gingham aprons minding cast iron pots over open fires—images to which my old-fashioned sensibilities are deeply attracted. Things were simpler then (by which my heart and mind mean 'better'); people had time for each other, not to mention trivialities like saltwater taffy and peanut brittle. When I am making candy, I get to pretend for a little while that there is no distance between this time and a simpler time.

But there I am drawn up again. I know better. There is no such thing as a simpler time. Ever since Adam and Eve first cobbled together the first clothing in history and hid themselves from the presence of God, life has been labyrinthine. It's no wonder the Bible is so full of injunctions to "fret not," "take no thought," and "be anxious for nothing." Even the most ordinary questions of survival can get thorny at times. I am forced to admit that "simpler times" are a mirage. There are only simple people (yet another illusion, perhaps) and complicated people and most of the time we're all a baffled blend of the two, vacillating between what we most truly love and long for, and what is demanded, asked, or expected of us.

Candy-making, on the other hand, cuts to the chase. All its decisions have been made ahead of time. It is straightforward. It is limiting. From instructions on timing and temperature one must not waver, even a hair's breadth. It is, in other words, utterly and truly simple. And while true simplicity will never be synonymous with "easy," I find this to be a great relief. A path has been cut through the thorns; women wiser than I have walked this way before.

The making of candy is one of the humblest—and surely among the most wholesome—of alchemies on earth. Like a refiner poring over a crucible of gold until he sees his own image reflected on the molten surface, the candy-maker watches her pot with a devotion bordering on tenderness. That everyday things like butter and cream, sugar, spice, heat, and time, should render such delectability is neither kitchen chemistry nor chance. It is nothing short of magic and nothing less than grace.

A WORD, PERFORCE, ON METHOD: If you have never made caramels before, it's important to remember that success lies in cooking the mixture at the right heat for the right amount of time. As with all candy-making, temperature is everything, but the requisite 248 degrees must not be reached either too fast or two slow. A digital candy thermometer will clear up this anxiety: all you have to do is set the temperature, clip it to the side of the pot, and keep an eye on the clock. Twenty minutes really is the sweet spot for my recipe. Less time will result in exceedingly sticky caramels, and more time will make them so hard you won't be able to get a knife through them when it comes time to cut the sheet of candy into squares. And don't be afraid to tweak the heat setting as the caramels cook. When mine are on the stove I'm constantly nudging the knob up or down to keep the temperature rising at a steady rate. It is worth mentioning, however, that those last fifteen degrees or so take longer than the rest.

Decide ahead of time where you're going to keep the caramels to cool for the 24-hour period, as you can't move them once they start to set. When it comes time to cut them, use a large kitchen or chef's knife, but try not to use a sawing motion, as this will stretch the caramels out of their perfect little squares. I highly recommend investing in some confectioner's grade cellophane wrappers, as this will not only save considerable time in the packaging of your candies, it will ensure that they stay fresh.

RECIPE: *Gingercake Caramels*

While wrapping dozens of caramels individually may seem like a chore, it can be done with relative efficiency once you get into a rhythm. To make it easier, purchase pre-cut cellophane from Amazon or your local craft store.

3/4 tsp. salt
1 tsp. ground cinnamon
1 tsp. ground ginger,
　or more to taste
3/4 tsp. ground nutmeg
1/4 tsp. ground cloves

2 pints heavy cream
1 pint light Karo syrup
4 cups white sugar
12 Tbsp. unsalted butter,
　cut into 1/2-inch cubes
1/2 cup unsulfured molasses

1 tsp. Madagascar bourbon vanilla extract

Coat a large, rimmed baking sheet (a 13×18-inch jelly roll pan works great) with cooking spray. Cut a piece of parchment paper 2 inches longer than the baking sheet and line the coated pan. Coat parchment and set pan aside.

Mix salt and spices thoroughly in a small bowl and set aside.

In a large, heavy-bottom stockpot, bring the cream, corn syrup, sugar, butter, and molasses to a boil over high heat, stirring until the butter has melted and all sugar has dissolved. Clip a candy thermometer to the side of the pot and reduce heat to medium-high. Cook for about 20 minutes, stirring frequently, until mixture reaches 248°.

Remove from heat and whisk in vanilla and salt-and-spice blend. Promptly pour into the prepared pan (don't scrape the pot!) and set on a cooling rack in a place where the caramels can remain undisturbed at room temperature. Let stand, uncovered, for 24 hours without moving.

The next day, coat a large cutting board with oil or cooking spray, and lift the parchment to unmold the caramel, inverting it onto the cutting board in a sheet. Peel off parchment and cut caramels into one-inch square pieces. Wrap candies individually in cellophane and store in an airtight container for up to a month.

MAKES 12 DOZEN CARAMELS

RECIPE: *Rachel's Mother's Toffee*

As with all homemade candies, the final temperature of the toffee mixture is as important as the time it takes to get there. You will need a candy thermometer and up to an hour of focused attention. The quality of the semi-sweets is also important, since the additives in less-expensive brands can cause the chocolate to separate from the top of the toffee when you break it into pieces. Also, be aware that the toffee will need to sit at room temperature for 24 hours to fully set.

Cooking spray for the pan
1 pound of butter, cut into ½-inch cubes
½ cup water
¼ cup light corn syrup
2½ cups sugar

2 12-oz. packages good quality semi-sweet chocolate chips

3 cups pecans, finely chopped

Coat a 12 x 17-inch rimmed baking sheet with cooking spray and set it on a wire cooling rack. In a large, heavy saucepan or stockpot combine butter, water, corn syrup, and sugar. Bring to a boil over high heat, then stir with a wooden spoon until thick, about 2 minutes.

Reduce heat to low and stop stirring. Clip a candy thermometer to the side of the pan and allow mixture to boil constantly for 35 minutes to 1 hour until it reaches 280°. It is very important that the toffee continues to boil at the lowest possible heat.

Remove from heat and pour immediately onto the prepared baking sheet without scraping the pan (or you will import any crystallized bits from the bottom of the pan into your toffee). Allow the toffee to cool at room temperature for one hour.

In the top of a double-boiler (or in a large, heatproof bowl set over a saucepan of water, snugly enough that the bowl remains suspended at least 2 inches above the waterline, and be careful not to allow any water to come in contact with the chocolate—even from steam—as this will cause it to seize or clump), melt the chocolate slowly until it reaches 90°. Pour the melted chocolate over the toffee and smooth to the edges with an offset spatula, topping with the chopped pecans. Allow the candy to set at room temperature for 24 hours.

Using a small spatula or the blade of a knife, gently lift one corner of the toffee and begin to break it into bite-sized pieces. Repeat with the rest of the candy. Store in an airtight tin lined with waxed paper, away from heat and humidity. The toffee may also be refrigerated or frozen for up to 6 months.

YIELD: 2 POUNDS

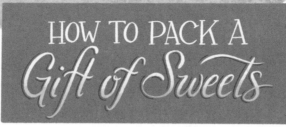

HOW TO PACK A
Gift of Sweets

People often ask what I do with the mountains of treats I make at Christmastime. "Surely you don't eat them all!" an acquaintance exclaimed after seeing a picture of my cookie-laden kitchen counters on Instagram.

I was quick to assure her to the contrary. The truth is, while our larder boasts an array of vintage tins, filled and at the ready for drop-in guests and afternoon tea, the greater part of the sweets I make are made to be given away. Some of them go to Philip's office by the trayful; others, brought out of their winter's nap in the chest freezer downstairs, are plated for neighbors, Christmas parties, or last-minute gift exchanges. A goodly supply of sugar cookies and gingerbread men are held in reserve for Christmas Eve, while dozens of cherry-studded Christmas Nut Cookies and delicately piquant Mince Pie Cookies are earmarked for our yearly Twelfth Night revel. And there are always gingercake caramels and buckeyes, boxed, labelled, and tied with organza ribbon, ready to be tucked into Christmas parcels for friends and family both near and far.

Packing homemade candies to gift or mail

MATERIALS:
Paperboard bakery boxes
Waxed or parchment paper
Blank stickers
Packing material for shipping

OPTIONAL:
Baskets
Vintage plates or trays
Paper lace doilies
Ribbon
Thrifted tins
Cupcake liners
Dry goods canisters
Plastic or cellophane bags

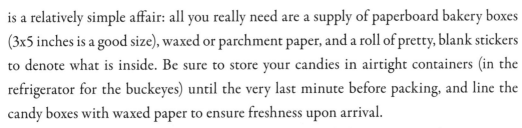

is a relatively simple affair: all you really need are a supply of paperboard bakery boxes (3x5 inches is a good size), waxed or parchment paper, and a roll of pretty, blank stickers to denote what is inside. Be sure to store your candies in airtight containers (in the refrigerator for the buckeyes) until the very last minute before packing, and line the candy boxes with waxed paper to ensure freshness upon arrival.

Homemade cookies can be presented in baskets, gifted on a vintage plate or tray, or simply stacked, interspersed with paper lace doilies, and tied with a length of slim satin ribbon. A half-dozen gingersnaps presented thus makes a fetching hostess or teacher gift. And a thrifted tin becomes a treasure when filled with gingerbread hearts and stars. One of the loveliest gifts I have ever received was an assortment of homemade cookies and candies nestled into cupcake liners, boxed and tied with a big green bow.

If you decide to ship your homemade cookies, you need to think about the rough handling they will experience in transit. Choose sturdy varieties, to begin with—if a cookie crumbles easily in your own kitchen it will be reduced to atoms by the time it reaches your recipient. Select containers that are both pretty and functional, such as cardboard bakery boxes or airtight tins—keep a look out for the latter on Etsy, or at your local thrift store. You can also repurpose canisters from dried goods, such as oatmeal or breadcrumbs; simply cover the outside bandbox-style with festive giftwrap,

wallpaper remnants, or original artwork. And for the freshest cookies upon arrival, ship them frozen.

If you are sending more than one type of cookie, different varieties will need to be separated to keep them from picking up each other's flavors. Resealable plastic bags are a good option, as are patterned cellophane bags tied with red and white baker's twine. Once you have arranged the cookies in your container of choice, pad the edges and spaces between with crinkle strips or crushed waxed paper. Shake it gently—if you hear any movement at all, add more padding.

Select a shipping box slightly larger than your tin and wrap the cookies tightly in an extra layer of packing material for a snug fit. Bubble-wrap is a good option, but you can also use an assortment of holiday tea towels or antique linens, gifts in and of themselves. Alternatively, crushed lengths of postal wrap or crumpled newspaper work well. Just be sure that, as within your tin itself, there is no room for things to shift about in the box.

Finally, before sealing it up, be sure to include a note or card detailing the contents. And, if you are unsure about food allergies, it's important to denote certain culprits like nuts, dairy, or gluten. As far as shipping options go, most cookies will do just fine via Priority Mail—remember to write "Fragile" on your package before dropping it off at the post office.

And, while you're at it, slip a tin of cookies into the mailbox addressed to your mail carrier.

This Rush of Wings Afar

I had been listening for them for weeks, ever since the first real shock of cold weather back in early November, expecting at any moment to be drawn up short by the most wistful and the most exhilarating sound I know of in nature: the wild, rasping cries of the sandhill cranes. We are fortunate enough to live in their migratory flight path, and Philip and I have a tacit understanding that whenever we hear the cranes we must stop whatever we are doing, no matter how important, and go outside to attend to them. I recall so many afternoons in late autumn, standing in the backyard with our heads thrown back in a compliment of complete silence, watching the black mass swirl and mount its heavenly way before pressing southward in a ragged "V." We always wait until they are completely out of sight and their calls have faded into the distance before heading back into the house. It's our homage to the passing of one season and the renewed familiarity of another.

That we can hear them at all astounds me, for it usually takes a few moments to locate the fine black specks of their bodies against the sky, and their far-off cacophony of chirrings and squalls must be deafening at close range. At such a distance, however, it has about it all the poignancy and bewildering exactitude of change ringing. Like bells clanging over a quiet landscape, the sandhill cranes fling forth a summons to new things deeply rooted in custom and an ancient rhythm. Their arrival thrills me every year, but that year they seemed awfully late.

It was one of those days when every second seemed to count, every hour so carefully planned as to press the last oil of productivity out of every moment. I had ironed, cleaned, worked in the barn, caught up on correspondence, and now I was baking. The last sugar cookies were cooling on the racks and I was measuring out the ingredients for gingerbread when I stopped as if I'd been tapped on the shoulder and caught my breath over that familiar ache of joy. I set down the jar of molasses, flew out the kitchen door into the keen chill of a December afternoon, and whirled about, searching the sky.

I think I felt them before I saw them, in much the way that a person senses observation. For just as I turned in their direction, they appeared with a gliding sweep above the proud hedge of hollies that border the kitchen yard. At first I was too fascinated to realize that I had never seen them at such close range: their bodies were grey, not black as they always seemed, and I could even make out the darker tips of their enormous wings. I wondered wildly for a moment if they were going to land in our pasture, until it became obvious that the slow and solemn circle was on the ascent. Perhaps they had taken off from the watering hole out front—perhaps had been there for quite some time while I was inside oblivious, up to my ears in flour and colored sugar!

I stood transfixed as they mounted heavenward, stately as a liturgical procession, with the occasional bird-shout of praise for good measure. As they reached a certain height and came into a level with the slanting rays of the departing sun, however, an absolute miracle transpired. Each time the wheeling throng passed through the light, a wash of glory set them ablaze, running over them like the ripples of some heavenly watercourse so that every wing was sheathed with silver and every feather bore a flash of gold. On and on they soared, higher and higher, passing from shadow to splendor in a recurring parable of unearthly beauty.

Soon after they forsook the charmed hold of light, and in another breathless moment or two they unfurled themselves into formation, a giant bracket with one leader at the fore and two lieutenants flanking him on either side. Thus they passed swiftly over my head and glided away over the pines to the south, trailing enchantment and inconsolable yearning in their wake. I was shaken as I went back into the kitchen and regarded my late occupation. It seemed almost silly to resume something as earthly as the baking of cookies after so heavenly a benediction. And yet, not silly. It had all been sanctified, somehow, in the purifying glow of a holy Advent which appropriates all willing things and makes of a flight of birds or a flour-dusted kitchen a sudden crossroad between the seen and the unseen. A "thin place," as the Celts might say, a lifting of the veil. I returned to my work with reverence, without another thought for efficiency. Even the doughtiest to-do list quails before the wavering of that curtain.

Philip and I talked that night about why I was so moved: why the advent of the cranes would bear such a palpable weight of glory to my waiting heart. Why their shrill, metallic cries would seem the very voice of one calling in the wilderness.

"It's because we know what they mean," he said.

He was right. The sandhill cranes mean that old things are passing away. But they also mean that everything is becoming new. Creation sings an endless song of death unto life, to which the cranes in their ritualistic flight bear witness, both going and coming. Even in winter, when their appearance signals darkness, decay, and cold, it nudges us on toward light, and life, and the warmth of true belonging. If the sandhill cranes are heading south, we know in our bones that they will return. One day, just when we have ceased to look for them, perhaps, a far-off cry will seize our hearts and the blood in our veins will leap like sap and we will lift our winter-weary heads to the sky and be met with the sight of wings uncountable.

Until then, their first advent leaves us with the sure and steadfast hope of their second.

Celestial fowles in the air,
Sing with your notes upon the height,
In firthes and in forests fair
Be mirthful now at all your might;
For passèd is your dully night;
Aurora has the cloudès pierced,
The sun is risen with gladsome light,
Et nobis puer natus est.

WILLIAM DUNBAR

Guard THE Nest

Long before I had Ruff House Christmases, there were Chestnut Drive Christmases. The plain, mid-century ranch house I grew up in was beautiful to me, though Mama's furniture was a hodgepodge of hand-me-downs from her grandparents and the original kitchen was sorely in need of an upgrade. I loved the cool brick floors on my bare feet, and the reassuring cypress rooftree overhead. I loved the two-sided fireplace between the living room and the den which always smoked, and the plate-glass windows running the length of the house making our shady backyard feel like an extension of the indoors. I have those windows to thank for my young parents having bought that house in the first place back in the 1970s. They were looking for a suitable home for their growing family, and the house on Chestnut Drive was the first one they viewed. It was February, and it had just begun to snow as Mama and Daddy walked in with the realtor. This house was, at the time, too small. Its simple lines and open floor plan were a far cry from the formal Colonial style toward which Mama's tastes leaned. It was built on a slab, so its floors were freezing, and the scrap of a front porch was little more than a stoop. Daddy, perhaps, was considering all these drawbacks in terms of their leveraging power. Mama, on the other hand, walked in the front door, saw that brick floor and that wall of windows and the snow coming down, and said, "This is my house."

To Daddy's credit, I'm sure he brought his native thrift to bear in the contract negotiations. But Mama's instinct was faultless; if ever a house had been waiting for a family, that house had been waiting for us. It was a perfect house to be a child in, with its one-level circuit of interconnected rooms and its massive backyard brimming with enchantments for the imaginative mind. It was a perfect house, years later, to invite our friends over for game nights, or chili nights, or moonlit croquet matches on the lawn.

Above all, it was a perfect house for Christmas. In the early years we put the tree in the den where a deep hearth encircled the table-height fireplace, but as time went on it migrated to the central living room where the colored lights could be enjoyed from all sides and reflected back in those wonderful windows. My siblings and I never hung our stockings on the smoke-blackened mantle, preferring to arrange them conspicuously along the top of the big Empire sideboard on Christmas Eve. That sideboard was also the perfect setting for the gingerbread church I made every year, with its gumdrop-topped steeple and stained glass window of crushed clear candies (I remember haunting the candy-by-the-pound aisle at Kroger for a perfect assortment of red, green, yellow, and orange-colored discs). Taking a cue from my beloved Tasha Tudor, I would set the church at one end of a mirror "lake" ringed with hills of white frosting, cedar-sprig trees, and leftover candle ends. Once I even managed to wedge a tealight into the open door of the church, and when lit, it made my crushed candies glow like real stained glass. The top of the sideboard was the only place in the house worthy of such a wonder.

Chestnut Drive Christmases were not fancy or expensive. Mama and Daddy made sacrifices, I know, to provide the three modest piles of presents we found in the living room on Christmas morning. But not even the thrill of gifts, breathless as it was, could quite match the pervasive excitement that settled upon our house in late November and lingered throughout the season. For though my Baptist-raised parents never observed Advent, Mama believed in the twin virtues of anticipation and savoring: Christmas started in our house on Thanksgiving night with the televised version of the lighting of the Rich's Department Store "Great Tree" in downtown Atlanta and the making of our Christmas lists. And it did not end until a day or two after New Year's, when Mama often indulged us in the rare treat of pizza delivery in the middle of the day while we undecorated the tree. I may have secretly yearned to keep things going in true Scandinavian fashion well into the middle of January. But I could not deny that it felt like Christmas in our home far longer than it seemed to in the houses of my friends.

Though it was past my expression as a child, I always intuited that Christmas was not merely an event. It was an atmosphere; a *place* we wanted to be. We wanted to be together, in the kitchen, around the table, in front of the television, adding to the annual mountain of movies and meals and rituals each of us felt Christmas could not be complete without. Daddy used to joke that we had to dispense with one tradition before adding another—the trajectory simply was not sustainable. The years, however, had a way of leveling things out on their own, welcoming worn-out things into the leaf mould of memory at the base of our family tree even as new growth sprouted in the branches above. It was an organic process, and one in which our parents allowed us to participate, for while traditions imposed upon a child can be tiresome, onerous even, traditions that flow naturally from the unique personalities and stages of life that comprise a household can be vessels of enduring joy, long after the tradition itself has gone by the wayside.

I know that Mama had her moments of overwhelm with the whole business; the first year we were homeschooling she threw in the towel in early December. ("I can homeschool," she said, "or I can do Christmas. But not both.") To the three of us, an extra week of school in June was a small price to pay for a whole glorious month of Christmas. For Mama, however, I imagine it was scarcely a break. I know she and Daddy were forced to consider practicalities like bills and aging appliances and ornery furnaces amid the poetry and magic we children experienced as Christmas; they had plenty to worry about, Christmas or no. But Daddy always made us feel like we were

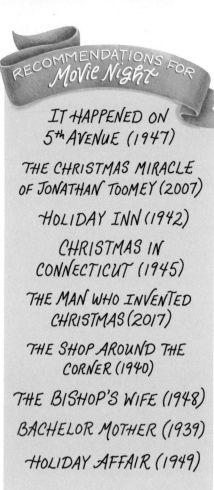

Recommendations for Movie Night

IT HAPPENED ON 5th AVENUE (1947)

THE CHRISTMAS MIRACLE OF JONATHAN TOOMEY (2007)

HOLIDAY INN (1942)

CHRISTMAS IN CONNECTICUT (1945)

THE MAN WHO INVENTED CHRISTMAS (2017)

THE SHOP AROUND THE CORNER (1940)

THE BISHOP'S WIFE (1948)

BACHELOR MOTHER (1939)

HOLIDAY AFFAIR (1949)

the best part of his day, and Mama always made us feel completely welcome in our own home. In both cases, this was utterly true; what I have only lately come to realize is that it is also quite rare.

All too often, children are made to feel like unwanted guests in a world of adult things: order they must not muss, dishes they must not break, conversations into which no one thinks to invite them. On the other hand, we've grown so rushed and fragmented that the very idea of a weeknight meal or a Sunday dinner—all sitting around the table at the same time, eating the same thing—seems almost quaint, certainly impractical. But to welcome one's own family, intentionally and without reserve, is to grasp the very heart of hospitality itself: already a rhythm and an order exists into which others might easily enter and savor a taste of true belonging. My mother was good at this; what may be less obvious is that anyone can be. It is tempting to suppose that hospitality must be forestalled until we have a bigger house, until the children are older, until we have a husband or a roommate or we have learned to cook. But hospitality does not depend upon such things; the raw materials are within reach for anyone who cares to claim them: generosity, presence, and love. Beyond these, the possibilities are endless, but without them, the most elaborate feast is a sham.

Our food—at Christmas or at any other time—was not elaborate. It was familiar, nourishing both heart and body. Mama was an excellent cook, and she loved to make things special: she cultivated our palates over the years with things like English trifle, and *pots de crème*, and steamed artichokes plated like stiff desert flowers alongside golden oases of clarified butter. But if you asked any of the three of us to name the foods which mean "home" to us, I'll warrant we would all point toward Mama's home-made whole-wheat bread, pot roasts stretched into vegetable soups, crowd-worthy vats of beans and rice, and boiled chickens picked bare for pots of featherlight dumplings bobbing in thick, brothy stews. Most of all, the holiday fare: the cornbread dressings and giblet gravies of Thanksgiving; the potato salads and coconut-sprinkled bunny cakes of Easter; the cinnamon rolls and cheesy egg casseroles of Christmas morning.

In our house, even popcorn felt special, because it often accompanied something fun—a noisily opinionated board game, perhaps, or a family movie night. I remember one evening in particular: it was Christmas, and the popcorn was popping and the teakettle was wailing and we were preparing to watch a movie together, one that my action-loving brother and my rigidly old-fashioned self had miraculously managed to agree upon—*Christmas in Connecticut*, probably, for he found it as funny as I thought it romantic. I was sitting on the hearth in the den, warming my back to a crackling fire, my lanky, teenaged legs tucked under my chin and the ruffled flounce of my flannel nightgown poked in around my toes. Everyone was getting situated, piling under blankets and arranging the couch pillows. Mama entered with a tray of steaming mugs, fussing over her shoulder at Daddy to hurry up, and Daddy loped in, pouncing upon his favorite chair with one of his blustery laughs as if he'd beat us all to the prize. Suddenly, I was seized with a wave of emotion that seemed to swell from the depths of my being and radiate outward with a force that took my breath. The sheer goodness of that moment and my love for the people in that room nearly choked me. I could not imagine a sweeter contentment, or a keener happiness. It felt like a wild, strange longing for something I already had. And it tasted like popcorn.

I never want to leave these people or this place, I thought, with all the precipitousness of seventeen.

"I love being *us*," I said from my perch on the hearth.

Mama set down her tray on the coffee table with a soft look.

"Me too," she said.

It was not an accident or a coincidence that home was such a safe place. For all the squabblings and eruptions that will inevitably occur in a household of strong-willed and passionate people, we genuinely enjoyed each other. Mama made a point of cultivating togetherness—"If you can't be friends with your siblings, you can't really be friends with anyone"—and one of the ways she facilitated this was through the shared imagination of reading aloud. We were all ardent readers, and while my brother and sister and I may have squirmed and yawned our way through Mama's rendition of *The Deerslayer*, no one could deny that *God's Smuggler* had us on the edge of our seats, or that Gene Stratton-Porter's Limberlost stories gave us a new reverence for the natural world.

One December, I came home from my part-time job at an old-and-rare bookshop with a small parcel. I wrapped it in festive paper and set it out on the Queen Anne occasional table in the living room. It was addressed to my family, and as soon as Daddy got home from work, Liz and Zach pressed him to open it. Inside, he found an old, dust-wrapped copy of Kate Douglas Wiggin's *The Birds' Christmas Carol*. I had written an inscription on the flyleaf:

To my family. To be read at Christmas.

I was not familiar with the story. I only knew it was one my employer, Mrs. Downs, could scarcely keep in stock—she was always searching out a copy for some customer or other, especially this time of year. But this one she had saved for me, discounting it so generously that my tiny paycheck scarcely took notice. We started it that night.

Things began merrily enough, with all manner of playful punning on the Bird family name and their "nest" of a Victorian mansion. The eponymous Carol was a little girl of tender sensibilities and cheerful demeanor despite her delicate health, and her birthday fell, appropriately enough, on Christmas Day.

By the time we reached the second chapter, however, the plot had taken a very Victorian turn. Young Carol, it seemed, would not survive the book. Daddy, whose tenderness of heart was second only to his sense of humor, barely made it through the final paragraphs.

"*Please* don't make me read that one out-loud again!" he spluttered when he came to the end, the corners of his wet eyes crinkling with a pained smile.

We didn't, but there were other holiday stories, most notably Truman Capote's shockingly poignant "A Christmas Memory," and Jan Struther's wartime passages from *Mrs. Miniver.* I remember my sister reading e. e. cummings's charming poem "little tree," and Mama sharing Peter Marshall's 1950s-era sermon "Let's Keep Christmas." Zach would demand a rap version of Clement C. Moore's immortal verse on Christmas Eve, which Daddy was only too happy to provide. And I loved a lyrical essay by Alice Van Leer Carrick called "Christmas in Our Town" because the author had such a winsome voice, and because the descriptions of her children made me think of my brother and sister and me.

After I married and became mistress of the Ruff House, I instinctively sought to facilitate the same comfort and contentment I had experienced on Chestnut Drive. Early on, however, I realized how much the emotional climate of our home depended upon the climate of my own heart: if I was rushed and bothered, darting about trying to shape perfection from a place of hurry and angst, the Ruff House itself felt out of joint, every odd angle and sagging clapboard amplified before my fretful gaze. If, on the other hand, I moved more slowly, honoring my love and my limitations, offering both my flawed humanity and my holy ideals to God, the very rooms around me softened with a new warmth and the myriad things that all needed doing at once seemed to scatter to the corners of my mind like shadows before the glow of a candle. I began to understand that this was what it meant to bring a Mary heart into the Martha realities of life—not to neglect responsibilities, but to orient them properly around a central Light.

This quiet nimbus was the only space to cultivate the life I imagined for Philip and me—the books and the conversations, the music and the silences, the memories and the laughter and the friendships and the fun. Beyond its pale clamored the falsely imperative, the tyrannous to-do list, the endless demands of a culture addicted to hurry and efficiency. But within that smaller iteration of a greater Light lay the heart of what made a house—any house—a home. Like the oil lamps of old, it needed tending to keep its light lively and its wick drawing life. And especially at Christmas, when opportunities and demands crowded in thick and fast, threatening to overshadow the very Light whose coming we all anticipate.

"Guard the nest," urges Eleanor Farjeon in her lilting "Carol of the Advent." Not against the messiness and imperfections and ruffled feathers of life, but for the very sake of it. Every nest must be filled with something—even discontent and discord are things, and emptiness a crowd which can throng the most well-appointed house. But it is a worthy care to keep the family gate, admitting only that which contributes to the well-being of those within. There are plenty of things that we cannot control in life, but the atmosphere of our living spaces is entirely in our hands. We can choose to fill them with expectations or impatience or envy; to crowd our calendars with worthy and unworthy commitments alike, proving to ourselves and the world around us that we are tired and productive members of a tired and productive society.

Christmas Read-Alouds

THE BEST CHRISTMAS PAGEANT EVER
Barbara Robinson

THE BIRDS' CHRISTMAS CAROL
Kate Douglas Wiggin

HOME FOR CHRISTMAS
Lloyd C. Douglas

SHEPHERDS ABIDING
Jan Karon

THE LITTLE SILVER HOUSE
Jennie Lindquist

A CHRISTMAS CAROL
Charles Dickens

THE SISTER OF THE ANGELS
Elizabeth Goudge

THE CHRISTMAS DAY KITTEN
James Herriot

LET'S KEEP CHRISTMAS
Peter Marshall

Or we can seek an older road, one whose ways are pleasantness and whose paths are peace. We can light candles and turn off the television set and learn to say no. We can ask for help.

"Gather my thoughts and order my steps," a wise older friend taught me to pray at the start of a busy day.

"Show me *your* ways, Lord," pleads the Psalmist, "teach me *your* paths."

Our God is unstinting in wisdom to those who ask. And though his answers will most likely run counter to the culture around us, they are the only sure foundation upon which to build a life—or a home. For there, amid dishes and dangling conversations, misunderstandings and unmade beds, the sacred invades the temporal with an irresistible invitation. We may say we want simplicity, or order, or beauty, or harmony. What we mean, of course, is that we want Christ himself, filling every corner, presiding over every meal, welcoming each weary heart with Lion of Judah-sized love.

I try to keep the calendar as open as possible in December, not only to clear the ground for Advent itself, but to make room for the quiet atmosphere in which its mysteries flourish like flowers in the snow. This is no time, I tell myself, for routine doctor's appointments and dental exams, not to mention committee meetings, some holiday parties, most correspondence, good intentions, or good opportunities. I am finite, and making room for the infinite amid the ordinary matters of life takes time. But I never cease to be amazed by how much time can be redeemed by simply eliminating the nonessentials. We are all living under the ancient goad of the urgent, driven along by the lie that the silent roar we hear between our own ears is the voice of the important and the imperishable. But it doesn't have to be this way. We can step in out of the wind. We can heed another voice.

Philip and I still read books together—he has narrated *The Birds' Christmas Carol* with much the same result as Daddy's—and we still seek to protect as many evenings as we can for games by the fire or one of our few really favorite Christmas movies. I like to think of a Ruff House Christmas as a small, snug outpost on the fringe of a darkening world, a refuge of belonging and simple, honest cheer for all who enter. But the Chestnut Drive Christmases laid the foundation of my ideals, not because my family was perfect, or because our house looked like a spread from a magazine, or because my parents wore themselves out trying to give us every experience or opportunity or up-to-the minute gift.

But because we were together. Because we belonged to each other and to our place and to our own story as a family. This was where Christ met me as a girl. And this is where he meets me now.

ADVENT
WEEK THREE

Stars, keep the watch. When night is dim one more **Light** the bowl shall brim, shining beyond the frosty weather, bright as **Sun** and **Moon** together. PEOPLE, LOOK EAST, AND SING TODAY:

LOVE, the

Star,

IS ON THE WAY.

Eleanor Farjeon, "Carol of the Advent"

Feasting with Friends PART 1

The iron gives a wheeze, chuckling a bit as it meets a limp square of old damask. I pull the corners taut and the starch hisses beneath the pressure and the heat. Around me, the windows of my little laundry are fogged with steam; at my feet, a small space heater chugs against the chill of a December afternoon. I fold the square and then fold it again, smoothing the iron firmly over the surface, admiring the way that pressure and heat and steam bring out subtle patterns in the cloth—stylized borders and subtly woven urns and scrolls and blowsy chrysanthemums. I place it atop a stack of crisp, white dinner napkins, then pluck another from the hamper, snapping it against the air and smoothing it onto the board. Once more, the iron laughs and sighs; once more the steam curls, incense-like. Once more the transformation of derelict crumple to a thing of usefulness and beauty.

Ironing, I realize, is rather antiquated these days. In a disposable society, where time is short and convenience abounds, ironing linens seems almost indulgent. Why take the trouble when there are paper options aplenty, and many of them quite pretty? No one is going to notice or care if their dinner napkin is freshly pressed or freshly liberated from a plastic wrapper. Ironing is, at best, an outdated nicety, at worst, a purgatorial chore.

I disagree, of course, on both points.

To the latter charge, I answer that, as in all housework, there is something inherently redemptive in the process, and therefore something truly good. To rend usefulness and order from the soiled and dejected is always a holy work, howsoever trivial it might seem on the surface. But we do not live on the surface of things, not really, no matter how we might skim along the glassy crust above the deeper meaning of our days. The place where we *really* live, where the humblest things serve the highest ends and the most menial tasks are quickened by love, is down amid the unseen ordinary where sacred significance thrums through the practicalities of daily life.

To the former claim, I can only say that while the mechanism of the household might churn along just fine without tablecloths and dresser scarves, pressed or otherwise, some layer of civility will have been lost, some mark of our care and concern for people and place casually forfeited to the fanatically casual spirit of our age. This may seem a slight thing, a loss hardly worth lamenting, but to me it betokens a far greater one: a diminution of everyday courtesy and occasional ceremony. As for me and my house, we will let this happen.

A freshly ironed napkin—like a freshly ironed pillowcase, tablecloth, or guest towel—tells someone that you have not thought merely of company, but of *them*. As my iron travels over the satiny cloth, I think of Joel, Cathryne, Michael, Edie. I think of flamboyant Katie and good-natured Rob. I think of Rachel, who embroidered my monogram on some of these very napkins, and of her husband, Gary, with his quiet, albeit penetrating wisdom. I think of Laura, my sister in all things Christmas, and of Luke, who always manages to slip a few bottles of Coca-Cola into our fridge and a pint of Kentucky's Finest into our butler's pantry on the sly. All of them, along with Philip and me, comprise the Notions Club. And all of them will be here Saturday night.

The Notions are our core of kindreds, united around the shared values of faith, fellowship, and excellent books. And while our monthly meetings all the rest of the year are jolly potluck affairs, December is of a different cast altogether. By mutual consent, it is always held at the Ruff House. And it is always a formal affair.

Although a flurry of emails will have confirmed the date ahead of time, a stack of large, ivory-colored envelopes goes out every November containing invitations worded in the traditional sense: *Mr. and Mrs. Philip Lloyd Ivester request the pleasure of your company . . .* And pleasure it is, from first thought of the menu to final embrace at the front door when the evening is over. I have occasionally been tempted to dispense with formal invitations; everyone has already inked it into their calendars and they know what to expect. They know how to get to the Ruff House and they know that, according to a loose jumble of unwritten bylaws, we always meet at seven. We never send out invitations to any of our other meetings. Nevertheless, I have never dispensed with the practice. For a decade and counting, the Notions have been summoned, not by a buzz, beep, or chirp on their cellphones, but by the sight of their own names, scrawled in black ink, couched between lines of printed black text.

A formal invitation not only communicates information—it expounds upon expectation. In five or six lines the stage is set for an evening of consequence. We will, we know, feast like those who know the meaning of food, not merely as sustenance to the body but nourishment to the soul. We will drink thankfully, every glass an oblation raised to the goodness of God. We will proceed through the place settings with unaffected ease, tacitly acknowledging that salad forks and soup spoons are there to serve—not intimidate—the guests. And, at the injunction of two short words at the bottom right of the page, we are assured once more of our inherent dignity: *Black tie.*

Philip likes to remind me that *Star Wars: Episode IV* does not end with rebel forces blowing up the Death Star. *Star Wars*, he says, is not an action film. It's a multigenerational saga depicting men and women (and robots and some seriously odd creatures) who possess motives and struggles and dreams very close to our own. We are invested in the franchise, for, with all their weird outfits, they are *like* us. They are pitted in a life-or-death fight against evil and undoing, struggling above all to believe in a Force which works mysteriously, silently, relentlessly, for good. If the original *Star Wars* concluded with an explosion and a round of high fives we would be seriously disappointed—we would want, not more films, but more formality. We feel it in our bones: such circumstance demands pomp–courtly robes, ceremony, medals. Princess Leia's "fancy" hair.

Likewise, when the Notions Club is bidden to the Christmas Dinner they are invited to don their finest. We have ridden the waves and billows of yet another year; we have lived to tell, individually and corporately, of the challenges and vicissitudes unique to 21st century life. We are battered from the fray, perhaps, and a bit more silver about the temples. But by the grace of God, we stand aright. Therefore: the tuxedoes and the pocket squares, the fancy updos and the sparkly evening bags. Katie will contemplate one of her Kate Middleton-esque fascinators; I will rifle through my grandmother's formals in the attic, while Laura will scour the aisles for something chic and midcentury. We will dress, not to impress one another, but to delight. Life abounds with the casual and the impromptu, and this is not to denigrate either one. We need to be at ease with each other and in our own skin; we need never forsake the assembling of ourselves for fear of informality, simplicity, or even shabbiness. We need, above all, to be together.

But we also need margins in life, clear demarcations between the common and the exceptional, the festal and the ferial. For just as we would eventually sicken of rich fare and courtly dress exclusively prescribed, so an endless succession of blue jeans and paper plates becomes not only slovenly, but boring. We were not made for boredom; we were made for wonder. Nature itself bespeaks this on every side, as do the great occasions of life: births, marriages, accomplishments, feasts. And if, occasionally, we are astonished by the sheer resplendence of our friends in evening dress, all the better. We are ragamuffins and fools exalted to royal status, not by our own merit, but because the Prince of the house has played the oldest trick in the storybook, switching places at the last minute with the beggar at the gate. In him we have become, without effort or entitlement, the children of a King. And while Christ's great humility should provoke us likewise to servanthood and sacrifice, there are moments in which it is meet and proper to acknowledge—nay, celebrate—this invisible lineage. To dress for dinner is both impractical and unnecessary—which is exactly why we should do it. Few things tap so effectively into the essential commedia of our human narrative like the sight of erstwhile bums arrayed like the lilies of the field. We might schlep around in workaday clothes all the rest of the year, blending in with the casual dictates of our day and rightly distrusting any exaltation of outward appearance over inner motive. But workaday is not our identity. At the formal dinner, for a few short hours out of thousands, we will live toward our destiny as lords and ladies of a renewed kingdom.

Dinner napkins done, I turn my hand to great-Grandmother Green's Nottingham lace tablecloth, stretching it carefully in advance of the iron. This cloth has seen regular service for over 100 years, and though the edges are unraveling a bit, and though new holes appear with each hand-washing, howsoever gentle, it remains the reigning queen of my linen closet. Like Grandmother Green before me, I reserve it for the great days in the year, but no Ruff House holiday or bridal tea or dinner of note would be complete without it. I smile, as the steam soothes out the puckers in each netted medallion. How many times have I flung this cloth over the table in the dining room? How many times have people I love

Music FOR A Christmas Dinner Party

CHRISTMAS WITH THE
GEORGE SHEARING QUINTET

THIS TIME OF YEAR
June Christy

A DAVE BRUBECK CHRISTMAS

A VERY SWINGIN'
BASIE CHRISTMAS
The Count Basie Orchestra

A MERRY MANCINI CHRISTMAS
Henry Mancini

SNOWFALL: THE TONY BENNETT
CHRISTMAS ALBUM

SOUND OF CHRISTMAS
Ramsey Lewis

SILENT NIGHTS
Chet Baker

drawn themselves up to place-settings lovingly laid, every plate centered among the rounds, each glass and goblet aligned down the length of its delicate surface?

To set a table is to prepare a place—no small thing in a world striving to estrange us from our true home, in God and with each other. We live like orphans much of the time, leaves driven before a tempest of transience and haste, hurried along from one crisis or commitment to the next, caring for others with very little margin to contemplate just how much we long to be cared for ourselves. But here, at the formal table, every provision has been made, every need anticipated. Like the guest in George Herbert's sonnet, we find, first to our reticence, perhaps, but ultimately to our relief, that "quick-eyed Love" has thought of everything. The napkins are ample and crisp, the soup bowls and bread plates foretell a good start, while the coffee spoons and dessert forks promise a happy ending. There are water goblets for our refreshment and wine glasses for our joy. There is candlelight, kindly to every face, and some form of centerpiece, artful enough for pleasure yet discreet enough for conversation.

Everything about the formal dinner is rooted in tradition, and the table setting is no exception. Tradition always has a "why." It may not be a good one—some traditions can be harmful, while others may have lost their way among thickets of stodginess and pride–but to say that something is traditional is to affirm that it originated for a reason. In the case of the dinner table, the "rules" were written in the name of courtesy and ease—the flatware is laid out in order of use, from the outside in, and there are pieces enough for every purpose (some of the older sets even have individual butter and salad knives). The glasses are on the right, to mitigate the bumping of elbows, and there should be salt and pepper to serve each end of the table—a long board begs at least three sets. "Serve from the right, retrieve from the left," may be a relic of Gilded Age dinners replete with staff in white livery, but it makes for seamless, almost invisible transitions in the meal, avoiding that disruptive tangle of arms and plates across the faces of guests in what my mother always derisively referred to as the "boardinghouse reach." Rules, of course, are only worthy insofar as they honor the guest—not the other way around. But the right rules, rightly applied, can make for a dinner that is less like a tennis match and more like a dance.

A better word for rules, perhaps, is ritual. Ritual is the handmaiden of tradition; despite its rather labored connotations at times, ritual is simply our way of catching hold of something fleeting in this life—some evanescent hint of ultimate truth—and anchoring its memory in something solid and repeatable. Remembrance is not enough; we must *do* something. We must inhabit remembrance in physical form. In this sense, ritual is our friend, helping us to engage with realities we could not otherwise articulate. It shepherds us along set ways toward an expressed hope and an expected end. This is true, of course, of our weekly journey to the Lord's Table. But it is also true, to a much lesser degree, of the dining table. In the Eucharist we taste the bread of heaven and the wine of salvation; at the dinner party we taste the restoration of all things. "Nowhere," writes Robert Farrar Capon, "more than in good and formal company do we catch the *praegustatum*, the foretaste of what is in store for us."

Knowing that what is in store is a wedding feast the likes of which the world has never seen, I lay my table for the Notions Christmas dinner with the very best I have—supplemented, as necessary, with the best I can borrow from my mother. We live in an age in which cultural ideals of "best" have gotten sadly tangled with "privilege" and "class," and excellence is often redefined as elitism. This is a modern development, an overcorrection, perhaps, for inequity and empty pretense. But like most overcorrections, it introduces a new set of dangers. For when all disparity between the ordinary and the extraordinary has been eliminated, our capacity for beauty is diminished. Beauty takes many forms; at the dinner table it may look like a single candle and a jug of flowers, for with thoughtfulness and care even the humblest meal and the most spartan setting are elevated to the exceptional.

On a French hilltop, I once was served a platter of cold scrambled eggs augmented by garden-fresh zucchini and a perfectly ripe *charentais* melon. All this was presented upon a plain pine table under an equally plain shelter, and it was truly one of the love-liest meals of my life, not only because I was tired and hungry after a long day of travel, but because our friend, Christophe, had taken great pains to make it beautiful. One minute we had been bemoaning the fact that we had reached our remote destination after the shops had closed and had, apparently, nothing to eat but leftover eggs, and the next we were clinking juice glasses of *Mouton Cadet* and marveling at our abundance.

So then, humble on the one hand, and yet on the other beauty may also reveal itself in a full service for eight, in the gleam of old silver and the glint of gilt upon a china plate. What matters, as in all things concerning our relations to fellow human beings, is *intent*. Grandmother Green did not lay her Sunday board with rose-sprigged Haviland because she thought she was better than other people, but because she esteemed both them and the day. To offer the best we have is to allude to the belovedness of others; to receive it, if only for the duration of a meal, is to accept that belovedness for ourselves.

For all the heft of my German iron, a sense of buoyancy seems to hover under my hand, as though the iron itself were propelled by glad intent. The days ahead will be crowded with preparation: hanging garland, setting the table, deciding upon a center-piece, not to mention the endless round of tasks that stave up the daily order of a home, Christmas or no. But in this moment, wreathed in the incense of starch and steam, it all rises like a living prayer.

Perfect Imperfection

Perfectionism is a lie," she says.

I nod knowingly, smiling at my friend across the table.

"What's more," she adds, "it's rooted in pride."

I wince, wrapping my fingers tightly about my coffee mug. I know she's right–agree with her, even. Still, it is a sore spot. How many times have I worn myself out over trifles, or sat down to a dinner party I was too tired to enjoy? How often do my cherished ideals chafe against the limitations of my actual life? An orderly home is a good thing, a backdrop for easy hospitality, and a beautiful one is a consolation for beauty's absence in other areas of life. It's never wrong to manage our homes with discipline and thrift, or to cultivate loveliness in our environment. It's always wrong, however, to do it for the wrong reasons.

My mother was the most hospitable person I have ever known. Perhaps this is because she never put the act of having people in our home above the actual people themselves. She was not flustered by the casual drop-in because she had her priorities in order: people first, place second. And she rarely went on a tear when guests were expected—if anyone was going to do that, it was me. (I was known, to the great exasperation of my family, to roam the house before a party with a cardboard box, picking up stray belongings and stashing them under my parents' bed.) We all had our weekly chores and deep-cleaning assignments, and on Fridays Mama would announce a "blitz," which was her word for a quick spree of tidying, lasting fifteen minutes or less. But comfort was what she valued, not a flawlessly clean house. Our home was beautiful in the sense of warmth and taste, but it really had less to do with the lovely brick floors and walls, the plate-glass windows, or odd bits of antique furniture than with the fact that it was so far from perfect we were all allowed to be absolutely at home. Mama collected what she liked and made do with what she had and put it all together in a way that just made people want to be there. And they wanted to be there because they knew *she* truly wanted them. That was the deepest beauty of Chestnut Drive: my mother's love.

At Christmas, it always helps to remind myself that perfectionism is the enemy of real hospitality. For the truth is, just like my mother's guests, people can tell if it's them you want, or the shadowy substitute of sparkling rooms and Pinterest-worthy tables. Beauty can disarm us in healthy and healing ways, but perfectionism is a threat. And it's not so much about the appearance of our homes as the attitudes and motives of our own hearts. *Have I exhausted myself over self-imposed standards, or have I poured myself out in love?* It's a difficult question, but one I must ask, again and again, probing that darker side of my heart's desires to keep me honest with myself and with God. And when I don't like what I find? Ah, then grace and mercy are waiting there to catch my wandering heart and shepherd me back into the paths of peace.

Alternatively, perfection can so hobble our hospitality that it keeps us from having people over at all. When we live in an imagined future of perfectly-realized surroundings or skills, we rob ourselves and those we love of the never-to-be-repeated gifts of the days we are in. For the "right now" is really all we have, and if we put off opening the treasure chest of the present moment until we think we are ready—until things, in other words, are perfect—we will find when we do only dust and ashes where priceless pearls once were. I am guilty of both faces of perfectionism. But I

must say, I think this side of it is the most insidious, because its pride is hooded in the most humble garb.

We all have our levels of comfort: some people cannot be at ease in a cluttered environment, while others are unable to relax in a perfectly clean house. Madeleine L'Engle once said that, while she was a haphazard housekeeper, she could not concentrate at her desk in the upper regions of her Connecticut farmhouse if she knew that there were dirty dishes in the sink downstairs. The point is not so much to identify our threshold, however, as to name our demons: are we being driven by cultural expectations, comparison to others, our own inner critics? Or are we allowing love to goad us along the peaceful path of imperfection? Acknowledging that things will never be perfect–welcoming the imperfections of life, in fact, as evidence of life itself–makes room for joy, decluttering our hearts and minds, as it were, from an unrealistic accumulation of "ought-tos" and "shoulds." Perfectionism always bears false witness, blinding us to the fact that a glorious mess lit by love is every bit as hospitable as a pretty room and a perfectly executed event.

A catchphrase that has come to help me combat perfectionism, and especially at Christmas, is "perfect imperfection." I try it out on my friend, smiling at her over my coffee cup. She likes it, too.

"But what does it mean?"

For me, it means saying no to myself. It can look like choosing my prayer book over my planner, or like a quiet list in the back of my mind of things I can let go of if I don't have time to enjoy them. I love poring over my books of Christmas recipes and crafts, but "perfect imperfection" can look like not pulling them out after a certain point in the season—or at all. It can mean taking stock of my time and my resources and my traditions and pronouncing them good enough. It means making space for people amid the comforts and the messes of my life alike.

It means, above all, refusing to let my ideals diminish my actuality. No matter where we look, we will always find someone more organized, more skilled in the kitchen, with a prettier house or a larger garden or a nicer wardrobe.

What is that to thee? Jesus says. *Follow thou me.*

My friend and I have walked with Jesus long enough to know how desperately we need his help to walk with him at all. And so, we commit ourselves anew to a mirthful inadequacy and an all-encompassing grace.

"To perfect imperfection," I say, lifting my mug.

"Perfect imperfection," she answers with a clink of white porcelain.

A *Word* ON YOUR "*Best*"

Your best things, by their very nature, are already in your house. Contrary to marketing ploys on every side, you do not have to go out and buy them. If your "best" consists of sensible pottery or mismatched plates, then, by all means, put them on your table with the loving abandon of the widow in the Temple, "who hath put in all that she had." Love always transforms the most ordinary elements of our lives with beauty and grace. If, however, you would like to build a collection of pretty things to use, not only for company, but to season your everyday life with a little additional loveliness, consider the fact that charity shops and yard sales tend to overflow with someone else's erstwhile "best."

On the other hand, if you have boxes of wedding china languishing in your attic, liberate them at once! Few things can make another person feel valued like placing a delicate porcelain cup in their hands or seating them before a place setting touched with a glint of gold. And if they must be washed by hand afterward, all the better, for they give us a moment to reflect on the time we have shared with someone important to us. In a throwaway culture, it is such a charming bit of resistance to temper our lives with things that need a little extra care.

WEEK THREE

HOW TO
Set the Table

For a meal of more than three courses a formal place setting is in order. And it has been designed with comfort in mind: flatware is used from the outside in, progressing naturally through the courses, and dessert cutlery is placed at the top. By the time coffee is served almost everything else has been cleared away, making room for cups and saucers, as well as dessert plates. If a dessert spoon is required it may be placed above, or in lieu of, the dessert fork.

Butter knife

Bread plate

Napkin (may be placed on the plate if space is tight)

Salad fork

Dinner fork

Place Card

Teaspoon

Dessert fork

Water goblet

Wine glass

Dinner plate

Soup bowl or Salad plate goes on Top

Cup and Saucer go here after dinner is cleared

Dinner knife

Soup Spoon

165

Feasting WITH Friends PART 2

It's two o'clock in the morning, and a clear, cold moon silvers the circles of frost on the kitchen windows. I wring out my dish cloth, pull the stopper from the sink, and remove my gloves with a sigh. It has been another rousing—even raucous, at times—Notions Christmas Dinner, in which my friends have been the chief and loveliest ornament of my home. I am well content. I have sent Philip off to bed, relieving him of his saturated dishtowel, and already a soft, whiffling snore issues from the bedroom. I'll be glad of a few hours' sleep myself ahead of early service at church in the morning. But there is one last thing I must do.

At the door to the den I pause, picturing the late cluster of tuxedoed men, the glint of Grandma's silver champagnes in the hands of friends, the laughter, the firelight. I remember, perhaps, how Joel read us an original story after dinner, or the toast Philip raised before. At the thought of Katie's latest outfit, I'll smile and shake my head; how on earth does a woman with eight children always manage to show up looking like a flamboyant fashion model? What fun we've had in our gaiety and garb, flaunting for just an evening in the face of life's hardships.

"Thank you," I murmur into the empty room.

It is not a vague expression, or even a prayer. It's a whisper of gratitude to the room itself for all the ways it has sheltered our joy this night. These walls hold the memory of our merriment; the very books and furnishings have borne witness to sweet ceremonies of friendship. I close the damper on the woodburning stove, pick up a crumpled cocktail napkin, switch off the lights. Knowing how I hate to see the Christmas tree turned off at night, Philip has it set on a timer programmed for an hour well-past any reasonable person's bedtime. Nevertheless, as I turn to go I hear the click of the little device and the room behind me goes dark.

In the kitchen, the parlor, the hall, I enact a similar little ceremony: a memory-laden pause, a slight setting to rights, a word of thanks. At the front door, I think of happy greetings and fond farewells, and my hand lights momentarily on the old brass knob in blessing.

At the door to the dining room, however, I linger. Here, of all places, does the fragrance of our fellowship most persistently cling. I can still see the loved faces consecrated by candlelight, hear the clink of crystal and the roar of honest mirth. I run my eyes over the empty wine bottles on the server, the splatterings of wax on the sideboard, the glowing remnants of a merry blaze on the hearth. Though the hours flew, they felt somehow timeless, linking this night to something beyond, something eternal.

In reality, the Notions Dinner began weeks before with the planning of the menu, a rite sacred in itself. Every year I sit down with my calendar, my planner, and a pile of cookbooks, invoking the Holy Spirit for what I like to call "a special dispensation of organization." Not natively an efficient person, I have learned from experience that a party of any stripe needs an extra layer of time-management, and that no request for wisdom is too small for God's notice. Indeed, if, as I proclaim, I'm endeavoring to clear space in a hectic time of year to treat my friends to a taste of their own belovedness in Christ, it's going to take something more than a garden variety to-do list. It's going to take a Tactical Plan.

As I flip through the familiar books, the temptation to experiment is strong. What about roast duck with an orange madeira sauce, or even a Dickensian goose glazed with quince paste and rosemary? I flirt with the thought of a crown pork roast, the bone ends capped with gold foil frills, or succulent little quails slathered in rich brown gravy. Reason suggests it's bad policy to practice on guests (even Julia Child fairly begged her readers to rehearse *cerises flambées* on their own families first), but I'm a bit of a rule-breaker—in the kitchen, at least—and I banish reason to the other side of the room. Eventually, however, anything-is-possible gives way to tried-and-true, and I find my way back home to the fact that the best kitchen policies are always rooted in love. Am I cooking to impress my friends, or to nourish them, body and soul? With regard to the dinner party, experimentation leads to ruination, or, at the very least, a goodly portion of regret. Best keep to the old roads.

Standing rib roast, I scribble at the top of the page.

Rib roast, also known as prime rib, is one of the juiciest, most flavorful cuts of beef. It is dramatic and elegant, can sate a crowd, and is incredibly easy to prepare. It is also invariably on sale at the local grocery at Christmas. All of this I know because I have made it for the Notions Dinner so many times that my recipe is one in which my heart can safely trust. It's called "standing" because the meat is roasted using the bones as a rack, and if you order it in advance, you can ask your butcher to prepare it "trimmed and tied," which means that the meat has been cut off the bones and tied back together, making for much easier carving. Do be sure and stipulate first cut, or loin end, for while there will be less marbling, the roast will be far more tender. You can make up for the loss of fat by tossing a couple of short ribs into the roasting pan at cooking time, which will also elevate your drippings to diamond status.

From rib roast the rest of the menu falls naturally in line: golden potatoes crisped up in those priceless pan drippings, individual Yorkshire puddings, creamy horseradish sauce, and springlike Brussels sprouts roasted with cayenne and a splash of maple syrup. And since there are vegetarians in our midst—a segment of society too often relegated to side dishes and bread at the dinner party—I like to think of a special main which will make them feel cared for as well as satisfied: in this instance, a savory pair of spinach and Stilton Wellingtons which can be made up the day before and popped into the oven with the puddings and potatoes.

A cheese course will be a pleasant interlude before dessert—something blue, something creamy, and something sharp, with dried apricots and figs for a lyrical counterpoint—and for the first course, a clear, bright consommé to whet the appetite without surfeiting it.

With dessert alone do I loosen the reins. Since sweets are generally prepared ahead of time (*cerises flambées* and its ilk excepted), space may be made for something a little exceptional: a frozen white chocolate mousse, for instance, or a raspberry-studded "tipsy" trifle. For this dinner, however, I ultimately side with a cranberry Sachertorte, a festive riff on the traditional apricot-filled Viennese specialty, since the cake can be baked and frozen and the icing glaze applied the morning of the party. I love the tang of a homemade cranberry sauce against the smoky sweetness of dark chocolate, and the requisite "Sacher" signature on top may be modified to suit the occasion (I once decorated a New Year's Sachertorte with the now-famous words of Eric Peters: "Ha, ha to the Old Year!").

The menu settled, I turn my thoughts to the calendar. And here is where the real strategy comes in. For while "make-ahead" is undoubtedly my best friend this time of year, the fact remains that things still have to be *made*. And for this, it follows, time itself must be made. In the early years, I bewildered myself with myriad last-minute tasks, things easy enough on paper, but which, in the fray of actual hostessing blew up in my mind all at once like a cacophony of alarm bells, timers, buzzers, and sirens. Some people can baste a roast, chop herbs, whip cream, toss vegetables, wash berries, make the coffee, and remember to turn on the Brussels sprouts, all while maintaining unflappable poise and intelligent conversation.

WEEK THREE

I am not one of them.

And so, knowing that our hearts' desire in this party is to be fully present to our guests, and that my focus goes out the window as soon as the doorbell rings, I endeavor on this quiet afternoon to entrust as much of that focus as possible to a few sheets of paper. Scrutinizing my recipes, I make note of the various steps and of anything—I mean anything—that can be done in advance. The consommé actually improves with a stint in the refrigerator, so I assign it to the day before the party. Likewise, the Wellingtons, the cranberry filling for the torte, and the batter for the puddings. The potatoes and the sprouts can be prepped the morning of with no ill effect, and the chocolate glaze on the cake will need several hours to set. With a little care, even the fresh mushrooms and chives for the soup may be chopped well in advance.

The roast, while simple enough, is going to need some cosseting: the evening before, it should be anointed with a piquant rub of mustard and brown sugar, and left to bask in the refrigerator overnight, tightly blanketed with foil. And once it's in the oven, it will want to be basted every half hour—with timers already going for vegetables, puddings, Wellingtons, and soup, not to mention the chirp of the digital meat thermometer, this could easily spell a recipe for chaos. Which is why I have come to rely on a visual for this last-minute play-by-play: the One Plan to rule them all.

The Plan will ultimately be typed up in bold and printed out to keep close to the stove, and to its care I commit anything for which I might otherwise repair to a recipe: not only the *what*, but the *when*. If I want to serve dinner at 8:00, I count back accordingly:

7:45 Roast out of the oven; 7:50 Warm consommé gently and add Vegetable Wellingtons to the oven with the potatoes; 8:00 Serve consommé (topped with sliced mushrooms and fresh chives) and turn Brussels sprouts to low. Heat muffin pan in oven for puddings for 5 minutes; 8:15 Carve roast . . .

And so on. Each basting, tossing, into the oven and out gets its own time slot. Which means that, when the time comes, I can tick it off the list and get back to sipping champagne with my friends rather than running around in the kitchen like a frantic squirrel.

I like to think of a dinner party as a well-crafted theatrical production which lifts guests out of the ordinary for a few brief hours, or a musical score in which each instrument contributes to something larger than itself. Which is why, when planning a dinner, I invariably think of Bach. It is a bit of well-known trivia that Bach always signed his compositions with the initials S. D. G.: *Soli Deo Gloria*, or, Glory to God Alone. What strikes me, however, is the way he opened them: before writing a note, the great-big-grandfather of classical music always applied the letters J. J. at the top of the page: *Jesu, Juva*. Jesus, help.

It may seem outrageous—sentimental, even—to ask Jesus to help me pull off a dinner party. But we serve a God of the intimate and particular, as well as the mysterious and sublime, a God who put on our flesh and lived with us, who sat down at tables and served meals. I don't want to do this without him, because without him it's just an event. With him, however, it is a means of grace. I want him to be glorified; I want the sacramental implications of this feast to break through to our hearts and minds. But I also want his companionship.

WEEK THREE

A day or two before the party I set the table in the dining room, strategically arraying plates and goblets, silverware and napkins to cover the holes in Grandmother Green's perfectly imperfect lace cloth. Since my old table only seats eight comfortably, I will pull a drop-leaf table up to the end to form a T and collect chairs for twelve from all over the house. Place cards may seem stuffy, but a dinner party of any size will only flourish with a bit of such forethought—ideally we want one conversation, with occasional commentary on the side, not a half-dozen pockets of unrelated banter, and so I strive to seat my guests accordingly. Interspersing men and women is a good place to start, and, with the exception of Philip and me at each end of the table, no spouses opposite or next to each other.

I love to use pineapples on the table, those age-old symbols of hospitality, settling them into floral foam atop Grandmother Hamrick's silver candelabras. But this year I've turned once more to old-fashioned sugared fruit, one of the fixtures of my childhood Christmases. Nothing could be simpler than a wash of egg white and a quick toss in a bowl of *Dixie Crystals* (if you don't believe me, I refer you to the instructions on page 193) but it transforms ordinary apples and oranges, lemons and limes, into magical versions of themselves. Arranged on a tray and studded with fresh holly it is a centerpiece worthy of the occasion, though it only takes moments to compose.

Stepping back to admire my work, I think how essential beauty is to a life grounded in all that is lasting. For earthly beauty always points beyond itself, beckoning us to consider greater realities for which these lesser symbols stand in pledge. Keats tells us that "A thing of beauty is a joy forever"—but a beautiful table? Soon these gleaming plates will be soiled with the remnants of a late feast, and this table will be littered with wrinkled napkins and unused coffee spoons; the work of days undone in an evening. The sugared fruit will eventually spoil and the crisp, bright holly will darken and curl. Nevertheless, they will have done their work, lifting our chins, as it were, with a finger of transcendence and a thrill of hope. For these things tell a story that is true, namely, that beauty matters because we matter. God will keep sinking that hook into our hearts for the rest of our days, luring us onward toward beauty's perfect fulfillment in himself. And I will keep trying, in my table-settings and in my homemaking, my high days and my humble days, to beautify in his image, alluding thereby to a beauty that will never fade.

Loveliness, I have learned, has nothing to do with our circumstances and everything to do with our intent. I experienced this in a poignant way after our house fire: we were displaced and disoriented, buffeted by seemingly endless waves of loss and devastation. There were piles of ruined belongings on the patio and in the yard, a dumpster steadily filling on the other side of the garden, and a generator out front chugging power to the air scrubbers which roared day and night through the empty rooms. And the Ruff House was in shambles, its darkened spaces haunted by the stench of burnt wood, rotting food, and waterlogged plaster. For the first two weeks, Philip and I sheltered at a La Quinta across town with our dog and five cats. Thanks to a rider on our insurance policy, however, we ultimately found ourselves ensconced in an RV in the backyard. It was a providential arrangement, permitting us to stay on site to care for our animals and oversee the restoration of the Ruff House. But we were in exile, facing a displacement of unspecified duration with our promised land in daily view, and God himself only knew what travailings of body and soul awaited us on our journey back home. I cracked the blinds of the camper that first morning and looked out across the lawn to the white clapboard bulwark of my home.

How long, O Lord?

Early on, we called our little bivouac "Camp Marah" after the place where the wandering Israelites found the bitter waters made sweet, and from the start we had tastes of similar mercies. To begin with, our friends stocked the camper for us with household necessities: sheets, towels, pots and pans. There were wooden spoons and dishcloths, stainless flatware and sturdy white porcelain—dinner plates, salad plates, bowls, cups, and mugs. Everything we would need to make a home in the wilderness.

WEEK THREE

No sooner had we gotten settled, however, than packages started arriving from all over the country—from people we knew and from people we had yet to meet. Inside we found delicate cups and saucers, gold-rimmed china plates, bread-and-butters, and salad dishes, each in a lovely pattern called *Phoenix*. In all, it amassed to a full service for six, and we were as touched as we were mystified. A couple of faraway friends, it seemed, had organized a conspiracy to gift us with fine china, knowing full well what a necessary grace it would be in such a time. It would be easy to assume that no one *needed* china in a camper—which is exactly why I needed it so much, needed it in a way I had not even recognized until I opened that first box and pulled that first beautiful plate from its wrappings. The mystical bird curving low over a bank of flowers spoke of rebirth and renewal, a coming beauty from ashes. But these physical things also witnessed to civility, to the hope and promise of beauty, not only in the yet-to-be-regained spaces of the Ruff House, but in *this* place.

The camper was too small to host Notions that year, but I was able to welcome Laura and Rachel for Advent Tea, and though I was obliged to keep things simpler than ever, it gave me joy to prepare Camp Marah for their visit. I laid the dinette with a Victorian tea cloth (the gift of a friend) and dainty cutwork napkins (a gift from my mother), and as I arranged the *Phoenix* plates and cups and saucers something began to stir beneath the surface of my weary heart like the first snowdrops piercing the hard crust of winter: we were called, I knew, not just to receive beauty, but to shape it, fashioning our surroundings to affirm the comfort and belonging for which we were made. This ideal was so deeply entrenched I almost took it for granted. But when circumstances unmoored me from all sense of the ordinary—sometimes, it seemed, from my very sense of self—my friends swept in from afar and held the line for me.

I stepped back and smiled. A few clippings of holly from the yard and a couple of mercury-glass votives completed the table, and a festive paper chain swung over the dinette. Across the room, a compote of glittered acorns caught the light from our brave little Christmas tree, and in our postage stamp of a galley a bright bowl of navel oranges made its own sunshine against the wintry day outside. It was beautiful—even the cheap vinyl surfaces and ugly laminate seemed touched with a new warmth, and the Advent wreath in the window shone with a greater light. Desperate as I was to get back home to the Ruff House, home was *here*, at a table set in love, in a few fragrant dishes simmering on the stove and a few candles against the gloom of the world.

Beauty was intrinsic to my sense of home—it always had been and it always would be. This experience, however, had refined my relationship with it in a profound way. For when every pretense of perfection had been stripped away, when my pride was slain, again and again, by overwhelming circumstances, and when any temptation to compare myself with others felt like a laughable luxury, beauty had remained, illumining my darkness with a gleam of hope. Once back home in the Ruff House I would resume my round of hospitality and homemaking, gardening and beautifying, with renewed resolve and a chastened reverence for all that home meant. But also, I realized, I had come into a new freedom to thumb my nose at perfectionism and toss my head at comparison. For beauty made no distinction between the longed-for and the less-than-ideal, and I knew in that moment that everything I valued mattered here at Camp Marah, or it mattered not at all.

WEEK THREE

Among my favorite moments of a party are those bright, breathless ones before the doorbell rings for the first time. I can almost feel the anticipation of the rooms as I light the candles and touch matches to Philip's carefully laid fires. And despite the quick tingling of panic, the fear of forgotten things, the sudden urge to flee and let the well-oiled machine of my dinner carry along without me, the sturdy silence of the Ruff House is reassuring.

A flash of headlights breaks like a beacon from the bend in the drive, and the dogs begin to bark. Philip and I smile at one another across the kitchen. The champagne is cold, the fires are snapping, the music is mellow but merry. Tonight, we know, we will taste *convivium*. We will raise toasts and take pictures and tell stories. Philip will carve the roast with an apron over his tuxedo and Luke will help plate the food and Gary will serve more wine. And I will sink, as usual, into my chair when dessert is underway with the relief of a conductor who has seen a symphony through to its final movement. When we adjourn to the den for second cups of coffee, I will rejoice that no one notices the time. And when we finally say our goodbyes, I will rejoice that there are such friends to be had in this life. For at the end of the night, the only thing that will last is the love. Philip and I know this, and we know that it is more than enough.

Thus I stand at the dining room door, watching the last embers fall, committing these golden hours to the bright host of memory with which this space is so blessedly haunted. It has been a perfect evening, but only in the sense that imperfection and human limitation have collaborated with Christ to set the table for true hospitality.

"Thank you," I whisper, and this time it really is a prayer.

"And goodnight, dear Ruff House. Goodnight."

A MENU FOR FEASTING with FRIENDS

CHAMPAGNE COCKTAIL

MUSHROOM CONSOMMÉ
MAPLE-CAYENNE
BRUSSELS SPROUTS

STANDING RIB ROAST
VEGETABLE WELLINGTON
YORKSHIRE PUDDING
HORSERADISH SAUCE
ROASTED POTATOES

CRANBERRY SACHERTORTE
ASSORTED CHEESES
DRIED FIGS & APRICOTS
COFFEE

SIPS & STARTERS

Be careful not to stuff your guests with appetizers and heady drinks before sitting them down to a big dinner. Simplicity is always best: a flute of dry champagne (make it a cocktail, if you must, with a sugar cube and a few dashes of bitters) and a bowl of roasted nuts will keep everyone happy without upstaging your main event.

Soak a couple of cups of raw almonds and a pinch of kosher salt in a bowl of filtered water on the counter overnight; after 24 hours, squeeze the tip of each almond to remove the skins and toss them in a bowl with 2–3 teaspoons olive oil, ¾ teaspoon kosher salt, and 1 tablespoon chopped fresh thyme. Spread on a baking sheet lined with parchment paper and cook for 35 minutes in a 300 degree oven, turning once. Then increase the heat to 400 and roast for another 10 minutes.

Or warm a pound of unsalted cashews at 350 degrees for 5 minutes, then toss them in a large bowl with 1 tablespoon melted butter, 1 tablespoon kosher salt, 2 tablespoons chopped fresh rosemary leaves, 2 teaspoons brown sugar, and ½ teaspoon cayenne.

Set either of these out on your coffee table and rest content that you have done right by your guests—and your dinner.

CHAMPAGNE COCKTAIL

SERVES 1

One bottle of champagne will serve roughly five guests.

- 1 sugar cube
- Angostura aromatic bitters
- Brut champagne or Cava, well-chilled
- Lemon twist for garnish

Douse the sugar cube with a few dashes of bitters and drop into a champagne flute. Fill the glass with champagne and garnish with a lemon twist.

MUSHROOM CONSOMMÉ

SERVES 12

Dried porcini mushrooms can be pricey, but are well worth it for the fully-matured flavor they bring to this dish. And, like many specialty ingredients, they are often on sale around the holidays. If you can't find porcinis you can use a bulk mix of dried mushrooms, but you will need to augment the seasonings significantly. This recipe benefits greatly from a night in the refrigerator, so begin the day before you wish to serve it.

- 2 cups dried porcini mushrooms
- 8 ounces fresh white button mushrooms
- 2 quarts vegetable stock
- 4 large garlic cloves, thinly sliced

2 tablespoons soy sauce or coconut aminos
Kosher salt and freshly ground black pepper
Fresh lemon juice
2 tablespoons chopped fresh chives
Cheesecloth for straining

Place the dried mushrooms in a large heat-proof bowl. Pour 4 cups boiling water over the mushrooms and allow to sit for 30–45 minutes to reconstitute.

Wipe the white mushrooms and break off the stems, setting them aside. (Do not be tempted to rinse them or you'll wash off their earthy bouquet.) Set aside half of the caps in a separate bowl, cover, and refrigerate. Roughly chop the remaining caps.

Place a colander over a large bowl and line with the cheesecloth. Strain the reconstituted mushrooms, squeezing the cheesecloth gently to extract as much broth as possible, and set aside. Rinse the mushrooms thoroughly. Measure the broth and add enough fresh water to total 8 cups.

In a large stockpot, combine the mushroom broth, the vegetable stock, the reconstituted mushrooms, the fresh mushroom stems and chopped caps, sliced garlic, and salt to taste. Bring to a simmer and cover, cooking over lowest heat for 30 minutes. Strain the consommé and return to the pot. Add the soy sauce or aminos and season to taste with salt and pepper. Refrigerate overnight.

At serving time, bring the consommé to a simmer and adjust seasonings, as necessary. Thinly slice the reserved mushroom caps and toss them gently with a few drops of fresh lemon juice. Garnish each bowl of soup with a few slices of mushroom caps and a sprinkling of fresh chives. Serve immediately.

MAPLE-CAYENNE BRUSSELS SPROUTS

SERVES 8

Roasting brings out the natural sweetness of Brussels sprouts and this method even converted Philip, who used to think he didn't like them! Following my mother's lead, I purchased a large, countertop roaster for overflow food when cooking for a crowd, and I often use it for my sprouts to free up space in my regular oven if I'm making several dishes at once. The method is exactly the same as that listed below for a conventional oven, only you will spread the sprouts in the bottom of the roasting pot and toss them there with the olive oil.

3 pounds Brussels sprouts, trimmed (halved lengthwise if they are large)

3 tablespoons olive oil

Kosher salt

Freshly cracked black pepper

3 tablespoons maple syrup

½ teaspoon cayenne pepper

Preheat the oven to 400 degrees. Combine the maple syrup and cayenne in a small bowl and set aside.

Line a rimmed baking sheet with parchment paper. Spread the Brussels sprouts evenly on the baking sheet and toss them in the olive oil. Season to taste with kosher salt and a few good turns of the pepper grinder. Roast for 15 minutes, stirring occasionally, until the sprouts are starting to get tender, then drizzle with the syrup mixture and toss well to coat. Continue to roast another 5–10 minutes until the sprouts are just beginning to brown and some of the outer leaves are crispy. Serve immediately.

STANDING RIB ROAST
SERVES 10

When ordering your roast, ask your butcher for 1 pound of meat per person (because of the bones), or roughly 1 rib for every 2–3 people. Also, if you decide to cook a smaller (or a larger) roast, keep in mind that under 5 pounds will need to roast 20 minutes per pound, while over 5 pounds it will take only 15 minutes per pound. You will also use less salt with a smaller roast; calculate roughly 2 teaspoons per pound. One of the great things about a standing rib roast is that you get a variety of doneness, which can suit the various tastes of your guests—however, the roast will continue to cook once you have taken it out of the oven, so plan accordingly. 125 degrees is a perfect target in my opinion because you will end up with a span from rare (120 degrees) to medium (140 degrees).

- 1 rib roast (8 to 10 pounds) with 4 to 5 ribs, cut, trimmed, and tied
- 2 teaspoons dry mustard
- 2 teaspoons brown sugar
- 2 teaspoons Dijon mustard
- Kosher salt and freshly ground black pepper
- 3 beef short ribs
- 2 tablespoons all-purpose flour
- 1 cup beef stock
- 1 cup dry red wine

The day before you plan to serve it, place the roast rib-side down in a heavy roasting pan. Combine the dry mustard, brown sugar, Dijon mustard, and 2 tablespoons kosher salt in a small bowl and brush or rub over all surfaces of the roast. Cover the pan tightly and refrigerate overnight.

The next day, remove the roast from the refrigerator and let it sit out on the kitchen counter until at, or near, room temperature, about 2 hours. (Do not be tempted to skip this step, as it will render a juicier roast at serving time.)

Preheat the oven to 450 degrees. Score the fat diagonally with a sharp knife in a diamond pattern (taking care not to cut the strings) and season with 1 tablespoon kosher salt and 1 teaspoon pepper. Add the three short ribs to the pan and insert a digital probe meat thermometer into the middle of the roast (do not allow it to touch the bone). Roast for 15 minutes (the roast should be sizzling volubly). Turn the oven down to 350 degrees and continue to roast, basting every 15 minutes with the pan drippings, until the meat reaches an internal temperature of 125 degrees.

Using a couple of pot forks, or two large serving forks, remove roast to a large serving platter or cutting board with a juice groove. Allow to rest 30 minutes. Remove short ribs from the pan and reserve for another use.

Pour off all but 2 tablespoons drippings into a large, glass measuring cup. Set the roasting pan on the stovetop over medium-high heat and cook for 1–2 minutes, until the fat begins to darken. Whisk in the flour, scraping up the caramelized bits, and continue to whisk for 2–3 minutes until the mixture is a deep, golden brown. Pour in the stock and wine and bring to a boil. Keep whisking until thick enough to lightly coat the back of a wooden spoon. Season to taste with salt and pepper and strain through a wire mesh strainer. Serve immediately with the roast, potatoes, and Yorkshire puddings.

INDIVIDUAL VEGETABLE WELLINGTONS
Makes 4

Stilton is a special blue-veined English delicacy often available at the local grocery this time of year. If you can't find Stilton, substitute with another semi-hard aged cheese like sharp cheddar or gouda.

I like to prepare these, up to the egg wash, the day before I plan to serve them. Store in gallon-sized plastic bags in the refrigerator overnight. At cooking time, preheat the oven to 400 degrees and arrange the wellingtons on the baking sheets. Brush with egg wash and cook as directed. Any excess filling may be reserved for another use—it's delicious in an omelet!

2 tablespoons olive oil, divided

1 16-ounce package frozen butternut squash, peeled and cubed

1 teaspoon maple syrup

1 teaspoon plus 1 tablespoon fresh thyme leaves

¼ teaspoon paprika

½ teaspoon kosher salt, divided

3 garlic cloves, minced

2 shallots, minced

4 cups fresh spinach leaves

¼ cup dry white wine

½ cup chopped walnuts

Freshly cracked black pepper

5 ounces Stilton cheese, sliced

1 14-ounce package Dufour frozen puff pastry

1 egg

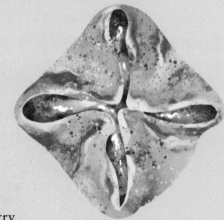

Thaw pastry in the refrigerator according to package directions.

Preheat the oven to 400 degrees. Toss the squash in a large bowl with 1 tablespoon olive oil, maple syrup, 1 teaspoon thyme leaves, paprika, and ¼ teaspoon salt. Spread the squash onto a parchment-lined baking sheet and roast for 30–35 minutes until tender. Set aside, leaving the oven on (unless you are planning to cook the wellingtons at a later time).

Meanwhile, heat the remaining olive oil in a large skillet over medium heat, then add the garlic and shallot, sautéing for 1 minute. Add the spinach leaves and sauté 2–3 minutes until completely wilted. Pour in the wine and cook for 3–5 minutes more, until the mixture is dry. Then stir in the cooked squash, the remaining salt, the walnuts, and the remaining thyme. Season to taste with salt and pepper.

Line a baking sheet with parchment paper. On a lightly floured surface, unfold and roll out the pastry to a ¼ inch thickness. Cut into 4 equal squares and spoon about ½ cup of filling mixture into the center of each, topping with a slice of Stilton. Fill a small bowl with water and place it near the work surface. Draw two of the opposite corners of pastry together and pinch firmly, dipping your fingers lightly into the water to help seal the dough. Repeat with the remaining two corners to form a pyramid shape, pressing firmly with damp fingers to seal. Pinch along all four seams in the same manner until the wellingtons are thoroughly closed.

Using a spatula, place the wellingtons on the prepared baking sheet. Beat the egg with 1 teaspoon of water and brush the wellingtons generously with egg wash. Cook for 25–30 minutes until puffed and golden.

WEEK THREE

INDIVIDUAL YORKSHIRE PUDDINGS
Makes 1 dozen

As with the red potatoes (next page) this is a job for those storied pan drippings from the Standing Rib Roast. These savory puddings mimic the crispy puff of a traditional Yorkshire pudding, but in single-serving size, just right for a dinner party. It's important that the milk and eggs are at room temperature before mixing up the batter so you'll want to take them out of the refrigerator a couple of hours ahead of time. And you need to get the drippings very hot before you add the batter—this will help them to rise as well as keep them from sticking to the pan. Bake them in the same oven as the Roasted Potatoes.

2 cups all-purpose flour

1 teaspoon kosher salt

½ teaspoon freshly ground black pepper

4 large eggs, at room temperature

3 to 3½ cups whole milk, at room temperature

6 to 8 tablespoons pan drippings from Standing Rib Roast

Preheat oven to 400 degrees.

In a large bowl, combine the flour, salt, and pepper. In a small bowl, lightly whisk the eggs and ¼ cup milk. Make a well in the center of the dry ingredients and pour in the egg mixture, whisking from the center of the well outward until all the flour is incorporated. Keep whisking until the batter is smooth and thick. Stir in about half of the remaining milk and let stand, covered, at room temperature for 30 minutes.

Pour 1–2 teaspoons drippings into each cup of a standard 12-cup muffin tin and place in the preheated oven. Heat for 5 minutes until very hot.

Stir 1 to 1 ½ cups milk into the pudding batter—you want the mixture to resemble heavy cream. Remove the muffin tin from the oven and ladle batter over the hot drippings, filling each cup about ⅓ full. Bake 25–30 minutes, until puffed, crisp, and golden. Serve immediately.

HORSERADISH SAUCE
Makes 2 cups

Look for prepared horseradish that doesn't contain additives, like Bubbie's or Woeber's brands. This recipe makes a lot of sauce, but if you have leftovers it's great on vegetables, or even used as a salad dressing.

  2 cups sour cream
  6 tablespoons lemon juice
  4 tablespoons prepared horseradish
  ½ teaspoon kosher salt
  ¼ teaspoon white pepper
  ½ teaspoon paprika
  ½ teaspoon cayenne pepper

Mix all ingredients in a medium bowl. Taste for seasonings, and chill until ready to serve.

WEEK THREE

ROASTED POTATOES
SERVES 8

This recipe makes mouth-watering use of the pan drippings from the Standing Rib Roast, a kitchen economy that is at once sensible and sublime. Roast the potatoes while the meat is resting and you're making the gravy, and everything will be done at the same time.

5 pounds Russet potatoes, peeled and quartered
Kosher salt
¾ cup pan drippings from Standing Rib Roast

Early in the day, place the potatoes and a few good pinches of salt into a stockpot and cover with water. Bring to a boil, then reduce heat and simmer, covered, for 5–7 minutes. Remove from the heat and drain in a colander. Once the potatoes are cool, score them on all sides with the tines of a fork. Spread the potatoes in a casserole dish large enough to accommodate them in a single layer and cover tightly with foil. Set aside.

About 1 hour prior to serving time preheat the oven to 400 degrees and drizzle the reserved pan drippings over the potatoes. Toss well to coat and roast until golden brown and crispy, 30–40 minutes. Serve immediately.

CRANBERRY SACHERTORTE

SERVES 12

To prepare ahead of time, this cake may rest (before filling and glazing) at room tempera-
ture in an airtight container for up to 1 day. To freeze, use two spatulas to gently lift the
cake onto a large plate and place in the freezer for 1 hour. Once it is frozen solid, wrap the
cake in plastic wrap and store in an airtight container or a freezer bag for up to 1 month.
Defrost in the refrigerator overnight, then allow to come to room temperature before filling
and glazing. Alternatively, the entire cake may be frozen using the above method, although
the glaze will lose its sheen. To defrost, thaw on the counter for several hours before serving.

CHOCOLATE CAKE:

8 ounces good quality semi-sweet baking chocolate, coarsely chopped

1 cup unsalted butter, softened

1 teaspoon Madagascar bourbon vanilla extract

¼ teaspoon salt

7 extra-large eggs, room temperature and separated into yolk and whites

1 cup fresh cranberries, chopped

¾ cup sugar

1 cup cake flour

CRANBERRY FILLING:

1 cup homemade (recipe at www.GladandGolden.com) or store-bought whole-
berry cranberry sauce

1 tablespoon dark rum

WEEK THREE

CHOCOLATE GLAZE:

>   12 ounces good quality semi-sweet baking chocolate, coarsely chopped, divided
>
>   ⅓ cup sugar
>
>   ⅓ cup water
>
>   5 tablespoons unsalted butter, cut up

FOR THE CAKE:

Preheat the oven to 350 degrees. Lightly butter and flour a 9-inch springform pan. Cut a round of parchment paper to fit the bottom of the pan; line pan and butter and flour the parchment.

Melt 8 ounces of the chopped chocolate slowly in the top of a double-boiler over simmering water (alternatively, place a heatproof bowl over a saucepan of simmering water with 2 inches between the bottom of the bowl and the surface of the water), stirring frequently. Do not allow the water to boil. Once the chocolate is thoroughly melted, remove from the heat and stir in the butter, vanilla, and salt until mixture is smooth and cool. Add egg yolks and stir until fully incorporated. Fold in the chopped cranberries.

In a large mixing bowl, beat egg whites at high speed until soft peaks form. Continuing to beat on high, sprinkle in the sugar, 2 tablespoons at a time, until the sugar is dissolved and the egg whites stand up in stiff, glossy peaks.

Slowly add the chocolate mixture to the beaten egg whites, folding it in very gently, alternately sprinkling in the flour about ⅓ cup at a time. You want to be sure that all of the chocolate and flour have been incorporated without deflating the egg whites, so be careful and take your time. Once blended, pour into the prepared pan and pass a rubber spatula gently through the batter to break up any air pockets.

Bake 45 minutes or until top is firm and cake springs back when lightly touched with a finger. Cool in pan on a wire rack for 10 minutes (the cake will shrink away from the sides of the pan and settle slightly), then carefully loosen the edges of the cake with a knife and remove the side of the pan. Invert the cake onto the cooling rack, remove the bottom of the pan, and peel off the parchment paper. Cool thoroughly.

Once the cake is cool, use a large bread knife to cut the cake in half horizontally. Place the top layer, cut side up, on a cooling rack set over a piece of waxed paper and prepare the filling.

FOR THE FILLING:
In a small saucepan, combine cranberry sauce and rum. Bring to a boil over medium heat, crushing any large pieces of cranberry with a spoon. Spoon the hot sauce over the cut side of the cake on the rack, spreading evenly. Replace the remaining layer, cut side down, on top of the filling. Allow the filling to set while you prepare the glaze.

FOR THE GLAZE:
In the top of a clean double-boiler, combine 8 ounces of the chocolate, ⅓ cup sugar, and ⅓ cup water. Heat over simmering water (do not boil) until the chocolate melts and the mixture is smooth. Remove from heat. Add the 5 tablespoons of butter and stir until melted. Cool at room temperature for 30 minutes, stirring occasionally, until glaze thickens.

WEEK THREE

Pour the glaze over the cake on the cooling rack in a circular movement, allowing it to run down and coat the sides of the cake. With a long frosting spatula, quickly smooth and level the glaze before it begins to harden.

Let the cake stand at room temperature for at least an hour to allow the glaze to set. (Do not refrigerate, or moisture beads will form on the surface of the glaze.) Once the glaze has fully hardened, carefully slip your fingers (or two wide spatulas) beneath the cake and lift onto a serving plate. Melt the remaining 4 ounces of chocolate in a small saucepan over medium heat, stirring constantly. Spoon the melted chocolate into a plastic sandwich bag, squeeze to one corner, and cut off the tip (about ⅛ inch) at a 45 degree angle.

Pipe your message on the top of the cake—you can use the date, a brief holiday greeting, the name of a friend or your group of friends. Or pay homage to the 16-year old apprentice chef who famously created this cake for the Chancellor of Austria in the 1830s with the simple appellation, "Sacher."

HOW TO MAKE
Sugared Fruit

My mother loved to have sugared fruit on the table at Christmastime. She said it reminded her of her grandmother, and now, with the cunning springboard of memory, it reminds me of her. To this day it evokes Mama's cherished red and green plaid cloth, her Spode Christmas Tree china, the dining room table spread for a caroling party or a family dinner or a Christmas Eve feast. It is forever linked in my mind with the anticipation of the holidays as well as the actual enjoyment, conjuring images of Mama bustling around the kitchen and my Aunt Sara arranging magnolia leaves and holly in the great, cracked Delft bowl on the sideboard, while my sister and I, a clean expanse of newspaper on the table between us, sugared the fruit for the Christmas centerpiece.

It always felt like such an important task, and it made us feel special for Mama to entrust it to us. The beauty, of course, is that it really is a simple project which, with a little patience, yields unfailingly satisfactory results—just perfect to occupy small hands for a space of time and to include them in all the preparations.

The Victorian-era convention of sugared fruit hearkens back even further to the glacéd and candied confections of the Medieval period. And while any fruit destined for life as a long-lasting centerpiece becomes, alas, inedible, it is possible to apply the same technique to berries, herbs, and even flowers, to create comestible adornments for cakes and desserts, not to mention your Christmas

MATERIALS:

Fresh fruit (e.g., apples, pears, oranges, lemons, limes, plums)
Half a dozen eggs
2 cups sugar
Waxed paper
Wire cooling racks
optional: white glitter

193

ham. You will just need to allocate ample drying time for the sugary crust to harden on the fruit before arranging in the actual centerpiece or decorating your food—24 hours is generally a good rule of thumb. And do consider the weather: you will want to select a day that is on the drier side, as too much humidity in the air can turn your sparkly fruit to a sticky, syrupy mess.

To sugar fruit for a centerpiece, select fresh, firm, produce with a smooth skin and no blemishes or bruises. Apples and pears work great with this method, as do oranges, lemons, limes, and plums—anything, really, which may be kept at room temperature without threat of imminent spoilage. You will also need about a half-dozen eggs, roughly two cups white granulated sugar (superfine or caster sugar works beautifully, although it is considerably more expensive—save this for your edible creations), waxed paper, and a couple of wire cooling racks. For decorative fruit only, you may also use a bit of white glitter, either tossed in with the sugar or dusted over the fruit before drying.

Separate the whites of half a dozen eggs, reserving the yolks for some other use (make lemon curd!), and whip them lightly with a fork to break them down a bit. At this point, you may dip the fruit whole into the whipped egg whites, or, alternatively, brush the whites over the fruit with a pastry brush. As soon as the fruit is fully coated, immediately roll in the sugar, dust with glitter if desired, then place on cooling rack with a sheet of waxed paper underneath to catch any drips. Once all the fruit has been coated, leave at room temperature until completely dry.

To assemble your centerpiece, consider any interesting pieces or serving dishes you might have on hand to create some structure: for example, a compote or candy dish placed in the middle of a round tray will provide instant height to lift some of your fruit into Victorian-style tiers, while another smaller tray on top of that will give you even more dimension. Alternatively, group the fruit in clusters around a few candlesticks, or arrange it in a single layer on a mirror or a large tray. Tuck a few sprigs of holly in and around the individual pieces—the dark glossy green and bright red look fetching against the subdued, sugary colors of the fruit—and you will have a centerpiece which Dickens himself would admire.

For food garnishes, use only fresh, whole, slightly under-ripe berries (cut fruit will not work for this method, as the exposed surface will absorb the sugar), and brush them gently with egg whites, using a pastry brush or a small, clean paintbrush. Roll in a cup or so of caster sugar and place on a waxed paper-lined cooling rack to dry overnight. Use immediately.

You can also sugar-coat sprigs of woody herbs, like rosemary or lavender, for a snow-dusted look. Fresh, supple bay leaves are lovely at Christmas encircling a festive main like roasted turkey or the aforementioned ham (bay leaves should never be eaten, however, fresh or dried), and for some extra color, throw in a few frosted kumquats—the sugar will temper the delightful tartness of the little fruit's edible skin.

Filling the Freezer

O f all the characters in Kenneth Grahame's timeless classic *The Wind in the Willows* the shy, home-loving Mole is the one with whom I most identify. But Mr. Badger is the one I most admire: Badger, with his kindly wisdom, his effortless hospitality, and his endless stores. When Rat and Mole stumble to his door in a snowstorm, they find Badger's kitchen smiling with firelight and stuffed with provisions, the rafters hung with hams and herbs, onions and baskets of eggs. The plentitude overflows into the guest room in hampers of apples and root vegetables, jars of honey and piles of nuts, while the many closed doors they pass en route from one part of his domicile to another hint at an even greater abundance tucked away against future need. In short, Badger's sett is a bastion of comfort and contentment, a tunneling fortress against loneliness and privation and cold. And it is a very good place to be if you are hungry. So well has Mr. Badger prepared for winter's contingencies that he is able to feed the weary wanderers— in addition to two young hedgehogs and a passing otter—at a moment's notice without so much as lifting a paw.

Mr. Badger's ethic of putting by in advance and pulling out at need has had a marked impression on my own domestic arrangement. Where some might prefer to collect teacups or decorative spoons, my tastes lean strongly toward cold storage. At last count I own and employ no less than two chest freezers, two upright refrigerators, and four refrigerated drawers, not to mention the freezer and refrigerator in our Airsteam travel trailer which I often put to use even when we're not camping. I love to see the hanging baskets in my larder brimming with sweet potatoes and garlic and firm onions wrapped in smooth, brown-paper skins. Putting up tomatoes and canning jelly is my very hot-and-bothered idea of fun, and I rejoice that "root-cellaring" is an active verb as I dream of burrowing badger-like into the red clay beneath the Ruff House.

I think of Mr. Badger as I ease a few foil-wrapped pans into the downstairs freezer a week or so before Christmas. It is a little gift to myself: three extra casseroles, wedged in among the pizza crusts and packets of meat, the quart jars of bone broth and the bags of last summer's garden bounty. For though my deep freeze threatens to burst this time of year, exploding vegetable wellingtons and cake layers and cookies all over the basement, this is a tradition with which I simply cannot dispense. Somewhere, amid all the messes and mixing bowls, the stock pots and saucepans and sinks-full of dishes that characterize my kitchen this time of year, I manage to carve out time for this squirrel-like fit of provisioning, this last, savory layer to cushion our household with simple abundance. For this food is not necessarily for other people—unless, of course, they happen to be around to share it. It is for us, a token of the holiday rest that awaits come December 26th, and a downpayment on the Twelve Days of Christmas.

Contrary to the early excesses and abrupt endings of our modern holidays, Christmas is a feast that can be kept, not just for a day, but for a whole stretch of days, each one bearing its own gifts of memory and merriment and tradition. But the Twelve Days, I have learned, do not just happen—like a well-loved guest, they must be prepared for. Early on, Philip and I realized that keeping the Twelve Days of Christmas was a culture we would have to cultivate if we wanted it to be a reality in our home, and like so many of the nicest things in life, it would need space and time and a little extra forethought. It would mean standing still while the rest of the world hurried feverishly along to

New Year's resolutions and post-holiday diets. It might look a little odd to the casual observer, steeped in the regrettable assumption that Christmas is over at midnight on the 25th. And it would most certainly require comfort food.

As much as I love to cook, however, by the time the last dish is dried on Christmas night I am ready to hang up my apron for a while. Originally I sought to pad the Twelve Days with a gentle array of easy dishes which could be whipped up in half an hour or less: a quick green curry, prepared ravioli swimming in canned marinara sauce, Welsh rabbit and tomato soup. Eventually, though, it began to dawn on me that not having to cook *at all* was the recipe for a real holiday. To read by the fire, or to tramp about in the frosty woods with Philip and the dogs well-past an hour in which dinner must be thought of is my idea of decadence. Better yet, to know that something hot, delicious, and homemade is only a turn of the oven knob away—ah, this is enough to color a whole day with contentment.

I want the dishes I prepare for the Twelve Days of Christmas to be both special and repeatable, anchoring us in a specific time and place. They need to be ordinary yet set apart, and comfortably unpretentious. For food doesn't just nourish, it communicates, whether we realize it or not, and the food I make for this week needs to say that it's still Christmas in our house, but that it's also all right to eat supper in our pajamas if we want to. The beauty of this time—apart from its lovely cluster of feast days and its deep-rooted traditions—is that time really does seem to slow to a crawl, while the expectations which often encumber the days leading up to Christmas have evaporated overnight. This time is for merriment of a mellower cast, for puzzles and hot chocolate and backgammon tournaments by the fire. It is a time for chicken and vegetables simmering under a flaky pastry crust and for meaty pastas crusted consolingly with copious amounts of cheese. It is a time, if ever there was one, for shepherd's pie.

It would be easy enough to pick up a frozen lasagna at the grocery, or a couple of Marie Callender's meat pies (and there is, for the record, absolutely nothing wrong with this), but while I'm already so busy in the kitchen it just doesn't seem all that daunting to make them ahead myself. And what compares with the simple goodness of home-made food, both in nourishment and taste? When we sit down to a dish which has been crafted in love, we receive the added benefit of the care with which it was made—even if we ourselves have made it.

For my pasta I have learned to rely on a sausage-studded baked ziti with a mildly spicy tomato sauce and layers of mozzarella, parmesan, and ricotta, while for the chicken pie only a buttery pâte brisée pastry crust will do—not only is it superlatively easy, but those tender, delicate layers simply coddle the white sauce and vegetables. And though Christmas week is no time for diet-conscious deprivations, I usually substitute the customary mashed potato topping of the shepherd's pie with a less starchy but no less toothsome version in cauliflower. Being the agreeable vegetable that it is, cauliflower has a way of absorbing the flavors of whatever you mix with it—in this case, puréed with 8 cloves of roasted garlic, a splash of chicken broth, and a goodly amount of butter it will render a creamy blanket of goodness worthy of the most winsome of pies.

I am tired as I trudge back up the basement stairs. The kitchen is a mess, and scarcely will these dishes be washed before others are dirtied. How these Advent days *do* seesaw, I think, between contemplation and preparation! And how it all images our innate need to both anticipate *and* savor our joys. A pleasure we don't have time to look forward to, much less space to sit with, is scarcely a pleasure at all. I smile, picturing myself curled up beside the fire with Philip, savoring steaming bowls of baked ziti, a stack of Christmas records on the Crosley. Ah, yes, our Twelve Days of Christmas will be provisioned indeed. Mr. Badger would be proud.

WEEK THREE

BAKED ZITI

SERVES 6

To make ahead, allow the casserole to cool after assembling, then cover with a layer of plastic wrap and a layer of aluminum foil. Freeze for up to 3 months. Defrost in the refrigerator overnight, then bake uncovered at 350 degrees for 45–60 minutes, checking every 15 minutes or so, until the sauce is bubbling and the cheese is lightly browned.

1 pound ziti or penne pasta

Kosher salt

1 tablespoon olive oil

1 pound bulk Italian sausage

1 large onion, chopped

4 cloves garlic, minced

1 tablespoon fresh rosemary, minced,
    or 1 teaspoon dried

1 teaspoon dried oregano

1 teaspoon dried parsley

1 teaspoon dried basil

1 teaspoon kosher salt

½ teaspoon freshly ground black pepper

½ teaspoon red pepper flakes

2 24-ounce jars marinara sauce

Freshly ground black pepper

8 ounces shredded mozzarella cheese

1 cup grated Parmesan cheese

1 cup ricotta cheese

200

Preheat the oven to 350 degrees.

Bring a large pot of salted water to a rolling boil. Add the pasta and stir, cooking according to the package directions until al dente, 9–11 minutes. Drain and toss with a small amount of olive oil to keep the pasta from sticking together.

In a large skillet or sauté pan, heat 1 tablespoon of olive oil over medium heat. As soon as it begins to shimmer, add the onions and sauté 5 minutes until translucent. Then add the sausage and brown well, breaking up any large chunks with a spoon until the meat is thoroughly cooked. Add the garlic, rosemary, oregano, parsley, basil, salt, pepper, and red pepper flakes, tossing to combine, and stir for 1 minute. Pour in the marinara sauce and bring to a simmer. Taste for seasoning and add salt and pepper as desired.

To assemble the casserole, spread a thin layer of sauce in a 9 x 13-inch casserole dish, then dot the surface with ½ cup ricotta cheese, a teaspoon or so at a time. Ladle a spoonful of sauce into the prepared pasta, combine well, then add the pasta to the casserole dish. Spoon the remaining sauce over the pasta, dot the surface with the remaining ½ cup ricotta cheese, and sprinkle with mozzarella and Parmesan.

Bake uncovered for 25 minutes until the cheese is melted and lightly browned. Let stand 10 minutes before serving.

SHEPHERD'S PIE

SERVES 6

To make ahead, allow the casserole to cool, then cover with a layer of plastic wrap and a layer of aluminum foil. Freeze for up to 3 months. Defrost in the refrigerator overnight, then bake uncovered on the lowest oven rack at 425 degrees for 30–45 minutes, checking every 15 minutes or so, until the filling is bubbling and topping is lightly browned.

8 cloves garlic, unpeeled

1 tablespoon olive oil

2 small heads cauliflower, cut into florets

⅓ cup chicken broth

6 tablespoons butter

Kosher salt

Freshly ground black pepper

1 pound ground beef chuck

1 medium onion, chopped

1 garlic clove, minced

¼ teaspoon dried thyme

2 tablespoons ketchup

1 tablespoon all-purpose flour

1 ½ teaspoons Worcestershire sauce

10 ounces frozen mixed vegetables

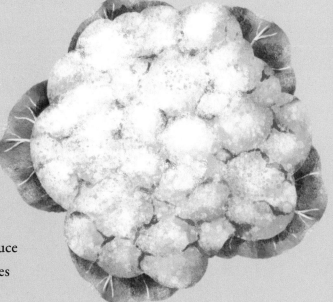

Preheat oven to 425 degrees.

Place the garlic cloves in a small, ovenproof dish and drizzle with olive oil. Roast the garlic for 15 minutes, until the skins are darkened and papery. Set aside to cool.

Place the cauliflower inside a steamer basket set in a large saucepan or stock pot. Add ½ inch of water and bring to a boil over medium-high heat. Reduce to low, cover and simmer for 10–15 minutes until the cauliflower is fork tender, then drain and transfer to the bowl of a food processor. Squeeze the roasted garlic cloves out of their skins and add to the processor, along with the chicken broth, butter, 2 teaspoons salt, and ¼ teaspoon pepper. Process for 15–20 seconds, until the mixture is smooth.

Brown the ground beef in a large, heavy skillet or Dutch oven over medium heat, breaking it up with a spoon, until no longer pink. Drain the fat off of the meat, if desired, or soak it up with a paper towel. Add the onion and garlic and cook until softened, about 5 minutes. Add thyme, ketchup, flour, Worcestershire sauce, 1 teaspoon salt, ½ teaspoon pepper and stir until combined. Pour in ½ cup water and add the frozen vegetables. Cook until vegetables have warmed through and liquid has thickened somewhat, about 4 minutes.

Transfer the beef mixture to a 2-quart casserole dish and spread the cauliflower evenly on top. Place casserole dish on a rimmed baking sheet and bake until warmed through and topping is lightly browned, 25 minutes.

CHICKEN POT PIE
SERVES 6

To make ahead, allow the pie to cool, then cover with a layer of plastic wrap and a layer of aluminum foil. Freeze for up to 3 months. Defrost in the refrigerator overnight, then bake uncovered at 375 degrees for 45–60 minutes, checking every 15 minutes until filling is bubbling and topping is lightly browned. If the top is browning too quickly, cover loosely with foil.

2½ cups all-purpose flour

1 teaspoon kosher salt

1 cup (2 sticks) cold, unsalted
    butter, cut into small pieces

6–7 tablespoons ice water

2–4 chicken breasts, bone-in,
    skin-on, 2 pounds total

3 tablespoons olive oil

Kosher salt

Freshly ground black pepper

4 tablespoons unsalted butter

1 medium onion, chopped

⅓ cup flour

2 cups chicken broth

1 cup heavy cream

10 ounces frozen mixed vegetables

1 egg yolk

For the pastry, combine the flour and salt in the bowl of a food processor and pulse until thoroughly mixed. Add the butter and process for 8–10 seconds, until the mixture resembles coarse meal. With the machine running, add the ice water, 1 tablespoon at a time, until the dough just holds together. To test, squeeze a small amount of dough between your fingers: if it is dry and crumbly add more water, but not to exceed 7 tablespoons, and do not process for more than 30 seconds.

Shape the dough into a ball and flatten into an elongated disk. Wrap tightly in plastic and chill in the refrigerator for at least 1 hour and up to overnight.

Preheat the oven to 400 degrees. Line a large, rimmed baking sheet with parchment paper and place the chicken breasts on the sheet, drizzling with the olive oil and seasoning generously with salt and pepper. Roast for 20–25 minutes, until a meat thermometer inserted in the thickest part of the chicken registers 165 degrees. Remove from oven and allow to cool.

Meanwhile, bring ½ cup water to a boil in a medium-sized saucepan. Add the mixed vegetables and return to a boil, stirring gently. Reduce heat to low, cover, and simmer 5 minutes until tender. Drain.

In a large saucepan, melt the 4 tablespoons butter. Add the onion and sauté until translucent, 3–5 minutes. Stir in the ⅓ cup flour, ½ teaspoon salt, and ¼ teaspoon pepper. Whisk in the chicken broth and the heavy cream. Cook, stirring constantly, over medium-low heat until the sauce comes to a boil and thickens, 10–15 minutes. Remove from heat.

Remove the roasted chicken from the bones and cut into bite-sized pieces. In a 3-quart casserole dish, combine the chicken and vegetables, then pour in the sauce and mix gently.

On a lightly floured board, roll out the pastry dough 2 inches larger than the top of the casserole. Place the dough over the casserole, folding the edges under and crimping the top edge. Cut several vents in the crust. Beat the egg yolk with 1 tablespoon water, then brush the crust with the egg wash. Place on a rimmed baking sheet and bake 40–45 minutes, until the sauce is bubbling and the crust is golden.

HOW TO MAKE
Literary Clothespin Dolls

Clothespin dolls are a fun and simple way to transform ordinary household items into something whimsical and imaginative. I have always loved the notion of making things with what one has at hand—the "Crafts" section of my childhood *Highlights* subscription was always the first place I turned when a new magazine arrived and I used to pore over those pages with a yearning akin to rapture. I scrounged Mama's craft stash for felt and bits of trim and raided her sewing basket for buttons and embroidery floss. Once I made an elf out of little green pom-poms with an acorn for a head and a snip of plaid ribbon for a hat; another time it was an infant Jesus nestled in a walnut shell with a sleepy-eyed paper head, a cotton-ball body, and a tiny scrap of calico for a blanket. When I fashioned a family of clothespin dolls for my dollhouse, coated thickly with tempera paint and graced with lopsided smiles, my satisfaction knew no bounds. Not only had I made them, I could play with them.

Around the same time, a small army of clothespin toy soldiers appeared on our Christmas tree, a gift from one of Mama's friends who had made them herself, and I remember the fascination with which I admired

MATERIALS:

Wooden craft clothespins
Acrylic paint, including flesh tones
Paintbrushes in varying widths
    (1/4-inch, 1/2-inch, 3/4-inch, etc.)
Permanent marker with an extra-fine tip
Scratch awl, such as used for piercing
    leather or wood
1/2-inch screw eyes
Craft felt in various colors for clothing
Bits of ribbon, tiny trim or lace,
    small beads
Scissors
Hot glue gun with an extra-fine tip
Elastic stretch cord (1 mm) or
    thin ribbon (1/8-inch) for hanging

the pom-pom hats, poseable pipe cleaner arms, and bits of miniscule silver braid marching down the fronts of the blue painted jackets. Here was a woman, I reflected, who knew her way around a craft store. And she knew her stuff when it came to clothespin dolls.

Those clothespin ornaments were irresistible to my brother and sister and me, spending far more time off the tree than on as they were recruited into various roles in our playtime. But Mama never seemed to mind. And the fact that not a one of them exists to this day is testament to the fun we had with them. For what good is a Christmas tree without a few toys in its branches, safe for small hands and entirely permissible?

The clothespin doll will blessedly never go out of fashion because how could so homely a thing be in fashion to begin with? And they are equally fun to undertake with a group of friends as with a clutch of small children. The possibilities are limitless— within the confines, of course, of a ramrod-straight body and wooden bead of a head. If you decide to make some clothespin doll ornaments, why not give them a literary flair, reflecting your noblest tastes in an endearingly humble way?

1. Paint the clothespin, beginning with the flesh tones. Thoroughly cover the head and neck area. Allow to dry, then paint the hair. Depending upon how your doll will be dressed, paint the rest of the clothespin to match the clothing, i.e. pants, boots, shoes.

2. After the paint has dried, draw the face with the permanent marker.

3. Make a hole in the top of the head with the awl and twist in a screw eye.

4. Using the templates provided (GladandGolden.com), cut the felt into clothing. Glue the clothing onto the doll with sparing amounts of hot glue, then trim the clothing as desired with ribbon, lace, or beads. Glue arms to the sides after the doll is dressed.

5. Thread a length of stretch cord or ribbon through the screw eye, knot tightly, and snip off the ends.

NOTES: Depending on the character you want to portray, you may wish to add fine mohair yarn or embroidery floss for hair. In this case, glue the hair to the top of the head after adding the screw eye in step 3. Detailed instructions for this can be found at GladandGolden.com.

Think about your character: do they have a distinguishing feature, color of hair, or article of clothing? Is there some tiny accessory you can glue into their hands to identify them? After you have decided on your doll's identity, shop your own house for items that will suit the needs of the particular character you wish to portray. For example, a mini-binder clip was the perfect shape and size to use as a base for Anne Shirley's carpet bag, and an acorn cap provided the crown for her hat. Tiny beads make excellent buttons, and larger ones can be glued to the back of the head to make a bun.

ANNE SHIRLEY:

Yellowish-grey or buff-colored felt
Anne's dress and hat templates
Card stock
1 small acorn cap, such as from a water oak
Fine jute twine (1.5 mm)
Craft glue
Power drill with a micro bit (#60)
Fine mohair yarn, rusty orange or auburn
Orange thread
1 mini binder clip (3/4 inch)
Scrap of colorful fabric (2 inch square)
Thin brown ribbon (1/8-inch)

1. Using the templates provided at GladandGolden.com, cut Anne's clothing out of felt and her hat out of cardstock.

2. To make the hat, carefully coil the jute twine over the top and bottom of the hat brim, securing with craft glue as you go. Repeat the process with the acorn cap, gluing the jute only to the top of the cap. When the glue has fully dried, attach the crown to the brim with a thin bead of glue. Dry.

3. Paint the features and dress the doll as instructed, then glue on the hat before attaching the screw eye. Drill through the hat with the #60 bit, then twist in the screw eye.

4. Cut the mohair yarn into three lengths, each about 10-inches long. Glue two lengths of yarn under the brim of Anne's hat, and one across the back of her neck. Braid the lengths, securing tightly with orange thread, then snip off the ends.

5. To make the carpetbag, remove the metal fasteners from the binder clip. Position the clip over the scrap of fabric and secure with hot glue, beginning with the bottom followed by the front and back. Trim off the excess as needed, then secure the two ends by folding the fabric in on all sides, like you're wrapping a gift. Cut two small lengths of 1/8-inch ribbon for handles and glue to the front and back. Slip the handles under Anne's hand and attach with a small amount of hot glue.

JIM HAWKINS:

Blue felt
Black felt
Jim's coat and hat templates
Small gold beads
Brown embroidery floss
Parchment paper
Fine-tipped pen

1. Using the templates provided online at GladandGolden.com, cut Jim's coat out of blue felt and his hat out of black felt. Paint the features and body as directed and draw the face. Attach the screw eye.

2. Dress the doll by centering the clothespin over the coat and gluing on each side to wrap the coat around the body. Fold down the collar and lapels, securing them, as necessary, with a small amount of glue.

3. Cut a yard-long piece of embroidery floss and fold it in half three times to make a hank roughly 12-inches long. Glue the midpoint of the hank to Jim's forehead, just beneath the screw eye, then pull the two edges toward the back of his head, securing with a little bit of glue on each side. Knot tightly into a ponytail with another piece of embroidery floss and trim the ends.

4. Make a small hole in the middle of Jim's hat with the awl. Apply a small amount of glue to the top of the head, then slip the hat over the screw eye, pressing firmly to secure. Working one at a time, fold up the edges of the hat, two in front and one in back, securing with a small amount of glue.

5. Cut a treasure map roughly 1-inch by ¾-inches out of a piece of parchment paper, using the fine-tipped pen to add details. Carefully burn the edges with a match, then attach the map to Jim's hand with a small amount of glue.

JO MARCH:

Crimson felt
Jo's skirt and top templates
Card stock and plain white paper
Needle and thread
Fine-tipped pen

1. Using the templates provided at GladandGolden.com, cut Jo's dress out of felt. Paint the features and body as directed, then paint the hair, making sure to give the suggestion of a rough, boyish haircut. Draw the face and attach the screw eye. Secure the dress top, then add the skirt.

2. To make Jo's book, cut a small piece of cardstock for the cover, about 1-inch by ¾-inch. Paint or decorate as desired. Cut three small pieces out of the white paper, slightly smaller than the cover. Fold all of the pieces in half and stitch along the fold 2–3 times. Use the fine-tipped pen to give the suggestion of writing throughout the book, then secure the book to the front of Jo's dress, just under her hand, with a small amount of hot glue.

The Empty Table

The year my mother died, the holidays felt like one more mountain to climb after a succession of seemingly endless ranges of exhaustion and grief. A couple of days before Thanksgiving I went over to Mama's house—it would always be Mama's house to me, though Mama had gone from it forever—and as soon as I opened the back door the emotions rushed over me again. There was the pool table, around which so many friends had gathered over the years; the velvet sofa, its down pillow backs permanently dented by Mama's black lab, Portia; the wild boar's head my Daddy shot with a bow and arrow, and which we ate on for months from small, white-wrapped parcels in the freezer. Every house has a scent—one of Elizabeth Goudge's homes smelled most memorably of "old wood, and lemon oil, and dog"; ours was always woodsmoke and cedar and candles and books— and this time the aroma greeted me as kindly as ever, if perhaps a bit reproachfully.

The truth was, I hadn't been over there in weeks. After nearly five months of ceaseless work, we had listed it on the market back in October, and I had vowed within my heart not to so much as lay eyes on the For Sale sign in the yard until I absolutely had to. Cleaning out the Chestnut Drive house was the hardest thing I had ever done, and yet, it was one of the most precious and meaningful experiences of my life. I felt like an archeologist excavating a happy past—a past that present sufferings had temporarily obscured. Time and again I sat in those silent rooms weeping over some unknown or unremembered evidence of our parents' love for us and for each other—cards and letters, prayer journals and Bible notes, book inscriptions and baby spoons and bits of broken china carefully glued back together. In a stash of gifts on the floor of my mother's closet one day, I found a plaque that I knew she had intended as a Christmas present for me: *Courage, Dear Heart*. After mopping my eyes, I hung it on a nail on the now-empty wall in the den beside the pool table, and it was the last thing I took out of the house with me when the realtor showed up with the lockbox and that odious sign.

Today, however, I braved the silence and strange emptiness for two items: Mama's woven cornucopia, which I'd spotted months back in the storage shed, and Great-Aunt Tiny's stylized painting of lantern flowers, which we'd left hanging over the fireplace in the living room. The former was requisite for my Thanksgiving table; the latter, I'd realized, would look lovely in my front hall.

Up in the storage house I secured my prize, and back in the living room I gently lifted Aunt Tiny's painting off of the brick wall. Then I wandered through the quiet rooms, closing closet doors realtors had left open, turning on certain lamps and turning off others. In the laundry room I remembered the shock of sorrow over cleaning out the utility closet, for, in a real home, of course, there is no such thing as the purely utilitarian. It's all sacred, right down to the corn-cob holders and picnic napkins, the dryer sheets and the brooms. The only things left in the kitchen were the teapot and three cups that our agent had asked me to leave for staging, and Mama's kettle on the stove, which looked so natural there that it had naturally been overlooked. I smiled, and left it.

Coming through into the dining room, however, I nearly choked over the sob that rose in my throat. There was Mama's table, her favorite piece of furniture in the house, its homely pine surface dark with varnish and age. How we used to tease and roll our eyes every time she pulled out her point-and-shoot camera, and later her cell phone, to snap yet another picture of us sitting around that table enjoying a meal together.

"We're going to have the most boring photo albums on earth," one of us would quip. *Who wants to look at a bunch of people eating?*

But Mama knew what the rest of us had to learn: that the best moments in life are not the exceptional ones, but the ones it was easy to miss altogether. I thought now of all the jolly feasts we had shared there together, the first time Philip had come for dinner, the holidays and special occasions, the homeschool mornings when it was littered with books and binders and mugs of cinnamon-laced coffee. I thought, more recently, of little teatimes with Mama, or lunches of our favorite Chinese takeout. I thought of her ubiquitous camera.

Even when Mama's illness had robbed her of the articulate conversation she was known for, it was still important for her to acknowledge the sacredness of this space, this domestic altar, as it were.

"Here," she would say, clutching the corners of the table with both hands and smiling at me with soft eyes. "Right here."

"I know, Mama. I know."

Packing up the photo albums a few weeks earlier, I had flipped through hundreds of pictures of us sitting around that table together, and it was far from boring. It was beautiful. One of the loveliest sights on earth, in fact, though I completely took it for granted at the time. In spite of the unreason of it all, I thought that we would always be going over there for dinners and everyday festivities, Christmas morning break-fast and just-because tea parties. I imagined that the big freezer in the laundry room would always be stuffed with dove and quail, rainbow trout and sweet white perch from Daddy's hunting and fishing expeditions. I assumed that nothing would ever change.

A few days later, Philip and I carried that table out under a sodden sky.

"Of course it's raining," he said.

"I don't mean to sound irreverent," I replied, as we squished across the backyard, "but this feels like the stripping of the altar."

I had a hard time settling into Advent that year. I was seized with a weariness that seemed to seep from the recesses of my soul out into the very limbs of my body. Even with the delightful prospect of a houseful of guests for both Christmas Eve and Christmas Day, I found myself paring back lists and tasks that would have been easy to manage in a less demanding year. I had the beautiful liturgies and traditions of my church to carry me, and the company of faithful friends both new and old with whom to make this sacred pilgrimage. I had my hymns and carols, my poetry books and my prayer book, a few cherished decorations sacred to Philip's and my story and a few newly assimilated treasures sacred to the story of the family in which I'd grown up. My heart was usually brimming with expectation this time of year. But as I sat in the glittering dark beside my Christmas tree in the mornings, I felt . . . *hollow*.

Every year I have asked Jesus to visit me and those in my care in a unique and specific way, to meet us in those places of our lives that most need tending. That year, however, Advent felt more like Lent, like a tenebraeic pall over the chambers of my heart. When I asked Jesus to come, to remember me with some healing image of his love in my mind or in my circumstances, all I could picture was a small, dark enclosure, like the cell of an anchoress buried in the walls of a church.

Then, one morning I thought of something else: *my mother's table.*

I'd snapped a photo back on that November day, but even as I reached for my phone to pull it up, I understood what it meant. That table was me: empty, barren, skinned to the bone with sorrow. I was completely depleted. And even as I was preparing to spread all these tables in the coming days for people I loved, *this* was a table I could not set.

"Please, Lord," I whispered into the silence of my den. "I'm not even sure what it means, but please set this table."

I had nothing to offer other than my emptiness. But it was enough—all that was required, in fact. I sensed that this picture was both an image and an invitation.

I would like to say that Jesus laid that board until it groaned, and, in a way, he did. It was one of the sweetest Christmases we had known, not just in spite of, but in the very face of, grief. The tender love of Christ was very real to me as I moved through my days and my preparations. It seemed, at times, as though a silent, sorrowful presence companioned me, holding space for my grief. At other moments I found myself laughing gently with the Lord over the fact that in years past I would have lost sleep over things like unfinished Christmas shopping and unwrapped gifts. But that year my mantra was exquisitely clear: the only things that mattered were that he was with us and that we were together. Perfect imperfection not only ruled over all my preparations, it carried me when preparations fell by the wayside. For everything else faded before a feast of such love.

And I began to understand what it means for God to prepare a table before us in the presence of our enemies, for what greater enemy is there than death? On Christmas night, my gaze traveled over the merry faces crowded around our table, each alight with a common joy and a shared hope, and I exulted over the kingship of Christ it signified. We could laugh and be silly, groan over awful cracker jokes, tell funny stories and savor special food *even when our hearts were breaking*, because we knew where the story was going. Someday, when all things were restored, death itself would die, for good and all.

In another sense, I knew that the setting of that inner table would be a long process, one with which I could cooperate, but not dictate. Mama always used to say that it takes us as many days to recover from a trip as those in which we've been away, and perhaps grief has a parallel. "Make us glad for as many days as you have afflicted us," the Psalmist entreats, and I like to think that embedded in this request is the tacit acknowledgement that "glad-making" takes time. Grief is a capricious thing, and it has a heyday with archetypical loss: we will never, God knows, outgrow our need to be parented. But God (two of the most consoling words ever stitched together) does not leave us orphaned. He comes to us in our most quiet need, mothering and fathering us back to gladness, trading our mourning for the oil of joy.

ADVENT
WEEK FOUR

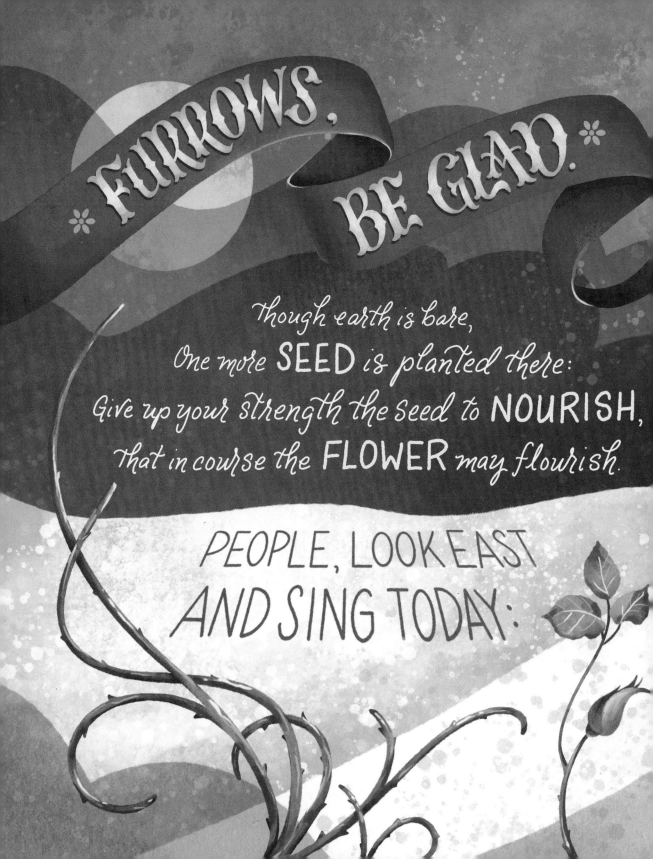

FURROWS, BE GLAD.

though earth is bare,
One more SEED is planted there:
Give up your strength the seed to NOURISH,
that in course the FLOWER may flourish.

PEOPLE, LOOK EAST
AND SING TODAY:

LOVE, THE ROSE, IS ON THE WAY.

Eleanor Farjeon, "Carol of the Advent"

Lo, How a Rose

It was late November, a time by which I had often completed most of my Christmas shopping, planned my holiday menus, mailed out invitations, and basically thrown myself heart and soul into the preparations for the season I love best. But that year I just wasn't up to it. I was worn out with sorrow, with protracted waiting and exhausted hopes, crushed under a disappointment that felt like a physical blow. Not exactly a recipe for a happy Christmas.

I was mad at God. It was all his fault.

I told him so, standing at my window, looking out over a diamond-shot dawn. Christmas, with all its gilded joys and tender associations, would only make things worse.

"I can hardly bear the thought that my Christmas rose has such a thorn."

I whispered it into the windowpane, and then I immediately thought how foolish that was, for a bright sadness had brooded over that stable in Bethlehem and a crown of thorns had drawn drops of blood as red as holly berries. I knew sorrow was a part of joy, as inextricable as the Cross from the Resurrection, and that any earthly hurt can make us keen to that loving heartbreak of God. The sorrow had just never been so tangible, so odiously unavoidable. And my thorn had such an ugly name: *Barrenness*.

It takes a good, stout Old Testament word to express the arid disgrace of it: the Bible is painfully good at looking things in the eye and calling them what they are, and those first faithful wanderers certainly knew a desert when they saw one. What better image of the desolation of disappointed hopes than a weary land hopeless for rain? For a long time I shied away from the word. I held it at arm's length and buoyed up my spirits with a sanguine hope for "next year." But on that late-November morning, options having dwindled and hopes all but extinguished, I stared into its lifeless expanse and realized with a horror that seemed to drain all the life out of me that this was the wilderness into which Jesus was asking me to follow him. It was the last place on earth I wanted to go. I wanted the desert of waiting to give way to desire fulfilled. I wanted him to be glorified, yes, but I wanted him to do it by giving me what I longed for.

The fact was, Jesus had let me down. Early in the newborn days of the previous January he had whispered a word to me, a potent assurance that seared itself on my mind in an unmistakable way. He had comforted my storm-tossed heart with a passage from Isaiah that echoed down through the centuries with a shout of triumphant hope and exploded into the very midst of the quiet room where I sat reading in my wasteland.

The wilderness and the solitary place shall be glad for them;

ran my trusty old King James,

and the desert shall rejoice and blossom as the rose.

The words were a cooling shower, steaming and hissing on the dry ground of my desert place of longing, and I sensed the silent movement of God's voice like a breeze among the brittle grasses:

It's all right to be sad about that. Now—let me make it something beautiful.

"Way to go, God," I wanted to say. He was really going to be glorified this time. And what better way to show himself strong than to make possible that which had proved impossible? To utter a resounding "Yes!" where circumstances had declared such an inexorable, "No." I could hardly wait to see what he was going to do.

And here I was almost a year later, disillusioned and disenchanted, in one of the darkest places I had ever known in my whole life. Nothing had changed—nothing but a heartbreaking flare of medical hope that had ended in ashes and a desire that had grown too heavy to bear. I felt bereft. I was bereaved and utterly forgotten, with no one to blame but the Author of the universe.

But there's one thing I've learned over the years when it comes to playing the blame game with God: he can take it. "Reviling is also a kind of praise," says the poet; "Pour out your grievances," says the psalmist. I have to believe that God prefers even insolence to apathy, feigned or otherwise—or worse yet, a pious stoicism. Complaint, at least, is personal; murmuring is abstract, which is why I think God must hate it so; it destroys intimacy. Astonishingly, in those moments when I've been most angry and honest with him, his benevolence has ended up appearing the most poignant. And in the first tender days of that particular Advent season, in the gathering glory of his great Giving and Coming, a bright-winged shadow seemed to gather and fall over me and a breath of wind began to stir through the barrens of my wilderness.

There is beauty in this place, he told me again and again, in precious and particular ways, and I clung to that idea like a drowning swimmer. If there was beauty here, I had to see it, for without its promise in my life I knew I would wither away inside. If there was no beauty here, there was no beauty anywhere—the thought chilled me to the marrow. But God's mercy is new every morning and visits us in a thousand unforeseen ways. The words of a favorite carol bore fresh grace to me the first time I heard it that year:

And so through every time of life,
to him who acts with reason,
The beauty of all things doth appear.

All things? Even this wasting patch of earth? Even this bewilderment of pain and desire? Even the hard-crusted face of suffering and surrender? *Yes, yes and yes!* came the answer on all sides, as if the very rocks and stones of my desert cried out in praise of God's harmony. Almost against my will, I went back and looked at that passage in Isaiah again—and I saw something I had never seen before. Those verses speak not of *exchange*, but of *transformation*. The desert is not merely traversed for a season and then gratefully left behind—it is remade, renamed, plowed and sown and domesticated. This from the hand of the God who "calls things that are not as though they were" and who makes new things out of nothingness.

The wilderness shall blossom as the rose.

"All right, Lord," I said. "Have at it."

And he did. On the first Sunday of that December we attended the Advent Procession at the cathedral downtown. The service is an ancient one, steeped in monastic tradition, wherein the choir travels around the church, singing at all the points of the compass, symbolizing the passage from darkness into light that our Lord's coming fulfills. I am such a visual person that this physical embodiment of the great Story is powerful to me, with all the anticipation building to the final glorious Latin hymn sung on the steps leading up to the altar. The most enlightening moment, however, was in the middle of the service, in the midst of a song I had never heard before. From the back of the cathedral came the springing of music and words, buoyant as birdflight:

People, look east! The time is near
Of the crowning of the year.
Make your house fair as you are able,
Trim the hearth and set the table.
People, look east and sing today:
Love, the Guest, is on the way.

An overwhelming longing seized me, deeper and more wordless than even my longing for a child, and I sat there in the pew with tears in my eyes and my heart pounding. A year ago I had imagined myself welcoming the baby we had long prayed for, but in that moment of blinding, choking joy, there in the holy hush of a cathedral with angels' voices filling the air, the Lord sang his own longing over me:

Welcome me! Prepare for me! Incarnate your love in practical ways—love your loved ones for my sake! Open wide your heart and your home and receive me more joyfully than ever before!

It was both a gift and a charge, a glad challenge my tired heart suddenly—miraculously—roused to meet. I felt as though strong wings were lifting me from beneath, as though a cup of joy had been held to my lips and a gentle voice commanded me to drink my fill, as though the wilderness itself was breaking into song all around me.

Furrows, be glad! Though earth is bare,
One more seed is planted there:
Give up your strength the seed to nourish,
That in course the flower may flourish.
People, look east and sing today:
Love, the Rose, is on the way.

WEEK FOUR

That moment threw a quiet mantle of wonder over the rest of the season, tingeing every act with a significance I had never known. A few days before Christmas I was up on a ladder wiring greenery onto a chandelier in anticipation of the loved ones that were soon coming, humming "Lo, How a Rose" under my breath (anything that had anything to do with roses seemed burdened with meaning that year), when suddenly I stepped down, clippers in hand, under the thrall of a singularly beautiful thought. I went straight to the phone, dialed my floral wholesaler, and ordered a huge box of blood red roses. When Philip came in with them later I literally danced around the table as he set the box down and lifted off the lid. They were breathtaking: an utter luxuriance of crimson and velvet, couched in a bed of tissue-soft wrappings. But ever so much more than that, they were to me both an image and an offering–an honor to the Author of this glad revel we were keeping in his name. Those roses were my personal statement of faith, my version of perfume lavished before the coming King.

I nursed them through two harrowingly warmer-than-usual nights and one down-right balmy day, but at the end of it I had the joy of spreading out on the porch with my floral supplies and clipping and wiring to my heart's delight. I made a big wreath of ivy to hang in our bedroom window and trimmed it with snowy white hypericum berries and sprigs of cedar flanking the perfect blooms. I tucked roses among the greenery over pictures and into the big arrangement of holly and pine in my grandmother's white porcelain compote. I laid them in beds of cedar along the mantle and I worked them into the wreath on the front door. And for the dining room, I fashioned them into rings at the bases of pineapples down the center of the table. I couldn't remember when I'd had such fun decorating, or been so pleased with the results. And this in a year when I wasn't sure I was equal to Christmas at all.

On Christmas Eve our home was bursting at the seams with family and friends-like-family. After the blessing, I read the beloved old greeting penned by Fra Giovanni in 1513 which has become a standard in our home. But never had the words seemed so appropriate:

There is glory and beauty in the darkness, could we but see! And to see, we have only to look.

I could vouch for that a hundred times over—but as I looked around the circle of beloved faces, I knew that every single one of them could testify to it as well. These were no untouched souls—many of them older and wiser than me by far—but faithful men and women of God who had taken his hand and wandered through deserts of their own. And every single one of them had come up with him rejoicing—*regardless of the circumstances*. They had seen a light in that dark place that the world could not offer or explain away. And they had never been the same.

The rooms rang with laughter and the snapping of fires and sounds of feasting and good fellowship that day. But loveliest of all to me were the sounds of the children, running through the hall, squealing in their games in the backyard. They lined up for the old-fashioned treat of oranges with soft peppermint stick "straws" and they pulled English crackers in the den by the tree. One three-year-old lass required my help to pull hers and when it gave way she toppled over backward in a cloud of white batiste and astonishment—I have to say it might have been the most beautiful sight of the day in a day full of beauty.

I will never forget that Christmas, or the fundamental shift that happened down inside of me. How it literally changed everything and how the wilderness flowered before my eyes. My desire had not abated a whit—if anything, it was heartier and haler than ever. But the wild anger had gone, and in its place there bloomed a fresh-flowered hope that all would be well: not because life is perfect or every desire will be fulfilled, but because Jesus *is*. Because he came among us, and he's still here when Christmas is over. *Thou meetest him that rejoiceth, and worketh righteousness.* In the years since, that has been the standard I have borne in all my preparations for Christmas: a torch flaming in the darkness and a voice in the wilderness. And he *does* meet us, in our most broken places, year after year, with the marvel of his Advent. And he *does* work wonders—miracles of quiet righteousness—even if they are so hidden in the depths of our hearts only he can see them. But wonders, no less.

Wondrous as a heart breaking with longing and joy at the same time; inexplicable as a barren place blossoming with roses.

Ah—with God, nothing shall be impossible.

HOW TO CARE FOR *and* ARRANGE
Roses

For centuries the rose has appeared in Christian poetry and texts as an image of Christ himself, and in many traditions the rose and the chalice are closely linked: just as the cup receives the wine, the calyx cups the petals of the rose, both of which represent the acceptance of divine grace.

If you would like to decorate with roses at Christmas, it's important to care for and condition them before using them in your arrangements. Long-stemmed roses tend to be pretty hardy, but in order to ensure a long vase-life, be sure to remove all broken stems, extra leaves, and lower buds as soon as you get them home. Give each stem a clean, diagonal cut with sharp clippers—preferably underwater to reduce oxygen intake into the vascular tissue—and place immediately in a vessel of clean, room temperature water. Store in a cool place, out of direct light, until ready to use.

When it comes to the actual arranging, the possibilities are limitless. Mass them together, cut at varying heights, in a special vase with cedar or fir as filler. Range a

RECIPE: Homemade Floral Preservative

2 Tbsp. white vinegar   ½ tsp. household bleach
2 Tbsp. sugar   1 quart warm water, filtered or distilled

Mix the vinegar, sugar, and bleach with the water (100–110 degrees). Warm water will move more easily up the stems of flowers, so use immediately.

series of small posies down the center of your table, or scatter them in vases around the house (be sure to place one by your guest book!). Place a single bloom in a bud vase for a special breakfast tray. Fill a compote with holly sprigs and trailing bits of ivy, nestling roses among the greenery.

To add them to a wreath or a garland, cut the stems about 4 inches long and force them into pick-shaped floral vials filled with water. Work the picks into existing greenery, making sure to keep the vials upright and the stems in contact with the water.

To make a pineapple pedestal arrangement, you will need a round, plastic floral foam container with a candelabra base, such as those used in tower vases. Wedge the base into a low candlestick; if it does not fit snugly, wrap the base of the container with floral tape until there is no movement. Fill the basin of the container with well-soaked Oasis foam and insert a tall floral pick into the center. Position a pineapple above the container and push the pick into the core. Cut the rose stems 3 inches long and tuck into the foam to form a ring around the base of the pineapple, filling in with greenery or white hypericum berries, as desired.

THE Second Greening

On the 23rd of December, my house is a mess. There are ivy leaves on the floor, a broom and a trash can in the front hall, a white sheet heaped with greenery in the dining room. There is a mountain of holly on the back porch and a good-sized hill of glossy green magnolia by the front door. Philip steps over a pile of ivy strands on his way out of the kitchen, while I dive under the sideboard in pursuit of rolling red berries. This may all seem like a setback after these weeks of preparation for Christmas, but it is actually quite intentional. For the second time in the season, and on a much more exuberant scale, I am bringing in the greens.

This second greening of my home is one I have learned to put off until the last minute. Much as I love to feel ahead of the game, my love of live greenery dictates a more leisurely approach to decorating. It feels lovely and Christmassy to hang boxwood wreaths in the kitchen windows in early December, and to make a few arrangements that can be kept in water. And, of course, I always do something special on the dining room table for the Notions Dinner. But I save the full crescendo of holly and ivy, cedar and fir, for Christmas itself. It is my own little act of resistance against the pressure we all feel this time of year to have everything picture-perfect before Halloween is over. I hate feeling rushed, particularly under a false sense of urgency. As Jung famously wrote,

"Hurry is not *of* the devil, it *is* the devil." And so, knowing all too well my own tendency to fall into that infernal trap, I force myself to slow down, to stand still a bit while the torrent of busyness and consumerism flows past me on all sides. Being the idealist I am, I could very easily spend the entire season of Advent in pursuit of an ideal that doesn't even exist—or, if it does, comes at the cost of all that really matters. Decorating with live greenery, however counterintuitive it might sound, keeps that from happening. Living greens are a limiting factor, and a guardrail to safeguard simplicity.

Another benefit of putting off the final decorating is that this greenery will last well into the Twelve Days, prolonging the sense of it still being Christmas, even if the rest of the world seems to have moved on. To my great joy, I am confronted on December 26th, not with a funereal display of dead holly and crispy cedar, but with a house fresh and fragrant as a forest. This, I have found, really helps to make the Twelve Days feel like an actuality, rather than a sentimental bit of wishful thinking. The sense of festivity prevails, and this at a time I can actually relax and enjoy it.

More than all of this, however, decorating slowly makes space for anticipation to gather in tangible form. Advent is a season of waiting and expectation. It is a time to acknowledge just how needy we are, and how helpless to help ourselves. With a super-human effort we have wrenched our gaze from the western horizon toward which all of society is trammeling in such haste and futility, and we have looked to the darkened east. We have sat in the night with our questions and our doubts, our wild longings and our hopes. We have prepared the way in our hearts and in our homes for this great Visitation. We have wrestled alike with the excesses of our culture and the inclinations of our own lesser natures. We have watched and prayed and tried to embody the meaning of the Incarnation in tactile ways.

And now, after all these weeks of waiting, there is a change in the air. The breeze has picked up ahead of the dawn, and a pearly mist appears above the treeline. Looking around at all these piles of greenery on the floor, I realize that my home is imaging what is actually happening: *the night is far spent; the day is at hand*. I feel like I am trimming my lamp as I tie a sprig of holly to one of the sconces in the hall. There is a hope made present in these rooms, an invisible reality taking visible shape, and the Ruff House thrums with the excitement of it all.

Although this great bowering and bedecking has bided its time, shielding me from the tendency to move too fast and do too much too early, still I must guard against excess—not of beauty, of course, but of expenditure. I have made time for this, but time is limited, and perfectionism has no place in so significant a task.

"Touch it once," I tell myself, nestling a spray of cedar behind the picture of Mary in the hall.

It helps to be reminded that there is no such thing as ugly Christmas greenery. The mere act of sticking a branch of holly over a picture wakens a room to merriment and mirth. A slip of ivy twined into a wreath or draped over the branching arms of a chandelier brings the space an immediate grace of simple cheer. I set a timer, not because this is a race, but because it is one of the final legs of a journey lovingly undertaken back in late November on that long-ago first Sunday in Advent, and with my blessed destination so clearly in sight I cannot afford to stray off into excess. I clip and wire within the confines of a morning, dragging my bedsheet of greenery all over the house and repairing often to the porches for more. I twist the long strands of ivy that Philip has cut for me into garlands for the guest room mantles, and I drape a spray of magnolia whimsically from the pediment of the grandfather clock in the hall.

In the dining room I really let myself go. Every picture boasts a crown of holly and the effect is perfectly Dickensian. I cock my head, and start to tweak a drooping twig, when my timer goes off. Two hours have flown in a happy spree of adorning, but now it's time to shake out my sheet and sweep up the littered remains. There will, I know, be one last little flurry of greens ahead of our Twelfth Night party on January 5th, but that seems like decades away from this satisfying moment.

I set things to rights, moving through rooms that speak of hope made present and longing fulfilled. The night is nearly over; the Dayspring is at hand.

HOW TO MAKE AN
Ivy Garland

If holly is the king of Christmas, ivy is its gracious queen. For centuries the two have been linked, in carol and legend as they often are in nature, growing together in harmony. The ancient Celts saw in the two plants living symbols of resurrection and eternity, and where holly has stood in Christian use as an image of Christ, the clinging ivy represents the fidelity of his mother, Mary.

MATERIALS:

5 or 6 strands of ivy
   of varying lengths,
   from 3 to 5 feet each
Paddle wire
Wire cutters or scissors

Ivy is, in my opinion, the most forgiving of all natural greenery to work with. It is resilient, flexible, and unfailingly good-natured. I like to tuck it into larger arrangements to give a softening droop beneath bolder focal points like holly or roses. It nestles agreeably among the arms of a chandelier, or threaded between candlesticks on a table. I love to wire single long strands of it to the finials of our four-poster bed, or to droop lengths of it from the curtain rod, following the deep swag of the curtains themselves.

Best of all, I like to make garlands, twining the vines upon themselves to create a lush swag in minutes. Every year, a day or two before Christmas Eve, I send Philip up to the secret corner of our property where the needlepoint ivy falls in great curtains and ribbons from the pines.

"How much do you want?" he will ask.

"Enough," I always reply.

Enough to make a few wreaths for the hall, adorn the bed, spruce up the dining room centerpiece, and soften the greenery over some of the pictures. And always enough to weave ivy garlands for the guest rooms, gracing the mantles with a festive touch that will last well into Christmastide.

1. If possible, soak the ivy overnight in a bathtub or large sink to hydrate it.

2. The next day, drain the ivy and spread it to dry on a large towel or sheet. Identify the cut ends and the growing ends of each strand (the growing ends are the ones you will want toward the extremities of your garland).

3. Starting with the longest piece, lay it out on the floor and find the midway point. Place another length of ivy alongside it, the cut end about 4 inches to the left of the middle, and secure with a small piece of wire.

4. Twist the two strands together, securing the ends, as necessary, with wire.

5. Repeat in the opposite direction with another length of ivy, taking care to overlap the cut end with that of the previous piece by at least 4 inches and twisting to the end of the original piece.

6. Continue to add strands of ivy, placing the middle of each new length over the starting point of the former piece and twisting in both directions, until the garland reaches a desired fullness.

7. Secure any loose ends with wire and gently pull any trapped leaves from beneath the woven vines.

On Gift-Wrapping

If I love all the mess and flurry in the kitchen and the frenzy of greenery all over the rest of the house, I absolutely detest the chore of wrapping gifts. I am not good at it, in the classical sense. My corners are never clean and my presentation is never original. My brother-in-law and his wife make a real art of it, with hand-drawn tags customized to each recipient and paper so pretty I'm always tempted to save a scrap of it in that year's Christmas folder. Laura is a past mistress of the vintage look, while Rachel's gifts are sheer confections of thoughtfulness and organza ribbon. I do try to keep things simple: as sedate and traditional a pattern as I can find (an increasingly difficult task in these days of loud designs and outlandish color schemes) and yard after yard of double-faced satin ribbon. This feature alone saves my packages from the humdrum, and it is a touch of extravagance I will continue to indulge in as long as my wholesale supplier of ribbon stands.

The real reason I dislike wrapping, of course, is that I put it off until the last minute. Efficiency experts will tell you to first knock out the task you least look forward to and then coast into the rest of your list on the energy that accomplishment provides. But, as my husband will tell you, I am about as efficient as a dandelion, and therefore, cresting into the fourth week of Advent, I find myself staring down, not only a list of things I want to do and can't possibly complete, but one great, big thing I dread.

It is a self-generating problem: when it comes time to wrap the gifts, I am faced with my inadequacies as a giver. No matter how thoughtful, or even sacrificial, they may have seemed on paper back in those expansive days of late November, I begin to second-guess myself. Are my nephews' presents as interesting as my nieces'? Did I give Rachel that same book last year? Does Philip even *want* a magnifying glass made from the handle of an antique carving set? And so I put it off, delaying this confrontation with my inner critic for as long as possible. At some point, however, the angst over the gifts gives way to angst over their wrapping, and I remember afresh that procrastination is really just a foil for anxiety.

So silly, I tell myself, *to give yourself palpitations over presents.*

But it's not just the presents. It's the pressure. We are transitioning out of Advent and toward the Feast of the Incarnation, and, sometimes, if I am honest, this makes me panic a bit. There is still so much to do—or, at least, I think there is. *One thing is needful, Martha.* But even this loving prick at my conscience feels burdensome; not only must I prepare for the blessed onslaught of guests, and all the food, clean linens, cherished rituals, and wrapped gifts attendant thereto, I must do it with a sacred intent and a holy simplicity. I must tune my heart toward the silent annunciations of Christ's coming. I must be still at a time when it seems like I can't stop moving.

The only antidote is to stop—literally and figuratively. It has been suggested by theologians that the injunction in Psalm 46 to "be still and know that he is God," is less a gentle recommendation and more a parental rebuke, much in the way that my Great Pyrenees, Luna, will simply sit upon a rambunctious puppy until it

settles. And so I plant myself, perforce, in my low armchair in the mornings with a chastened resolve and a new desperation. In the early days of Advent, my devotions were a resting place, a green pasture of possibility and anticipation; now they are a lifeline, connecting me to the Captain of my soul.

It is here alone, in the darkness of my den, before an unseen throne, that my limitations and my expectations make peace with one another—or, at least, settle into an uneasy truce. Here my weariness is seen and my ideals are given audience. Here the frantic bird of my mind comes home to its rest. I lift my loved ones, and all the things I want to do for them, to the one in whose Name all this doing is done. I remind myself that I am an earthen vessel filled with heavenly treasure, and that all my imperfections only serve to let that glory through. Even my unease over Christmas presents finds a safe space in this quiet hour, a healing touch of grace whispering that people rarely remember the gifts, but they never forget the love.

A few days before Christmas, I knuckle down to that pile of presents. We make a little party of it, Philip and I, with sherry-laced cocoa and smooth, jazzy Christmas music, and his good-natured attitude begins to rub off on me. He does all the wrapping, with his engineer's specifications on creases and corners, and I tie all the ribbons, the satin spooling out into lustrous puddles in the firelight. There are, as yet, miles to go before that glorious moment on Christmas Eve morning when the doorbell rings and the preparations officially cease. And, I confess, it is at this point in the season that I begin to look longingly toward the quiet oasis of the Twelve Days. But even now I can rest, in imitation of my Creator, who contemplated the work of his hands with sacred satisfaction. All of these gifts of time and treasure, all of these preparations, all of my inadequacies and limitations and hopes for this holiday, all of these imperfections— they are not just good enough. They are *good*.

PANTRY ITEMS
for Drop-in Guests

With a few salty and sweet bites in your larder and a couple of cured meats and cheeses in your refrigerator, you'll be ready to spread a board for guests at a moment's notice. Here are a few suggestions:

Jars of pickles, such as cornichons or sweet gherkins

Crackers
(whole grain and table water)

Salted nuts

Mini toasts

Marinated olives

Roasted red peppers

Pepperoncini

Raw honeycomb

Fruit preserves

Grainy mustard

WEEK FOUR

HOW TO BEAUTIFY YOUR
Table or Mantel

Holiday centerpieces and mantels don't have to be elaborate. Even the slightest touch of sparkle or color looks festive at Christmas. If you have an outlet nearby you can trail a strand of twinkle lights along your mantel, threading it among clippings of greenery. If not, bring out the candles—in fact, bring out the candles, anyway! I am a firm believer that candles are meant to be lit—my mother considered a pristine white wick to be a mark of, if not poor taste, at least a hint of indifference. The best way to make candles both serviceable and decorative is to light the wick the minute you put them in your candleholders, even if you won't be using them right away, and then blow them out immediately. This gives your candles credibility. And when it comes time to actually light them they'll go right up with the touch of a match.

In addition to light, think about structure. I like to shuffle things up a bit, gathering items from other rooms that might suit a Christmas spread. Sometimes the bust of a girl from one of the upstairs bedrooms makes an appearance on the dining room mantel; with a slip of ribbon around her resin locks and a sprig of cedar behind her ear she looks fetching and fresh. Or I will move Mama's big, cracked Delft bowl from the side table to the sideboard, where, overflowing with roses and holly, it takes centerstage against the dark wood and the mirror behind. Greenery on its own adds structure, of course, but the benefit of a vessel is that you can tuck a jar of water or a brick of floral foam inside and keep your cuttings fresh for days, if not weeks.

I tend to be a purist about red and green, but the season abounds in color and hue. Even the produce department at the local grocery is a feast for the eyes, with its blood-red pomegranates and scarlet radishes, its jolly mandarins and silvery artichokes. If I purchase a bag of Meyer lemons for a recipe, I can't bear to hide them away in the refrigerator; any that aren't used up reside—for a couple of days, at least—in a pretty bowl on the bar cart or kitchen table where their presence looks like sunshine itself. Satsumas make another lovely (and edible) decoration, particularly if they have the stem and a few satiny leaves attached. Much of the fruit and many of the vegetables in season this time of year can double-shift as mantel or table ornaments, if only temporarily. Create a Dutch still life with mounded produce, unshelled nuts, and blood oranges sliced open to reveal their raspberry-tinted flesh. Fill a few glass jars or votive holders with cranberries and a jaunty flourish of fir like a cocktail garnish. Perch pears atop low candleholders and thread kumquats into a dainty garland.

Above all, have fun! There is no right or wrong way to decorate (unless, of course, you forget to light those wicks), and the only thing that matters is that the sight of your rooms makes you happy and your guests merry. Use what you have in love and Christmas itself will take care of the rest.

THE Christmas Eve Brunch

Tradition is a funny thing. On the one hand, it dictates that a thing must be replicated, in a certain way, in a certain order, at a certain time, with a certain degree of consistency and intention, over and over, or it never achieves its traditional status in the first place. We must fight for it, sacrifice other things to its pre-existing claims, say no to competing opportunities in order to preserve its sacred boundaries. Traditions thread lives together in ways that bypass language and go straight to the heart of our beings. Tradition-less, we would drift through our days unmoored from any sense of belonging to a place and to a people. We would be rootless—nameless, in a way—without these golden bonds of repeatable, relational experience. In a world of "I," "me," and "my," tradition anchors us in a story of "us" and "we."

On the other hand, like a living thing and in the name of love, tradition has to be kept on a slack lead. It must be held as gently and reverently as one might cup a baby bird in the palm of one's hand, a bird that might—and ultimately will—take flight at any moment, leaving only the memory of its bright, vibrant presence in our midst. Even the best earthly traditions are temporal; they have a beginning and will come to an end someday, and whatever their duration, their course is littered with lesser firsts and lasts along the way. It is only by living within these larger limitations, that we open ourselves to the gifts of our present reality. If we don't protect the bird, it will die; if we clamp down our hand over its eager development, we will kill it.

Another hallmark of tradition, especially where family ceremony and celebration are concerned, is that it often appears on the scene without any intention of pluming into a full-blown ritual at all. Tradition often fledges as a good idea, a passing word, an invitation, perhaps. And that's just the delight of it all—we have no idea what cherished and indispensable things are waiting just around the corner of our days. What may seem like an exception may flourish into a tradition we simply cannot picture life without. And of none of our traditions is this truer than that of the Ivester-Boggs Christmas Eve Brunch.

For over twenty years the Ivesters and the Boggs have gathered at the Ruff House on Christmas Eve. The tradition started decades before that, when Philip's parents, Janice and Harold, and Luke's parents, Luther and Carol, started to take turns visiting each other on Christmas Day. Luther and Harold had been college roommates, and the friendship that flourished between the men and their wives was staunch and devoted. It was only natural that they would spend so venerable a day in the company of such friends. But the Ivesters and the Boggs have never been just friends. They are, and always will be, family.

"Janice had us to their place first," Carol tells me after all these years. "And it was so much fun that Luther said it needed to become a tradition."

When the Ivesters moved an hour northwest of Atlanta, the distance between the two families shrunk from across town to around the corner. Living moments apart, the holiday visit became a brunch and it was moved to Christmas Eve. When, a decade later, Janice and Harold moved across the state to be near Philip's older brother and his growing family, the relationship weathered the distance unharmed. But the brunch took a direct hit. Two hours one way was just too far for anyone to travel on the 24th of December.

The next year, we all felt the lack. Luke's sisters, Louise and Lori, were now among my dearest friends, and Carol had welcomed me into "the families" as one of her own.

It made me sad to think that I had only just begun to taste so sweet a tradition before it came to an end.

On the day after Christmas, Philip and I sat by the fire, reflecting upon our second holiday as a married couple. It had been lovely and special and quiet. But a little *too* quiet, we agreed. I wanted the rooms to ring with mirth and good cheer. I wanted the Ruff House full of people I loved.

"Philip," I said suddenly, with widened eyes. "We are right in the middle."

"Hey, you're right!" he replied.

Like the heart of a compass, the Ruff House was centrally located. We were an hour from Janice and Harold, and an hour from Luther and Carol. We were even less from Louise and Lori and their respective families, and Philip's brothers made the drive out to our place all the time. If Janice and Carol didn't mind my appropriating their tradition—and if everyone wanted to spend their Christmas Eve with us—we just might be able to resurrect the tradition of the Brunch.

Everyone loved the idea. And by the time the next Christmas had rolled around, I had decided that the Christmas Eve Brunch was to be the pinnacle of the year and the very height of loveliness for my home. Although my rooms were still rather spartan, I decorated them with abandon, robbing the American holly and the cedars around the house of branch after branch of fresh greenery. I polished my silver and ironed linen napkins for each anticipated guest, right down to two year-old Isabelle. And when everything else was done, I set the table with my wedding china, rather dizzy with the thought that I was to be mistress over so momentous an occasion. Louise thanked me for taking up the mantle. But *I* was the one full of gratitude. That all of these households should entrust one of the best days of the year to my care was nothing short of beneficent.

That first year there were just over a dozen of us, in addition to a clutch of small children. In the years since, our numbers have swelled well into the thirties, pushing past forty at times, as families have grown and visiting in-laws have joined our ranks. Early on, I would catch our impish friend, David Brooks, peering wistfully into the kitchen windows each year, and now David and his wife and four children are as much a fixture as any Ivester or Boggs. And our niece, Anna Kate, has broken ground on the fourth generation with a tiny son. The sight of her leaning to place him into Harold's arms at our dining room table, the light from the window behind touching her head with a gentle nimbus, is among my favorite moments in all my years of hosting the brunch at the Ruff House.

In this much time, it's no wonder that a crop of lesser traditions has sprung up beneath the branching arms of this greater one. One year I placed a huge, cut-crystal bowl on the children's table and a candy dish of "King Leo" soft peppermint sticks close at hand. Cutting circles in the tops of the fruit with a sharp paring knife, I showed them how to suck the juice through the striped candy "straws," and the response was sweetly keen. Everyone wanted to try it, then nearly everyone wanted to try it again as I frantically bored holes and unwrapped peppermint sticks. The resulting sticky fingers and chins were a testament to the enduring nature of the simplest things, and the next year when my nephew Wesley wanted to know where the oranges were, I scrambled to raid one of my centerpieces and to ferret a few peppermint sticks out of the pantry. It was then that I vowed in my heart never to host another brunch without the oranges. It still gives me a pang to think of that first year that no one asked for them, when the "children," now in high school and college and beyond, walked past them on their little side table, preferring another cup of coffee or a saunter around the yard to a peppermint stick in an orange. I was sad for a moment. Then I heard my niece's baby whimper from the other room. I looked across the kitchen at David's small daughter, Violet, who was finishing her second cinnamon roll at the kitchen table, and smiled.

"Violet, would you like a peppermint stick in an orange?" I asked.

"Shu-ah," she said, in a sticky voice. "What's that?"

"I'll show you."

Other traditions have been more or less fluid. Many years, I've used Christmas crackers—those hollow tubes crammed with candy and treats and silly jokes and paper hats—as place cards. When I do, I make sure to stuff the children's with tiny silver bells and plastic horns, and the resulting parade is a cacophony of holiday bliss the parents are only too happy to usher outside. Lori brought a couple of bottles of champagne one year and introduced mimosas into the mix. David often manages to sneak gingerbread men off of the tray in the dining room and scatter them in odd places around my house: peering down from the top of the grandfather clock in the hall, or peeking out from behind a silver bowl in the china cabinet.

But nowhere is tradition firmer than in the menu. The beauty of Janice's and Carol's original intent was that it would be a joint effort. Now, with so many cooks represented in our lineup, we are able to spread a feast with relative ease. In the early years, the ladies would call me each in turn, politely wanting to know what they could bring. It was a pretense we all kept up for a while, full knowing that the original food assignments had become each woman's lot in perpetuity, world without end, amen.

People literally walk in the door now talking about Louise's grits, anticipating that first savory mouthful. These grits are so anticipated, in fact, that Louise has been obliged to first double and now quadruple her recipe in order to supply the demand. We love our grits here in the South, but if someone told me that they were an innocuous side dish, lumpy at best and bland at worst, I would simply tell them that they have not met Louise's. Hers are a masterpiece of simple indulgence, so creamy and rich and thick it took her years to convince me that they did not have cheese in them.

Lori anchors the meal with her famous strata, a baked concoction of eggs and cheese and meat, varying from time to time with spinach or other vegetables, but always puffed and brown, crispy on top, hot and pillowy within. In recent years she has taken up Janice's habit of preparing an extra meatless version for our vegetarians, and it is safe to say that if Lori wants leftovers she must needs cook for an army. Edie brings her enormous blue glass bowl brimming with colorful fruit lovingly arranged, and it simply would not be Christmas Eve without Carol's apple-cranberry casserole, a tart holiday take on the oat-and-sugar-crusted crisp.

I have tried in vain to replicate Janice's coconut cake, a delicacy I fear we have lost with her. But I can still see Harold coming in the door with that Tupperware carrier, and I am still haunted by the memory of dense, sweet cake encased in light-as-air white frosting. I remember how the flavors blended with the citrusy brightness of the ambrosia she always made to go with it—in itself a labor of love—and my heart rallies to try again.

My lot, however, falls to the cinnamon rolls, a once-a-year indulgence bathed in buttery caramel glaze. I discovered early on that if I divided my recipe among three disposable aluminum pans, I could make them well in advance, freeze them before the last rise, then thaw and bake them off on Christmas Eve morning. There is just nothing like the scent of cinnamon rolls to tell people that they are loved and welcome; mingling with the fragrance of open fires and the aroma of sausages browning away on the stove it is among the most felicitous greetings on earth. It broke my heart one year to realize that, having added the optional chopped pecans to the cinnamon-sugar filling, I had inadvertently cut Isabelle off from one of her favorite treats; henceforth a note in the margin of my recipe reminds me to dispense with the pecans in the name of nut allergies.

On Christmas Eve morning there is coffee to make, there are sausages to fry, candy dishes to fill, as well as last minute touches to be made to the arrangements and centerpieces. But it is my own personal and venerated tradition to be ready by 10am. The brunch doesn't start until 10:30, but, ready or not, I stop by the stove and turn on the radio. There I hear the rustle and stir of a great congregation settling into their seats, and, after one breathless moment of silence, the ethereal treble solo of "Once in Royal David's City,"

Music for Week Four

BRIGHTER VISIONS
BEAM AFAR
Don Peris

THE HOLLY AND THE IVY
Clare College Choir, John Rutter

A COLONIAL CHRISTMAS
Early Music New York

THE CHRISTMAS SONG
Nat King Cole

THE CHERRY TREE
Anonymous 4

BELLS OF DUBLIN
The Chieftains

THE DORIS DAY
CHRISTMAS ALBUM

wavering down the vaulted aisles of King's College, across the miles and over the ocean, right into my own kitchen where I stand rapt and teary-eyed to receive it. I have listened to the live broadcast of Nine Lessons and Carols from Cambridge, England, since I was a teenager. But this opening moment, and the great Bidding Prayer that follows, are my favorite parts of the service. And while the rest of the carols and readings may carry along joyously in the background of our party, these must be attended to in silence and reverent care, remembering those of our number who "rejoice with us, but on another shore and in a greater light." Somehow, those words always manage to span the supposed gulf between heaven and earth, assuring me that the communion of saints is not just a future hope but a present reality.

After that I just have time to dry my eyes, light the fires, and pop the cinnamon rolls into the oven before the doorbell rings. Michael and Edie are always first, peering and waving through the big fir wreath on the front door. But by the time Ross and Lori and their three children arrive, followed shortly by Andy and Louise and their four, the doorbell has been dispensed with and the front hall is a melee of merry greetings. In the kitchen, I wade through the throng, directing people where to put their dishes and hugging everyone I meet. In the bedroom, a mountain of coats is heaped upon the bed and a pile of mudboots, betokening adventures in the barn after the meal, amasses by the front door.

When it's time for the blessing, the hall is the only place that can hold us all. There is a burning at the back of my throat as I stand halfway up the stairs trying to capture everyone within the frame of a single picture.

"I never take this for granted," I always used to say, back in the days when our company only increased and never diminished. For we are living now, as Wendell Berry has said, in the "presences of absences." Before Luther, and then Harold, joined "that multitude which no man can number" we always asked one or both of them to pray for our meal and our time together. Now that honor rests upon Philip, and his voice trembles for a moment midway through. It is hardly perceptible, but I notice, and I know what it means. It is what we are all thinking. We—Philip, Andrew, and Michael, Luke, Louise, and Lori, and our respective spouses, are the older generation now. We seat Carol, queenlike, at the head of the table in the dining room, flanked on either side by Philip and Michael, who attend her with the courtesy of cavaliers. All around her the conversation flies up and down the table. From the parlor, the kitchen, the front hall, comes the clink of china cups, the crackle and hiss of open fires, the laughter. We laugh, even with empty places at our table and aching spaces in our hearts, because we know these are just the "shadowlands," as C. S. Lewis has said. Someday, for all of us, this school term of life will end. Then the *real* holidays will begin.

After the meal, little girls tromp up to the garret to raid the dress-up trunk while bigger girls wander over the pastures or play duets on the piano. In the backyard a game of pass is underway. Down at the barn, the ducks come fussing and flapping out of their house as Charlie Brooks's head appears in the doorway with a grin every bit as impish as his father's.

Before everyone has had time to even consider another mouthful, I announce that the pudding is imminent. Young and old alike descend upon the kitchen to see the yearly marvel of hot, molded cake a-dance with mystical blue flames, and its enchantment rarely disappoints. I used to make a very English plum pudding, to befit the antique mold Philip gave me for Christmas years ago, but it finally occurred to me that the children were merely sifting through the crumbs in search of the prized silver thimble. Its flavors were a little too Victorian, perhaps, for these very American children. So I devised a more familiar version reminiscent of gingerbread, and this, to my relief, is a dessert that is done credit to. I dish out servings, pretending not to notice when my spoon meets the little thimble amid the sweet, spicy depths, and that plate always goes to a child, who is delighted to find the treasure in his or her piece of cake. Nothing more than a trinket, bearing nothing more than the distinction of possession and the silly promise of good luck in the coming year. Yet the magic holds, again and again.

And thus the years have accrued, as our numbers have swelled and ebbed and begun to swell again. All so distinct, and yet all so very much the same.

Except, of course, that awful year when nothing was the same.

The Christmas after the house fire was a hard one. We were snug at Camp Marah while the restoration of the Ruff House was well underway. And we had managed to carry some semblance of tradition into this wilderness with us—the Advent wreath swung from a hook in the camper ceiling and the interior was festive with tea lights and bits of greenery. I had even hung a big wreath on the door of the camper, and there was often a simmer pot of oranges and cloves on the back burner of the tiny stove. But I was homesick for all the moments that meant Christmas to me: the cookie-baking and the candy-making, the menu-planning and the table-setting. I missed my guest rooms, lovingly prepared; my chest freezer, stocked with treats; the ring of my own doorbell.

Most of all, we missed the Christmas Eve Brunch. Back on that faraway June day when we had first moved into the camper, Louise and Lori had arrived on the scene with arms full of groceries. After they put everything away, we sat down in the vinyl-and-laminate space and looked at one another rather dazedly.

"I think we can cram everyone in here for the brunch," I said with a light laugh.

But we all knew it was impossible. And there was nothing funny about a Christmas without the Ivester-Boggs brunch.

As Christmas Eve drew near, I occupied myself with managing contractors and making decisions, flinching away from even the thought of what I would be doing were

I back home in the Ruff House. A couple of days before Christmas I went inside to survey the day's work. The contractors had gone and the quiet rooms were grey with winter light. I stepped over piles of debris, skirted the chop saw mounted on a makeshift table, looked up at the hollowed-out recesses of my front hall. It was hard to believe that the banister had ever been draped with garland, or that the tall archway, stripped of its trim, had ever known the feathery festoons of white pine and cedar. The kitchen was a desolate shell, the den a repository of extra lumber and electrical supplies. We were making progress, and hopefully this time next year we would be home and more grateful than ever. Nevertheless, I went back to the camper feeling sorry for myself. This was simply a Christmas to be gotten through.

We got through it. On Christmas Eve we grilled our traditional steaks, and on Christmas Day we went to my mother's for breakfast casserole and *bûche de Noël* from the French bakery. On Christmas night I collapsed on the little Camp Marah couch with a sigh. It had been hard and sweet and exhausting and tender, and now I wanted to sleep for a week.

The next morning, my phone rang. It was Lori.

"We don't want to impose," she said. "But the kids would really like to come over. It doesn't feel like Christmas without a visit to the Ruff House."

I hadn't acknowledged it until that moment, but a secret fear had crouched beneath my sorrow all season: what if, in taking a year off, everyone discovered something else they would rather do on Christmas Eve? What if this tradition had finally had its day?

But eight year-old Kitty put my heart at rest.

"I cried a little bit on Christmas about not coming here," she told me, standing in my backyard the next afternoon. "It wasn't nearly as good."

Lori confided that her young son, Drew, had prayed on Christmas night that Philip and I would be back in our house "really, really fast—maybe even before Christmas is over." Evie said, with one of her gentle smiles, that coming to our place was her favorite thing about the season. Hallie and Isabelle sauntered over the pasture and Virginia played with the dogs and Philip threw the football with Thomas. Then we gathered outside the camper for store-bought sugar cookies and hot cider in Styrofoam cups. A friend had sent me a box of soft peppermint sticks for Christmas, and when I produced them, Kitty asked solemnly if she might please have an orange.

These children had seen in their innocence what I had missed in all my so-called experience. They didn't care about the trappings and the trimmings so much as the memories and relationships they represented. It wasn't the flaming pudding or the beautifully set tables, or even the homemade cinnamon rolls that were requisite, but the *people*. The traditions were the container, the casket for the jewels. But the jewels themselves were right here in my backyard, under this kindly benediction of December sunlight.

We would move back into the Ruff House the following year, and there would be a return to the mountain of coats on the bed, the array of dishes on the kitchen counters, the pile of boots by the front door. But it would prove so much *more* than it would have been without that wilderness sojourn and the wisdom of children. For they had brought me home to the original simplicity of the thing. Tradition, like liturgy, grants form and substance to unseen reality, and it carries us when circumstances or emotions belie what is actually true. Luther and Carol, Janice and Harold, understood this. And they knew that tradition is always the servant of relationship. They probably never dreamed how their simple holiday gathering would become the anchor and the highlight of our year. But they absolutely recognized the treasure they had in one another. We were, I knew, enjoying the fruit of a fidelity that preceded us and which, if we stewarded it well, would continue long after we were gone. We do not keep our traditions so much as they keep us.

MENU FOR Christmas Eve Brunch

LANIER'S CARAMEL CINNAMON ROLLS
LOUISE'S CREAMY DREAMY GRITS
CAROL'S CRANBERRY-APPLE CASSEROLE
MEATLESS MAKE-AHEAD EGGS
LINK SAUSAGE
FRESH FRUIT
STEAMED GINGERBREAD PUDDING
JANICE'S COCONUT CAKE *with*
SOUTHERN AMBROSIA
ASSORTED JUICES
COFFEE

LANIER'S CARAMEL CINNAMON ROLLS
MAKES 36

You may not need the full amount of flour listed here—sometimes my dough will only accept 6 ½ cups, while other times it takes the full 8 cups before it starts to pull away from the sides of the bowl. The main thing is to add the flour ½ cup at a time and to watch the dough carefully. You don't want it to be too sticky, but if it is too dry your rolls will turn out hard. The perfect balance is a dough that just sticks to your finger yet loosens easily from the side of the bowl when you turn it out (you will incorporate a little more flour at kneading time). Also, take care not to heat your water above the recommended 105 degrees or it may kill the yeast and your rolls won't rise.

DOUGH:

2½ cups warm water (105 degrees)

2 tablespoons (two 0.25 ounce packages) active dry yeast

½ cup sugar

½ cup buttermilk powder

1 egg

1 ½ tablespoons Madagascar bourbon vanilla extract

⅓ cup vegetable oil

1 tablespoon salt

7 to 8 cups unbleached all-purpose flour

GLAZE:

1 cup (2 sticks) unsalted butter, cut into ½-inch pieces

2 cups packed light brown sugar

½ cup light corn syrup

¼ cup water

FILLING:

> 6 tablespoons unsalted butter, melted
>
> 1½ cups packed light brown sugar
>
> ¼ cup ground cinnamon
>
> 1 cup dried currants
>
> 1 cup chopped pecans (optional)

To proof the yeast, pour ½ cup of the warm water in a small bowl and sprinkle the yeast over it. Add a pinch of sugar and stir to dissolve. Let stand at room temperature until foamy, about 10 minutes.

In the large bowl of an electric mixer fitted with the paddle attachment, combine the remaining 2 cups warm water with the buttermilk powder and stir to combine. Add the remaining sugar, egg, vanilla, oil, salt, and 2 cups of the flour. Beat hard for 1 minute, then stir in the yeast mixture. Add the remaining flour, ½ cup at a time, until a soft, shaggy dough is formed that just clears the sides of the bowl. (Be careful not to add too much flour, as this will dry out your dough.)

NOTE: To mix by hand, combine the proofed yeast with the remaining 2 cups warm water, sugar, egg, vanilla, and oil in a large, heavy mixing bowl. With a large balloon whisk, incorporate 1 cup of flour, buttermilk powder, and salt into the wet mixture and whisk hard for 1–3 minutes until the batter is smooth and creamy. Switch to a wooden spoon and add the remaining flour, ½ cup at a time, beating vigorously between additions until a shaggy mass is formed that just clears the sides of the bowl.

Turn out the dough onto a lightly floured surface and knead for 1–3 minutes (3–5 minutes for a hand-mixed dough) until soft and springy, dusting with flour 1 tablespoon

WEEK FOUR

at a time, if necessary, to keep it from sticking. The dough should be moist and soft, with a smooth texture. Spray the inside of a large mixing bowl with cooking spray and place the dough in the bowl, turning once to coat the top. Cover tightly with plastic wrap and let rise at room temperature until double in bulk, about 1 to 1¼ hours. Combine the 1½ cups brown sugar and ¼ cup cinnamon in a small bowl and set aside.

About 10 minutes before forming the rolls, prepare the glaze. Grease the sides and bottom of the baking pans with cooking spray. In a small, heavy saucepan, melt the butter, brown sugar, corn syrup, and water over low heat, stirring constantly. When melted, remove from heat and immediately pour into the prepared pans, dividing the amount equally and spreading the glaze over the bottom with a rubber spatula. Set aside.

Turn out the dough onto a lightly floured surface and divide into three equal portions. Working with one at a time, stretch and roll each portion out into a roughly 12 x 16-inch rectangle. Leaving a 1-inch border around the edges, brush the surface with ⅓ of the melted butter, then sprinkle evenly with ⅓ of the sugar-cinnamon mixture, ⅓ of the currants, and ⅓ of the pecans, if using. With dry hands press the filling firmly into the dough, then roll up, starting from the long edge. Pinch the seam to seal.

With a serrated bread knife, gently slice each roll into 12 equal portions, about 1 inch thick. Place the slices evenly in the baking pans, cut side down, and cover loosely with plastic wrap.

If you plan to bake the rolls right away, let them rise at room temperature for 45 minutes, until risen and even with the rims of the pans. Preheat the oven to 350 degrees and bake until the tops are just beginning to brown, 25–30 minutes. Remove from the oven and let stand 5 minutes before inverting onto a serving platter or baking sheet, taking care not to touch the hot glaze. Let cool 10–15 minutes and pull apart to serve.

To bake them at a later time, cover the unrisen rolls with a loose layer of plastic wrap and refrigerate overnight. Remove the pans and allow the rolls to rise at room temperature, 30–45 minutes, then bake as directed.

To freeze unbaked rolls before the last rise, cover the pans with a layer of plastic wrap and then wrap tightly with aluminum foil. Prior to baking, let them stand, uncovered, at room temperature for about 6 hours, or until doubled in bulk, then bake as directed. (Be sure to use aluminum pans for freezing to prevent breakage and freezer burn.)

LOUISE'S CREAMY DREAMY GRITS
SERVES 8

Louise always makes these grits on Christmas Eve morning and brings them to my house in a big stock pot wrapped with towels to keep warm. If they need to be reheated you may do so over the lowest heat possible, covered. This recipe can easily be doubled for a crowd.

4½ cups chicken stock or canned low-salt chicken broth

1½ cup whipping cream

1 stick (8 tablespoons) butter

1½ cup quick-cooking grits

Salt and pepper to taste

WEEK FOUR

Bring stock, cream, and butter to a simmer in a heavy medium saucepan over medium heat. Gradually whisk in grits. Reduce heat to low, cover, and cook until grits are creamy and tender, stirring occasionally, about 6 minutes. Season to taste with salt and pepper.

CAROL'S CRANBERRY-APPLE CASSEROLE

SERVES 8–10

Fresh cranberries are only in season from September through November. But since this dish works just as well with frozen cranberries, you might want to pick up an extra bag and pop them in your freezer when you start seeing them in the stores around Thanksgiving.

2 tablespoons flour

¾ cup sugar

3 cups peeled, chopped Granny Smith apples

2 cups fresh cranberries, rinsed

12 tablespoons unsalted butter

2 cups rolled oats

½ cup brown sugar

1 teaspoon cinnamon

Mix flour and sugar in a medium bowl. Toss apples and cranberries with the flour/sugar mixture and pour into a 2-quart casserole dish.

Melt the butter in a medium saucepan. Add oats, sugar, and cinnamon and mix until well-combined. Layer on top of the fruit, and bake, uncovered, for 45 minutes.

MEATLESS MAKE-AHEAD EGGS

SERVES 8

There are widely varying opinions on a perfect scrambled egg; some people like them firmly set, while others prefer them on the runnier side. This recipe of my mother-in-law's strikes a nice balance between the two while providing a satisfying option for the non-meateaters.

12 eggs
½ cup heavy cream
½ teaspoon kosher salt
⅛ teaspoon white pepper
2 tablespoons unsalted butter
1 cup sour cream
1 cup shredded cheddar cheese

Beat the eggs and the heavy cream in a large bowl. Stir in the salt and pepper. Melt the butter in a large skillet over medium heat. Pour the eggs into the skillet and cook, stirring, until the eggs are scrambled and set to your liking.

Remove from heat and stir in the sour cream. Spread into a greased 9 x 13-inch glass casserole. Sprinkle with the cheese, cover with foil, and refrigerate overnight.

The next morning, allow the casserole to stand on the kitchen counter until it reaches room temperature, roughly 1 hour. Preheat the oven to 300 degrees. Cook, uncovered, for 20–25 minutes, until the cheese is melted and the eggs are hot.

WEEK FOUR

STEAMED GINGERBREAD PUDDING
SERVES 8

A pudding mold makes for an attractive and traditional-looking dessert. But if you don't have one, you can use a 2-quart heat-proof glass or ceramic bowl. Prepare as directed and cover the surface of the pudding with buttered parchment paper. Then wrap the bowl thoroughly in two layers of plastic wrap and two layers of aluminum foil, taking care to overlap the pieces so as to prevent steam from entering once the pudding is cooking. Set the bowl on a rack or inverted saucer in a large stockpot and steam as directed.

Don't forget to drop a silver thimble or other lead-free metal trinket into the pudding batter before steaming!

2 ¾ cups unbleached all-purpose flour

2 teaspoons baking powder

2 teaspoons ground ginger

1 teaspoon baking soda

½ teaspoon salt

2 teaspoons ground cinnamon

½ teaspoon ground allspice

¼ teaspoon ground cloves

¼ teaspoon ground nutmeg

2 large eggs, room temperature and lightly beaten

1 cup milk

1 cup dark molasses

3 tablespoons unsalted butter, melted

½ cup finely chopped crystallized ginger

Unsalted butter and granulated sugar for the mold
3 tablespoons brandy
Whipped cream

Butter the inside of a 2-quart covered pudding mold and sprinkle with sugar, shaking out any excess. Cut a piece of parchment paper the size of the lid. Butter the inside of the lid, press the parchment paper into the lid, and butter the paper.

Sift together the flour, baking powder, ground ginger, baking soda, salt, cinnamon, allspice, cloves, and nutmeg and set aside. In a separate bowl, whisk together the eggs, milk, molasses, and melted butter. Stir in the crystallized ginger. Add the wet ingredients to the sifted dry ingredients and stir until well combined.

Pour the batter into the prepared mold and attach the lid securely. Tie a length of kitchen twine tightly around the mold and place the mold on a rack or inverted saucer in a large stockpot, lid side up. Fill with enough water to come halfway up the sides of the mold. Simmer, covered, over low heat for 1½ hours.

Carefully remove the mold from the pot and allow to cool for 5–10 minutes. To unmold, cut the twine and lift off the lid, peeling back the parchment paper. Run a sharp knife around the edges of the mold while the pudding is still warm, then invert onto a flame-proof serving plate and lift off the mold. If the pudding sticks, gently tap the mold with a wooden spoon.

To set the pudding alight, warm the brandy in a cast-iron skillet over medium-high heat until it just begins to steam. Immediately remove and ignite the brandy with a match or a torch lighter. Pour over the pudding and serve with whipped cream.

WEEK FOUR

JANICE'S COCONUT CAKE
SERVES 12

My mother-in-law was famous for this cake; she made it for birthdays and special occasions as well as for Christmas. And she always seemed able to magically produce it at a moment's notice. While the method is relatively simple, however, it's important to note that the preparations need to begin two days ahead of time in order to give the flavors a chance to blend properly.

If this is your first time making a whipped-cream frosting, keep in mind that the trick is to start with a cold mixing bowl and beaters and to whip the cream at high speed with an electric mixer until stiff peaks stand up when you lift the beaters out of the cream—too little time and your frosting will be runny, while too much time will turn your cream to butter and the frosting will separate.

This cake can also be frozen after frosting. Wrap loosely with plastic wrap and place in the freezer for 2 hours until firm. Replace the plastic wrap with aluminum foil and wrap the entire cake once more in plastic. Defrost overnight in the refrigerator and let stand at room temperature for 2 hours before serving.

> 1 14-ounce bag sweetened coconut flakes
>
> 2 cups sugar
>
> 16 ounces sour cream
>
> 1 box yellow cake mix, plus ingredients indicated in the mix instructions (water, eggs, oil, etc.)
>
> 1 pint heavy cream
>
> ¼ cup powdered sugar
>
> 1 teaspoon Madagascar bourbon vanilla extract

Beginning two days before you want to serve the cake, mix the coconut flakes with the sugar and sour cream and refrigerate overnight.

The next day, prepare the yellow cake according to the package directions and bake in two 8-inch round cake pans. Cool on wire racks for 10 minutes, then invert and cool completely. Place a mixing bowl and beaters in the freezer to chill.

Slice each cake round horizontally in half, to produce a total of 4 layers. Reserving 1½ cups of the coconut mixture, spread the remainder evenly between the cake layers. Whip the cream and powdered sugar in a cold bowl with cold beaters until stiff peaks form. Fold in the vanilla, then stir the remaining coconut mixture into the whipped cream. Frost the top and sides of the cake, and let stand, covered loosely with plastic wrap, in the refrigerator overnight.

SOUTHERN AMBROSIA

SERVES 6

The jury is out in our family on whether to include cherries in a proper ambrosia or not. Philip's mother wouldn't think of it, while Mama wouldn't consider leaving them out. The great thing is that with sweet navel oranges in season it's good either way; for the best flavor select oranges with smooth, thin skins that feel heavy in your hand.

  8 medium navel oranges
  ½ cup shredded, sweetened coconut
  1 10-ounce jar stemless maraschino cherries

Cut a slice from the top and the bottom of each orange to reveal the flesh. Holding them over a bowl to catch the juices, slice off the peel with a sharp paring knife from the top downward, following the shape of the fruit to remove all of the white pith. Segment the oranges, dropping them into the bowl with the juice. Remove any seeds and stir in the shredded coconut. Drain the cherries in a colander and add to the orange mixture. Cover and refrigerate for at least 8 hours before serving.

HOW TO MAKE
Christmas Crackers

T he custom of Christmas crackers dates back to the 1840s, when Clerkenwell confectioner Tom Smith upgraded the tissue-wrapped Parisian bon-bon by layering strips of paper coated with silver fulminate against an abrasive surface to create an explosive little crack when opened. Supposedly, the pop was inspired by the snapping of a log fire, but the addition of paper hats and trinkets was the contribution of Smith's son, Walter, who scoured the globe for little novelties with which to stuff the popular treats. All these years later, the English cracker is an abiding staple in Christmas celebrations, both in Britain and beyond.

As Christmas approaches, I begin to see them everywhere, from the grocery to the discount stores to the farmer's market. But I've always been disappointed with the quality of the contents: far from Walter Smith's Japanese or European novelties, crackers these days are characterized by cheap plastic gewgaws and tasteless jokes. The solution, as with so many things in this over-manufactured and highly-commercialized world, was to make them myself, and I was amazed, the first time I tried, at, not only how simple they were, but how fun it could be to customize the crackers for my guests.

The year that Rob and Katie came with their eight children for Christmas Dinner, Philip and I sifted through the dollar bin at a local antique store for pins and pendants for the girls, fobs and figurines for the boys. When Rachel and Gary brought their newly grownup daughters for a champagne and candlelight affair one Christmas night, I filled their crackers with lip gloss and sample-sized spritzers of perfume. And if I decide to make them for Christmas Eve, there will be homemade candies or tiny wooden ornaments for the adults, and inch-square molded animals for the children.

I've charged Philip with sourcing the jokes, which he does from an internet archive of eye-rollingly bad Victorian wisecracks, and even these are tailored to their recipients as we giggle over who will read which nonsense around the table come Christmas. The paper hats are requisite, not only to add a touch of feigned formality to the reading of the jokes, but to dignify each person present with a touch of endearing absurdity. As most of our photos will attest, once the crackers have been opened, people will wear their tissue-paper coronets well into the afternoon or evening. Few sights are dearer to me than that of my dining room table littered with cracker contents and the remnants of a feast and encircled with beloved faces talking earnestly under the adornment of a lopsided paper crown.

Sweeping up the detritus of pulled crackers is yet another of the visual signals of Christmas to me. It means that merriment has been made and that wholesome fun has been had. I have learned over the years that in order to make the most successful cracker, it is important to keep both ends of the "snap" free from the glue that holds the rest of the apparatus together. It is also best to instruct the uninitiated to pull, not the paper wrapping, but the snap itself to make sure that the cracker opens with a pop rather than an anticlimactic tumble of tissue and treats. The most successful crackers are those that end up exploding all over—and under—the table, sending people scurrying after their contents.

MATERIALS:

Thick wrapping paper,
   cut to 8x12 inches
Cardboard tubes (paper towel
   or bath tissue rolls work well),
   cut to 4 inches long
Glue gun
Scissors
Curling ribbon
Cracker snaps *
Tissue paper crowns *
Small gifts or trinkets, one for
   each cracker
Jokes or riddles

1.   Center a cardboard tube on a piece of wrapping paper. Apply a small amount of glue to one of the long edges of the paper and roll the tube over the glue.

2.   Place a cracker snap in the center of the wrapping paper and roll the tube and paper to within ¼ inch of the paper's edge. Apply a thin bead of glue along the exposed edge and roll the cracker over the glue.

3.   Gently crimp one end of the paper close to the tube, taking care not to flatten the rolled edge. Tie a 10-inch length of curling ribbon around the crimp and knot it securely, snipping off the loose ends.

4.   Fill the cracker with gifts or trinkets, a paper crown, and a joke. Repeat step 3 to close the end, making sure that the snap remains centered and the ends are exposed.

*Find a resources list for these and
other materials at GladandGolden.com

The Animals' Christmas

Who are all these stockings for?" a mystified acquaintance wants to know.

It is a reasonable question. We hang our Christmas stockings on the kitchen mantelpiece, and while the "P" and "L" monograms on the two in the center give away their respective owners at a glance, they are flanked by smaller versions less obviously affiliated: there is an "O" and a "W," a "B," another "L," a "J." There is a medium-sized "C," a pint-sized "C," and a tiny "P."

"They're for our cats and dogs," I say with a laugh. *Oliver* and *Wemmick. Bonnie, Lucy, Josephine. Caspian* and *Calvin. Pip.*

I made them long ago, and though new pets have come to fill the places many of these beloved originals have so gently vacated, I never seem to find the time to update them. Caspian's stocking, tearfully laid to rest in my hope chest, was brought out of retirement for Luna. Balliol inherited Lucy's, while Fiona enjoys the stocking I stitched for the immortal Bonnie. Maybe one year I will think of it in October, when the first cool morning sends my mind winging toward Christmas and anything seems, not only possible, but absolutely doable. There is a good chance, however, that I won't think of it, or that I will be so busy planting collards and kale in the garden or updating the barn medicine cabinet for the winter that I will dismiss the idea with a laugh. At any rate, the animals don't seem to mind. Just as long as those stockings are stuffed with squeak toys and catnip mice come Christmas morning—a new collar for Laddie, perhaps, who has lost his again, or an elk antler for Luna—no one will complain.

I love treating my animals at Christmas. They give us so much in the way of companionship and delight that it would seem strange to me *not* to spoil them a bit this time of year. Caspian used to sit patiently, staring up at his empty stocking from the moment I hung it up, all but drooling over the memory of last year's marrow bone. And I will never forget the year that Luna got a stuffed unicorn and Bonnie got a lion. They regarded each other's toys for an uneasy moment. Then Bonnie daintily lifted the unicorn from between Luna's massive paws and sat down with it in her mouth a few feet away. Luna, seizing her chance, pounced upon the lion, and both dogs settled blissfully with their new toys. (I should have known Bonnie needed that unicorn—she was a magical creature, herself.)

The first year that we had chickens, I whipped up a batch of cornbread in a cast iron skillet and took it to them for their supper on Christmas Eve, still warm and topped with a sprig of holly. The custom caught, and as our barn family has grown, so too have amassed other seasonal rituals. There are two pans of cornbread now, divided between the ducks and the peacock and my current flock of chickens. The goats and sheep always get a big basket of apples, which I divvy up and portion out over the Twelve Days of Christmas, and armloads of Eastern red cedar, which is their particular treat. Some years I clip the greenery into shorter lengths and cram it into grapevine forms to make edible wreaths; other times we just mount a couple of massive branches in their stalls for them to munch on at their leisure. Either way, it is with an absolute frenzy of greedy joy that the animals see us coming on Christmas Eve. We wade in among the throng, holding basket and branches over our heads, and once everyone is in their stalls, the ecstasy only intensifies. We have to take care that our fingers are not mistaken for apples, or that Duncan gets his fair share of cedar from Juliet and Cordelia. But it makes us so happy

WEEK FOUR

to see them tearing into their treats with such relish. Every person has their own unique scents and sounds associated with holidays and special times, those recurring alchemies that connect the years with a golden thread. For me, the fragrance of sliced apples and crushed cedar masticated between strong little teeth will always mean Christmas Eve. It is with a tender smile I turn out the light, leaving them to savor in silence. Only Hermia gazes after me with a gentle look in her limpid eyes.

"You're welcome, sweet girl. And Merry Christmas."

Christmas Eve

The evening sun was at our backs, throwing a long, hand-in-hand shadow on the road before us as we walked back down the hill toward the slate-roofed cottage crouched amid a fold of the Scottish hills. Behind us, a windswept down; before, a heather-strewn valley tumbling toward a dark, tree-lined snake of a stream. It was high summer and we were on our honeymoon, having buried ourselves as effectually as possible in a remote corner of the Angus Glens. We were young, wildly in love, and with the rest of a shared life opening before us with all the beautiful possibility of this valley at our feet. We had been talking about that life all week. *What values did we want it to reflect? Which relationships were foremost, and what were our priorities? How could we invest in God's kingdom and what were our dreams?*

"What about Christmas?" I asked.

"What about it?" Philip replied, the lilt of a laugh in his voice.

"Well, we need to decide what we want it to look like. You know, what will really mean Christmas to *us*."

Philip's laugh was outright now. "It's July."

"And before we know it, it will be December, and we'll be pulled all over the place wanting to be with everyone and do everything. I just want to make sure we start off on the right foot."

Philip nodded solemnly. "I see your point."

He squeezed my hand and smiled down at me, his eyes soft with the same wonder that my heart had been reveling in all week: life was no longer "him" and "me." It was *us*.

I remembered Mama talking about the first Christmas that she and Daddy were married. They were impossibly young, in college, and quite poor. They could not afford decorations, nor much in the way of gifts, and, just to add insult to injury, Mercer University was located roughly halfway between their respective families. Mama wanted to be in Marietta, where my grandmother made much of the holidays in her lovely old Greek Revival, while Daddy was the only son of doting parents in south Georgia. The pull was strong in both directions. But with a Solomon-like acuity commendable in such barely-adults, they made a hard decision. They stayed in Macon on Christmas Eve, alone together in their pretty little rented room with its plasterwork mantle and wavy glass doors and creeping damp, and they made decorations for a tiny tree and exchanged dime-store presents.

The next morning, they got up and drove to Vidalia for Christmas morning in time for the tidal wave of aunts and uncles and cousins that marked a gathering of Daddy's side of the family. And the next year they got up and drove to Marietta. But that simple Christmas Eve had established something. Claudia and Harris were not just a part of families—they *were* a family, a young household with its own memories and seeds of tradition and sacred spaces. For even though my parents were not Christians at the time, they understood that their two stories, flowing from different backgrounds and upbringings and geographical locations (Mama always avowed that north Georgia and south Georgia were different countries), had merged into a single narrative sealed by an unbreakable promise. That promise was not always easy to keep, particularly in those tumultuous early days of immaturity and impecunity—Mama often said it was a miracle they had survived. And it was a miracle, a dispensation of grace that carried them on toward their true story together in Christ. But even in this infancy of their marriage Mama and Daddy intuited the need to begin building their home on its own unique foundation, influenced by, but separate from, the homes in which they'd grown up. It was this prescience, I think, which knit them together when times were good and held them fast when times were hard.

"Children don't make a family," Mama said to me before my wedding. "You and Philip will *be* a family."

Little did either of us imagine at the time how dearly I would come to cling to that pearl of wisdom. Needless to say, it would carry me over many a rough passage of longing and hope deferred. I did know, however, that Mama was right, not only because she was a woman of great discernment, but because she had lived it out. It was her example, all those years ago back in Macon, Georgia, that gave me the courage to call her a couple of days before my first Christmas as a married woman to say what Philip and I had decided on that Scottish hillside: we were going to spend Christmas Eve alone together at the Ruff House.

There was a brief silence on the other end. My parents' home was scarcely a ten-minute drive from ours, and Mama knew more than anyone else just how entrenched my heart had always been in our Chestnut Drive traditions. We all loved Christmas Eve best, inheriting, perhaps, Mama and Daddy's early reverence for it. And Mama had taken such pains over the years to make it the most special night of the year. It was nothing elaborate: early on, Mama had realized that special didn't necessarily mean fancy, and that simplicity was the golden key to a holiday everyone actually enjoyed. The magic lay in the sweet predictability of it all, the gentle assurances of familiar scenes and scents, tastes and sounds. The consolation that, even if all the face of the world had changed beyond the pale of our front door, here within was a peace the world could not give and treasure it could not take away.

It took a bit of experimentation to land upon the ultimate Adams family Christmas Eve dinner, but once it was settled it may as well have been graven in marble: grilled ribeye steaks, sautéed mushrooms, and baked potatoes slathered in butter and sour cream. To this day, any of these scents or tastes in isolation whisk me winging back to the candlelit spaces of that long, low ranch-style house on Chestnut Drive. I feel the cool brick floors under my bare feet, see the Christmas tree twinkling back at us from its reflection in the plate-glass windows, smell the smoky fireplace. Mama would have the primitive pine table spread with her favorite holiday cloth, a red and green plaid threaded with gold, and all the taper candlesticks would have their little ring of silk holly. And just before we sat down to eat, Daddy would put the Frank Sinatra Christmas album on the turntable and that first jingle of sleigh bells would send a silver thrill of delight through my frame. Liz would be next to me and Zach across the table, their faces radiant with anticipation in the candlelight, and one of our long line of family dogs would be poised at Daddy's feet, awaiting a morsel or two of succulent fat. It was all so perfect I could have wept (and, oftentimes, when it was all over, I did).

It was really rather brilliant of Mama to settle upon a main which could be cooked somewhere other than her overworked kitchen. For all I know, it may have been Daddy's suggestion, for he loved a perfectly prepared cut of meat with the gastronomic precision of a Frenchman. At any rate, I remember many a rainy Christmas Eve watching him dart back and forth from house to patio, umbrella bobbing, flashlight glancing, until the meat had been cooked to his exacting satisfaction: medium for my siblings and me, medium rare for Mama, barely seared for himself. The fact that when we were children steak was an uncommon treat, limited only to Christmas Eve and the odd bite from

Mama's or Daddy's plate all the rest of the year, made it an instant special occasion meal. As we got older and our palates were educated toward the rarer end of the doneness spectrum, it became a real gourmet experience, exquisite in its very simplicity.

For dessert, Mama often made her famous Tipsy Trifle, a confection rendered with ease, thanks to Bird's Custard Powder and a store-bought pound cake—under all those lashings of cream and custard and sherry and jam one would be hard-pressed to tell the difference between that and homemade. Once, when our friend Delphine was visiting from Paris she made a *bûche de Noël*, that famous genoise rolled around chocolate buttercream and iced to look like a Yule log. But oftener than not, it was trifle, served in Mama's footed glass bowl and topped with decadently out-of-season fresh raspberries.

After supper I would play a few carols at the piano in the living room; we might even sing if it didn't feel too contrived. Mama couldn't carry a tune in a bucket, and that sweet, slightly nasal voice of hers wandered aimlessly a pitch or two up or down from the rest of us, but it was so familiar a sound it carried with it all the comfort of a golden-voiced lullaby. Next came the readings: Clement C. Moore's immortal *'Twas the Night Before Christmas*, so well-known we could all recite it under our breath, followed by the Nativity story from the second chapter of Luke. Daddy was a great connoisseur of Bible translations: my childhood bedtimes were attended by the Egermeier's *Bible Story Book* of his childhood, with its vivid full-page illustrations and chapter-sized accounts, while Daddy preferred the Thompson Chain-Reference for his personal use. Family devotions, consisting of the five Psalms and one Proverb a day approach, were a job for the Amplified Bible, delighting, no doubt, Daddy's love of language and the expansive legal precision of his attorney mind, but our bookshelves were crowded with literally dozens of others— NASB, NIV, NLT, ESV, NKJV, all with attendant study guides and commentary.

For Christmas Eve, however, there may as well have been only one translation in existence: the 1611 King James. I think that the rest of us would have thrown back our heads and howled had he even considered venturing into experimental territory here. But he never considered it. For over twenty years I had sat in that living room, with my family all around me and the winter night blanketing our un-curtained windows with a darkness that only served to emphasize the warmth within, listening to the majestic cadences of the King James Bible rolling out in my Daddy's mellifluous Southern tongue.

And it came to pass . . .

My eyes would range over the beloved room with its beloved faces, toward the tree with its piles of intriguing parcels, into the dining room, where the table was set for tomorrow's breakfast, and back to the fireplace with its glowing heart of red embers, until the scene misted before me with unshed tears. There was nowhere else I would rather be, no other people to whom I would rather belong, and there was just something about Christmas Eve that made the goodness of it all so palpably present. Holiness seemed to hover in the very rafters and in the corners of the room, gathering us all in a joy that felt impenetrable. Nothing evil or scary or sad could ever happen on a night like this, I used to think with all the innocence of inexperience. I know better now, of course. But still the magic of those untouched evenings at home consoles me with the hope that someday nothing evil or scary or sad will ever happen ever again.

Daddy would pray for us, and then, even well into our teens, we would set out a glass of milk and a plate of red and green sugar-dusted cookies for that shadowy old sprite of our childhood and a carrot for his reindeer—always this little nod to memory and make-believe. And always the buoyant anticipation of the next day. I remember two-stepping all over the house one year with my sister, singing "Tomorrow Shall Be My Dancing Day" at the tops of our lungs for the sheer gladness of it all. But tomorrow would not be the high note of our happiness; tonight was the real crescendo, pausing time and bringing heaven so very near. There was nothing like Christmas Eve on Chestnut Drive.

And all of this I was willing to forfeit—had forfeited already, in fact, when I said the easiest "yes" of my life. Not that Philip and I would never participate in the rituals and rhythms of each of our families, of course, but we would also begin, out of the gate, to start shaping our own.

"All right, sweetheart." Mama's voice wavered somewhat. "I understand that you and Philip need to make your own traditions."

I know it wrung her heart to say it, and there were tears to be shed, both on and off the phone. But she had set her hand to the same plow, and no matter how devoted she was to the way things had always been, she wasn't going to impose that devotion as a wedge between her household and mine. Tradition is an excellent container, guiding a group of people into a regular rehearsal of their story and an experience of their belonging. But tradition without agency becomes a fetter. As Jesus pointed out with such scathing incision, the Pharisees had rendered God's Word powerless in their lives by the very traditions they had erected around it; it is easy to see how tassels and phylacteries and elaborate rituals could ultimately replace what they sought to protect. What may be less clear is that our family traditions, no matter how precious, have the potential to do the same thing.

That first Christmas Eve at the Ruff House was a tender one. We had, as yet, no grooves to guide us, no joint history from which to draw. I may have cried a little bit, content as I was, when seven o'clock rolled around and I knew that Daddy was putting the steaks on the grill. Resolute to forge our own little way, however, I made clam chowder for supper, simply because it was something neither of our mothers had ever cooked, and because so Northern a ubiquity seemed glamorous and fancy and special. We sat by the fire and opened our gifts to each other and listened to Ella Fitzgerald. I played a few carols on our new piano. And at midnight, Philip read the Nativity story from my worn little King James. It felt like Christmas Eve—just maybe on a different planet. In a different galaxy.

The next year I cried because the memory of the first was so sweet. But Philip and I had had a serious talk about tradition in the interim, namely with regard to food. The very thought of Christmas Eve just made my stomach growl for a good steak—why not shift things up and make it filet mignon instead of rib eye? I could add a splash of wine to the mushrooms; we could swap out the baked potatoes for mashed redskins with rosemary and cream. Perhaps even a small *bûche de Noël* from the French bakery in town. There was no reason, we agreed, to deprive ourselves merely for the sake of being different. It was our prerogative to glean from our favorite traditions of our families as we shaped traditions of our own.

On Christmas Eve, perforce, we pulled a card table near the wood-burning stove in the den. Philip grilled the steaks while I made the mushrooms and the potatoes. And just as we sat down to eat, I ran over to the turntable in the corner and queued up the Frank Sinatra Christmas record. As I sank into my chair the first jingle of bells brought that familiar shiver of joy and my eyes filled with tears. I took a bite of meltingly tender meat and my past and my present met in that moment with a fitness which seemed nothing short of heavenly. I smiled at Philip across the table as our dog, Caspian, nudged my hand for a morsel of meat. There was nowhere else I would rather be; no other person to whom I would rather belong. It was Christmas Eve at the Ruff House, and the joy of it all felt impenetrable.

We learned over the years that filets are better suited to a stovetop than a grill; now we sear them in my great-grandmother's cast iron skillet to lock in the juices and finish them off in the oven for the perfect medium rare. And I dispensed with the wine in the mushrooms, realizing, as Mama knew all along, that even the most ordinary white buttons provide an earthy bouquet of their own, requiring little more than a goodly dollop of butter and judicious dashes of salt and freshly ground pepper. I also circled back to the baked potatoes, finding the sight of a mashed potato pot in the sink on Christmas morning to be an unwelcome one. For just as a picnic can elevate ordinary bread and butter to nectar and ambrosia, a baked potato on Christmas Eve is delectable merely by association. I would much rather spend the night sipping Bordeaux by the fire and opening presents with Philip than washing dishes.

Regardless of such slight tweaks to the menu, for two decades and more, Christmas Eve at the Ruff House has looked pretty much the same; even at Camp Marah we ate our steak dinner by candlelight and opened our presents by the tree, and what may have been lacking in magic was more than made up for in memory and hope. (I could not, however, bring myself to listen to Frank Sinatra. That year, it was Over the Rhine's *Blood Oranges in the Snow*. On repeat.) We've had the occasional guest from time to time, but for the balance of those years it has been Philip and me, content to savor the quiet evening alone together, a small family cloister amid the bright and bustling community of the holidays.

The year that Daddy died, however, everything was different, even at the Ruff House. It was like a great light had gone out, leaving us all to grope in a murky dark for some sense of the people we had been before this loss. I remember walking into the room shortly after he had gone and feeling the bottom falling out of the world. Even as it did, however, something caught me, invisible and yet more solid than the small piece of ground that had apparently stayed beneath my feet. It was the Gospel–from the manger, to the Cross, to the empty tomb–and I saw it all in a succession of such clarity it made the room swim before my eyes. I had believed it for years, had built my life upon its claims, but standing at my father's deathbed, it went through me like a flash of lightning: death did not get to write the ending here. Daddy *was* because the story *was*—and it was all absolutely true. I was at once drowning in grief and borne up by joy.

But the holidays were hard. Chestnut Drive was a house of mourning, as was right and fitting. And the Ruff House bore its own unseen standard of sorrow beneath the greenery and ribbons and the packages under the tree. No one had told me how exhausting grief was, how effectively it drained the last reservoir of one's energy and made even the smallest decisions feel like moments of life-altering destiny. All through that preceding autumn I had muddled through what commitments I could muster, forgetting appointments and dropping balls right and left, knowing that Christmas would have to be scaled back out

WEEK FOUR

of sheer necessity. It came as a surprise, however, to find that some of our cherished traditions caught and carried us over the waves and billows of such a tender holiday, as though the faithful practices of years past had come alongside us now as faithful companions, shepherding us back toward the deep magic of days gone by.

Philip and I invited Mama to the Ruff House for Christmas, and she came, with her presents and her brave smile and her black lab Portia. I'd prepared her guest room with a tender care, weaving an ivy garland for the mantle and gathering a few sentimental oddments from the rest of the house, those I knew she would particularly like. On Christmas Eve we had tea from my cherished Georgian set and read from Milton's "Nativity Ode" by the fire. Then I opened a bottle of champagne and Philip put the steaks on. We dragged the kitchen table into the den to accommodate us all, and just when it was time to sit down, I turned on the Frank Sinatra Christmas album. We looked at one another with soft smiles and Philip asked the blessing.

It was a gently merry meal, despite our aching hearts, as if all our kindly Christmases past were gathered there in the shadows of the room. Mama gazed around at the cheerful fire, the sparkling tree, the two of us, and slipped Portia a bite of meat under the table.

On December 26th, she sat in the low armchair in our den, one last cup of coffee in hand, Portia at her feet. Behind us, a genuinely happy holiday; ahead of her, a daunting new year of widowhood. But she was smiling, even as the tears slipped from her eyes.

"Thank you for giving me this Christmas," she said. "You will never know what it has meant to me—what the two of you mean to me."

It was all she could manage. But any temptation to congratulate myself on daughterly benevolence was immediately dispelled by the sweet irony that it was she, in a way, who had contributed to all of these Ruff House Christmases in the first place. All we had done was to invite her into a precedent she had set; all we had given her was the fruit of her own faithfulness.

TO AN OPEN
HOUSE IN THE EVENING
HOME shall men COME,
TO an OLDER PLACE than EDEN
AND A TALLER town than ROME
TO THE end OF THE way OF THE wandering STAR
TO THE THINGS THAT cannot be AND THAT are,
to the place where
GOD was HOMELESS
AND ALL MEN
ARE AT
home

G.K. CHESTERTON

RECIPE: Claudia's Tipsy Trifle

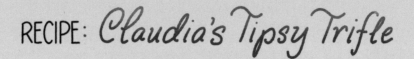

Bird's Custard Powder is an instant British confection which is increasingly available in the U.S. Make sure to purchase the original Vanilla Flavoured version. And you will need to allow ample time for the sherry, jam, and custard to soak into the cake—ideally overnight—before spreading the whipped cream on it at serving time. Absolutely stunning in a trifle bowl!

Bird's Custard Powder
2 Tbsp. sugar
1 scant pint whole milk
1 16-oz. all-butter pound cake, cut into 3/4-inch cubes

1/2 to 3/4 cup cream sherry
3 cups fresh raspberries
3/4 cup raspberry jam
1 cup heavy cream
1/4 cup sugar

Prepare the custard on the stovetop according to the package instructions, but only use 2 tablespoons of sugar and a scant pint of milk. After the custard begins to set (you will want it to be on the thick side), remove from heat and cover with plastic wrap touching the surface to prevent a skin from forming. Refrigerate for several hours until thoroughly chilled.

To assemble the trifle, place half of the cake cubes in the bottom of a trifle bowl or 3-quart serving dish. Sprinkle with half of the cream sherry. Place half of the raspberries on top of the cake and spread half of the jam over the berries. Pour half of the custard over the jam. Repeat with the remaining cake, sherry, raspberries, jam, and custard, reserving some of the berries to decorate the top of the trifle. Cover with plastic wrap and refrigerate several hours or overnight.

At serving time, whip the cream with the ¼ cup sugar in the bowl of an electric mixer fitted with the whisk attachment (or with a handheld mixer) on medium-high until soft peaks form. Spread the whipped cream over the surface of the trifle and dot the top with the reserved raspberries. Serve immediately.

SERVES 8

THE Ring OF Bells

It was my last Christmas at home. We were all pretending otherwise, for although Philip had yet to propose, it could happen any day. My sister firmly believed it could happen on Christmas Day, as evidenced by the jewelry-sized package she had seen Philip slip under our tree after dinner on Christmas Eve. And she was in good company—Louise and Lori were convinced I would get a ring, as was our friend, Delphine, who was visiting from Paris. I, for one, knew I would not. Philip was far too free-spirited to be backed into a corner by other peoples' expectations. He would, I felt sure, ask me to marry him at a time everyone was *least* expecting, allowing the fires of anticipation to die back a bit to a simmering blaze of impatient certitude.

We had our steaks on Christmas Eve and our readings by the fire, our music and Mama's trifle. Then Philip went home, promising to be back first thing in the morning, and our household began to prepare for bed. I could hear Mama in the kitchen, making ready for the morning and singing softly in her off-tune way. Zach was polishing off the hot water with one of his long showers, and Liz and Delphine were giggling over something back in Liz's bedroom. I knelt by the tree and rattled Philip's little box. I was so happy, and so much in love, that it had never really occurred to me that an entire chapter of my life was coming to an end. For so many years things had gone on as they always had, each Christmas distinct yet so very much the same, but never with so precious a burden of longing and joy. This time next year I would be Philip's wife—we had already begun to talk, hintingly and hesitatingly, of honeymoon plans—and the promise of it colored the present moment with a contentment I had never known.

This is the best Christmas of my life, I thought. *Well—to date.*

For some reason I glanced across the room to where a small end table once stood beside a sofa long-since departed. Mama had redecorated the living room with furniture from her mother's house—an English roll-arm couch, a walnut sideboard, an oak pedestal table with ball-and-claw feet. It all looked so harmonious, especially as she'd reupholstered the sofa and chairs to match the blue drapes. But suddenly I wondered what had happened to that end table. It was where we always used to put out a glass of milk and a plate of cookies for Santa on Christmas Eve, taking care (with a carrot or two) not to neglect the reindeer. It was a perennial astonishment on Christmas morning to find that glass drained and plate emptied of all but a few grains of colored sugar and a bitten-off carrot top. Of course we all knew that Daddy had bitten off that carrot, and that he'd likely taken care of the cookies and milk as well. Such trifles never interfered with our excitement, however. Whether it was Santa Claus or "Daddy Claus," as he liked to call himself, the magic was the delight of the game itself.

When was the last time we had played that little game?

The question seemed suddenly important. The life of a family is littered with "lasts": the last time a child is tucked in for the night, or a small hand taken to cross a street. The last lost tooth or trip to the pediatrician. The last bedtime story; the last homeschool morning. Life went by so fast, strewing precious things to the wayside right and left.

Mama had an uneasy relationship with "lasts"; she hated them, in fact. But she was of two minds when it came to their manifestation. "Do we want to know or do we not?" she and her friend Wendy used to ask one another, circling around the question with clear-eyed pathos. Is it better to face a "last" head-on, absorbing the sweet with the sad? Or should it be allowed to slip quietly away without sullying its essence with too much attention? The reality, as Mama and Wendy agreed, is that we rarely have much choice in the matter. Heeded or unheeded, the lasts will come. And the best we can do is to ground ourselves in the present moment and release them as gratefully and graciously as possible.

I stood up, gazing around the room with a new intensity, as if seeking to memorize every line and pattern, every surface and ornament. Then I went back to my pink-and-blue bedroom where Delphine was already in bed. She looked up over her book as I came in and her rosebud mouth curved into a smile.

"I like Christmas with your family," she said.

"Me, too," I replied, somewhat absently.

I climbed into the other twin bed and pulled up the quilt, running my fingers over the familiar chintzes and ginghams of the pattern. It was a green "Lone Star" made by my grandmother with pink flannel backing, and even in summer its weight was comforting and welcome. Grandma had given that quilt, and the blue and white one on Delphine's bed, to a disadvantaged family "down in the country," and as soon as Daddy heard of it he went straight out and bought a mountain of fine new blankets. These he took to the family, giving them in exchange for Grandma's precious quilts, the only two she had ever made before losing her vision. I smiled at the memory. I was branch, leaf, and fruit of a sentimental tree.

Delphine was just reintroducing the question of the engagement ring when I heard something outside. I put a finger to my lips. The window shades were down, but there was an unmistakable shiver of silvery music on the other side. It was one of the most familiar sounds of my entire life, but I couldn't for the life of me remember the last time I'd heard it.

The jingling continued along the side of the house and my sister appeared in the doorway of our adjoining rooms. Her eyes were wide and we stared at one another in silence.

"What is this?" Delphine demanded, as the chimes concluded with a final flourish.

Her evident alarm made us laugh.

"It's Daddy," Liz said, wiping her eyes.

Daddy, with his strap of antique sleigh bells and his great, tender, whimsical heart.

"He always used to ring those bells outside when we were little," Liz went on. "To make us think that Santa was here."

I was glad she was able to explain; I couldn't trust myself to say a word. But Daddy was right—some lasts ought to be acknowledged with a laugh and a lump in the throat, honoring the future with a loving glance at the past. We chatted for a few minutes after that, reliving childhood memories. Then Liz went back to her room and I switched off the light, pulling Grandma's quilt over my shoulders like an embrace.

I was right about the ring, by the way. The package under the tree contained a pair of silver hoop earrings, and Philip proposed on an otherwise ordinary night in the middle of January, catching even my sister off guard.

HOW TO *Love Yourself* WHILE *Loving Others*

In the midst of all the service and sociability which can characterize a hospitable holiday, it's easy to forget—or neglect—our own needs. But as every motherhood mentor will remind us, we cannot give from a place of depletion. Secure your own oxygen mask, in other words, before helping other passengers. Beyond bubble baths and Dove chocolate hearts, there are many small ways to show love—I would even say hospitality—to ourselves at a time when we feel like we just don't have time. For hospitality itself stems from the word "hospital," implying that anyone on the receiving end of it deserves a little extra care. Including you.

Here are a few ideas:

1.   A 10-minute nap. Even if you don't have time for a proper snooze, lying still on your back, with as much of your body touching the bed as possible and in a state of complete relaxation, is wonderfully restorative.

2.   Take your vitamins. And, while you're at it, go ahead and beef up your immune system with an echinacea supplement, black elderberry syrup, or a cup of ginger tea with honey and lemon.

3.   Drink plenty of water. Dehydration is sneaky (you know you're getting dehydrated when you cease to feel thirsty) but it can make you lightheaded and fatigued.

4.   Prepare a proper tea—teapot, cup, saucer—for yourself and sit down to drink it at the same time every single day.

5. Keep an Advent devotional or book of poetry by the bed that you can dip into for a few minutes first thing in the morning or last thing at night.

6. If you have overnight guests in the house, let them help with the preparations. A visitor feels like a member of the family when they're treated like one.

7. Keep mealtimes simple in the days leading up to Christmas. 'Tis the season for cereal night, snack suppers, and (gasp) frozen pizza.

8. Above all, be gentle with yourself. Listen to the voice in your head and make sure it's kind. We are told, after all, to love others as we love ourselves. Are you as nice to you as you are to the people around you?

9. And go ahead and take that bubble bath if you like that sort of thing. It certainly won't hurt.

Christmas Eve in the Barn

Sometimes we eat Christmas Eve dinner in our pajamas; other times we're still in our dress clothes from the brunch. Regardless, nearing midnight we bundle into coats and scarves, call for the dogs, and head out across the lawn to the barn. I have always loved the quaint legend that farm animals are granted the gift of speech on Christmas Eve in token of their being witness to the birth of Christ. Some traditions claim that the beasts kneel on their forelegs at the stroke of midnight in homage to the King of Creation, now so miraculously present with us, while others attribute Latin words to the sounds of each creature: *Christus natus est!* shouts the rooster, while *quando?* asks the duck and *ubi?* poses the cow. Only the lamb can tell them when and where, baaing out "Bethlehem" in a high, clear voice, while the faithful donkey is joyously adamant: *Eamus!* he says. Let us go!

I know the animals cannot talk, of course, though part of me still wants to believe it each year as we steal over the grass in the darkness. Perhaps, just this once, we will catch them at it before our presence silences them for another year. But as we enter the barn, the only sounds are a rustle and stir from the henhouse, an anxious quack or two from the ducks, a sleepy bleat from a goat. Philip switches on the stall lights and we slip in among the sheep, who are instantly on their feet. They regard us with calm, curious eyes, remembering, perhaps, what this is all about.

The tradition is simple enough. First, one of us will play Morten Lauridsen's breathlessly tender "O Magnum Mysterium." Even issuing from a cell phone, the music is sublime: ethereal and serene with its interwoven harmonies and mounting transcendence, yet reassuringly grounding as it swells to its magnificent assertion. I always like to read the English translation of the Latin, just to make sure we are all fully present to the astonishment of it all:

> O great mystery,
> and wonderful sacrament,
> that animals should see the newborn Lord,
> lying in a manger!

I love to watch the gazes of my sheep, trusting, almost human in the depth of their perception, as they circle around us, nudging our hands and pressing their heads against us with a confidential ease. The goats poke their long, aquiline noses through the slats between the stalls, flapping their pendulous ears as they toss their heads from side to side with an investigative air, wondering, no doubt, if we've brought them more apples. My sheep can be skittish, and my goats are downright naughty. Nevertheless, it is easy for me to picture these friendly beasts of ours gathering around the manger and looking on with silent worship of their Creator and ours. The sounds and smells anchor us in the reality that our Savior was born in a barn, while the ascending Alleluias of the music lift our hearts toward the glory with which he will come again.

After the last strains have died away, Philip will read Luke's account of the Nativity from my little King James. We are silent for a moment, sitting with the mystery, marveling at such love. Then, with a scratch of Juliet's long nose and a kiss atop Hermia's wooly head, we turn to go. We latch the stall and switch off the lights and there is a quiet stirring behind us as the animals drop to their knees and settle back into recumbent positions. I pat my leg for the dogs to follow and we set off for the house, the Christmas tree in the window a merry beacon and the smoke from our chimney a warm invitation. A few fireworks boom in the distance as neighbors celebrate in their own way, and a cold, clear moon silvers the world around us with radiance.

Halfway across the yard there is a noise from the barn: a cluck and a flapping of wings before my rooster, Diggory, lets out a shriek of triumph: *Christus natus est!* he cries.

"*Christus natus est!*" we shout in reply.

CHRISTMASTIDE

Angels, announce with shouts of mirth CHRIST who brings new LIFE to earth.

Set every PEAK and VALLEY humming with the word,

the LORD is COMING

PEOPLE, LOOK EAST AND SING TODAY:

Love, the LORD, is on the way.

Eleanor Farjeon, "Carol of the Advent"

Christmas Morning

I part the curtains with a smile. The sun, not yet level with the treetops of our eastern glade, is flooding the understory with golden mist, and the trees themselves, wakened by the breezes of dawn, sway gently as if in time to some silent lay. The window panes bear the etching of a light frost, though the tenderness of that advancing radiance looks more like May. Suddenly, it is not enough merely to look; I open the casement and lean out, breathing in the springlike air. It is crisp and cool, scented by dew and brimming with birdsong. The robins, whose *cheerily-cheerily-cheer-up!* can seem almost quotidian in less keen moments, sound like gospellers of glad tidings, while, brooding down among the branches near the creek, a mourning dove tunes his carol in a minor key. From somewhere far-off to the west comes the tremulous warble of a white-throated sparrow, the fragile notes drawn out with love and longing, and near at hand a cardinal bustles among the deutzia bushes, chitting to its mate of domestic matters with what seems like a new eagerness.

Such a temperate morning is not uncommon in our climate, even in the depth of winter. But this is no common morning. Last night, after our midnight ramble to the barn and before going to bed, we wished one another a drowsy "Merry Christmas," and the night wheeled on above our sleeping house with a holy hush, the very stars remembering, perhaps, the baby's cry that shook the universe to its core. I love to think of the angels bending low in wonder over that miraculous manger, even as they filled the sky with supernal music. *But could it be*, I thought, as I sank into my pillow, *that their eyes were dimmed with tears?* Christmas Eve is imbued with bright sadness. It's the very thing that makes it so sacred, the burning reality that the outstretched arms of the infant in our household crèche prefigures a Cross upon which all the weight of the world will be borne.

But now it is Christmas Day and this roseate dawn speaks only of joy. "The darling of the world is come," as Robert Herrick has said. And all nature seems to know it.

Christmas Breakfast

Christmas makes me hungry.

It's true—one of the first heralds to my senses that the holidays are near is what Winnie-the-Pooh would call a "rumbly in the tumbly." And the least fragrance of familiar food snaps me effortlessly back to the Christmases of my childhood. Take the aroma of pork sausage browning away in a skillet on the stove: regardless of the time of year, I will always think of Mama cooking the sausage for her Christmas morning casserole on Christmas Eve afternoon. We had that casserole every year, as far back as I can remember, and we cherished an almost fanatic affection for its spicy, cheesy, perfection. Mama kept it so special to Christmas, in fact, that the smallest bite is a treasure-house of memory, triggering a cascade of times past so pleasurable it almost brings pain. There were only two occasions upon which Mama made her Christmas casserole when it wasn't Christmas: the first was the morning after I returned from a mission trip to Moscow. I was seventeen years old and I had never been out of the country (it was only the second time that I had been on an airplane), and though I had found the Russian people to be among the kindest and most generous I had ever met, I was rather stupefied by the bleakness of post-Soviet Russia. I had left Georgia in early spring, when the trees were yet bare, and I had been tramping through streets banked with muddy, grey snow for two weeks. I will never forget opening my bedroom shades that first morning home to a green world so clean and sweet it almost hurt my eyes. And there, stealing under the door and beckoning me toward the kitchen, was the scent of Christmas morning. In an instant, I knew how missed I had been and how loved I was.

The other occasion was the day my best friend got married. She was engaged to an Australian, and, in order to keep the groom from seeing the bride before the wedding, Mama had invited Paul and his groomsmen, Hamish and Squigg, to spend the night at our house. We sat around the breakfast table that morning, blinking at one another, while Mama heaped plates and poured coffee and chattered like an eager bird. Nothing, it seemed, but Christmas was good enough for Paul and Rachel's wedding day.

The recipe itself was sacrosanct, and Mama guarded it jealously, fearing, no doubt, a dilution of its nostalgic potency through overuse. When I asked for it after I was married, she flatly refused. It took Philip to wheedle it out of her, and though I now possess both the original recipe card and the box it was housed in, it's Philip's hastily scrawled version to which I turn every year (Mama's is so splattered and smeared it is all but illegible).

Not that I need the recipe, of course. My mind wanders back to Chestnut Drive as I measure out milk and eggs. I slice the bread into cubes, remembering the way Mama would take the casserole out of the refrigerator when she started the coffee and tuck it into

GLAD & GOLDEN HOURS

the oven when we were opening presents, so that by the time we were finished it would beckon us to the breakfast table with whiffs and curls of aromatic triumph. It's a dish particularly suited to making ahead; the only deviation I have ever made from Mama's instructions is to prepare mine a few days before Christmas and pop it into the freezer, transferring it to the fridge before I go to bed on Christmas Eve. Either way, it's a simple way to have a lovely, hot breakfast on Christmas morning without having to lift a finger.

It's truly miraculous the way certain foods have the power to hold certain memories. Scientists tell us that the emotional center of the brain is closely tied to both taste and smell in a way which predates our verbal ability, but I think it's far more poetic than that. I think that God gives us these sure and certain pathways as a consolation for the fleetingness of our joys. Such a profound gift! That vanished times might live again, howsoever briefly, and that beloved people and places might be restored to us in a single aroma or bite of food. And while it's not something we initially have much control over, I do think it's something we can cultivate, especially in the lives of the children in our midst.

Mama was so good at this that her dogeared recipes and cookbooks are among the treasures of my household. On Christmas morning at the Ruff House, the fragrance of spicy sausage and eggs goes wafting through the rooms and up the stairs until my sister's guest room door flies open and a glad shriek emits from the upper regions: "Breakfast casserole!" Knowing that my brother on the West Coast will be putting his version into the oven about the time we're getting up from ours makes me smile. Someday this dish will likely send the same thrill of delight through his little ones as it does through all the rest of us.

We read the collects for the Feast of the Nativity from the *Book of Common Prayer*, and Philip leads us in a personal blessing. Then the eager clatter of cutlery and china, the playful squabbling over corner pieces, the leftover fruit from Christmas Eve. Like Mama before me, I make sure everyone's plates are heaped high before serving myself. But when I do finally sit down and take the first bite, it is a Proustian moment. No longer am I hostess, an accidental matriarch striving to live into an inherited role for which I will never feel quite qualified. I am five years old, cradling a babydoll with cheeks of roses and eyes that open and close. I am seven, with a jewelry box that pops open to reveal a twirling ballerina inside, and ten, wriggling our miniature schnauzer into a new Christmas sweater she hates, and fourteen, with a new Laura Ashley dress I adore. I am nineteen, proud of the hand-lettered poem I framed and gave to Daddy and the embroidered pillow I stitched for Mama. Twenty-four, and smiling across the table at Philip.

One Christmas morning, when Philip and I had only been married a couple of years, we both woke up violently ill. It turned out to be just a stomach bug we had picked up from one of our young nieces, but going to my parents' was out of the question. Mama sent Daddy over with a basket of ginger ale, soda crackers, and Disney movies; he left it on the front mat, rang the doorbell, and fled. I was initially too sick to care much about missing Christmas, but by that evening the sorrow of the thing began to sink in. It would be a whole year before the magic and warmth of it came around again! A year until the silliness and fun and shining thankfulness of Christmas morning with my family. I was bereft.

Twenty-four hours later, we were sufficiently recovered to make the six-mile journey to Chestnut Drive, and when we walked in the door, I could not believe my senses. I was assailed with fragrance and memory, hailed by the very essence of Christmas itself, for Mama had made a complete replay of the proceedings. The smoky fireplace was a-dance with a merry blaze, the tree was mounded with presents. And the Christmas morning casserole was just coming out of the oven. Daddy said the blessing and we all clattered up from the table to serve our plates. I took a bite, and all of my Christmases were present to me at once, including this sweetly recovered one, gathered into a single memory whose meaning is love.

RECIPE: *Mama's Sacrosanct Christmas Morning Casserole*

1½ pounds pork sausage
9 eggs, slightly beaten
3 cups whole milk
1½ tsp. dry mustard
1 tsp. kosher salt
½ tsp. black pepper

3 slices of sandwich bread, white or whole wheat, cubed
1¾ cups grated sharp cheddar cheese

Brown the sausage, breaking it up into chunks. Drain on paper towels, then spread on the bottom of a greased 9x13-inch casserole dish. Combine the eggs and milk in a large mixing bowl and sprinkle the mustard and seasonings evenly over the top before whisking to blend. Stir in the bread cubes and grated cheese and pour evenly over the sausage.

Cover tightly and refrigerate overnight. Bake uncovered for one hour at 350°.

SERVES: 6-8

CHRISTMASTIDE

RECIExPE: *Homemade Danish Orange Rolls*

Philip and his brothers absolutely love the Pillsbury Orange Cinnamon Rolls you can buy in a can from the grocery store, but here's a homemade version that tastes even better. Begin the day before you wish to serve them, as the dough must be refrigerated overnight.

½ cup water
¼ cup unsalted butter
¼ cup butter-flavored
   vegetable shortening
Scant ½ cup sugar
¾ tsp. salt
2¼ tsp. (1 envelope) active dry yeast
½ cup warm water (105-110 degrees)

1 egg, slightly beaten
3 cups all-purpose flour
8 Tbsp. unsalted butter, softened
½ cup sugar
1 Tbsp. freshly grated orange zest
½ tsp. cinnamon
2 cups powdered sugar
4 Tbsp. orange juice
   (roughly 2 oranges)

Bring ½ cup water to boil in a small saucepan. Remove from heat and add the butter and shortening. Stir until melted, add the sugar and salt and cool to lukewarm.

Place the ½ cup warm water in a large bowl and sprinkle the yeast over it, stirring to dissolve. Add the butter mixture and the egg and stir to combine. Add 3 cups flour and mix until the flour is thoroughly incorporated. Cover tightly with plastic wrap and refrigerate overnight.

2½ hours before serving, turn the dough onto a lightly floured board. Divide in half and knead gently for 10-15 seconds, then roll each half out into a 12×8-inch rectangle. Combine the softened butter, the remaining ½ cup sugar, the cinnamon, and the orange zest and spread evenly over each rectangle, leaving a ¾-inch border on all sides. Roll the dough up lengthwise. Using a serrated knife with a gentle, sawing motion, slice each roll into 18 equal pieces.

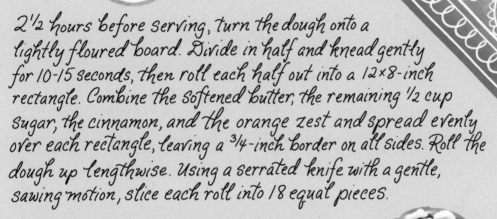

Place the rolls in two 9×13-inch greased baking dishes and allow to rise in a warm place until almost doubled, 1½ hours.

(ALTERNATIVELY, you can proof and shape the rolls the night before, after giving the dough a 12-hour stint in the refrigerator. Allow them to rise until nearly doubled, then cover loosely with plastic wrap and refrigerate overnight. The next morning, take them out of the refrigerator and let them sit at room temperature for 30 minutes, then remove plastic wrap and bake as directed.)

Preheat the oven to 375°. Bake the rolls for 10-15 minutes until lightly browned. Combine the powdered sugar and orange juice and drizzle over the warm rolls before serving.

YIELD: 3 DOZEN

Christmas Dinner

I was getting rather self-conscious over my sadness. It was the same sadness that took up residence in my heart each year, the thing I had to name in prayer again and again: the silent grief that yet another twelve months had carved away that much more of the likelihood of certain things turning out the way I wanted them to. But this old grief was darkened by the shadow of a new one. A few months previous we had admitted my father to a skilled nursing facility for a cruel disease none of us understood, and my mother was alone now on Chestnut Drive. My days were consumed with doctor's appointments and difficult conversations; my nights were marked by fearful dread and a weariness that would not let me sleep. Though I tried to make it special and different, Thanksgiving had left me melancholy. Christmas felt like a minefield.

As Christmas drew nearer, a desperation began to swell, something independent of the holidays and yet deeply connected to them. Caught between my longing for a child and the slow, grinding sorrow of Daddy's illness, I realized there was something more—something I could scarcely name or even imagine, but which left me absolutely impregnated with desire. I sat with the immensity of it all as it stretched and grew, straining my heart with its bright burden, until suddenly–I knew. I didn't just want to *be* a mother. I wanted to *mother*.

Already I had sensed a holy invitation to parent both of my parents through a heartbreaking situation. But this felt even larger, more limitless, not a temporary post, but a permanent vocation. I remembered years ago making casual reference to my infertility to a friend on the phone with far more flippancy than I felt. It was the ultimate self-consciousness, the thing that made me feel cut off from other women, excluded from a society of maternity and from that joy the Bible speaks of which makes one forget there was ever such a thing as suffering. I tried to move the conversation along, but she interrupted me.

"Wait a minute," she said. "This doesn't often happen to me, but I feel like the Holy Spirit wants me to say something to you." She paused. "You are *not* infertile. I don't know what that means, but I know it's the absolute truth."

I thanked her rather awkwardly and changed the subject. Of course I was infertile—I had the doctors' visits and the disappointed hopes to show for it. Now, however, her words came winging back to me. Maybe—just maybe—God was calling me to a fruitfulness I hadn't considered before. Maybe there were other ways to mother than bearing children. Maybe motherhood was not so much a status as a calling, a secret, silent conspiracy between a woman and her God, an invitation to populate the world with love simply by offering herself as a vessel.

It felt like an annunciation. It blazed over the ordinary opportunities and decisions of life with sharp, sweet clarity. I wanted to nurture bodies and souls, to push back against the darkness and sorrow of the world with candlelight and music, good food and noble thoughts. I longed to create safe, beautiful spaces where people could encounter the mystery of the Incarnation and the beauty of their own belovedness. I wanted to affirm that families didn't have to look like each other, or even be related. And as Christmas crested on the horizon like a fair ship with banners flying, I wanted to greet it with joy, to celebrate, not as a distraction from all this sadness, but a declaration that death—of people or of dreams—is merely a passage to new and greater life.

CHRISTMASTIDE

I longed, in short, to pour out my desires and my gifts and my resources in a reckless torrent of love. The only trouble was that there didn't seem to be anyone much in need of what I had to give. I dreamed of the Ruff House full to bursting on Christmas, a home to many on that blessed day. But everyone I knew, it seemed, had something else to do or somewhere else to be. I was stumped.

I was actually starting to get a bit testy about it, though I had made it a matter of ardent prayer, when an idea occurred to me with such winsome appeal I nearly laughed aloud. Before self-consciousness or social anxiety could stop me, I sent an impulsive text. And then I writhed with uncertainty. Of course they had plans—Katie and Rob had close extended families of their own. Besides, why would they want to pack up their eight children, leaving behind a trove of new toys, no doubt, to spend Christmas with us?

When I told Philip what I had done, he was surprised for the same reason I was uncertain. We waited together for the warm and friendly and apologetic "No."

But, "YES!" Katie texted back.

We couldn't believe it. My phone rang and Katie and I squealed and rhapsodized like young girls. It seemed that Katie's mother would be out of the country, visiting her sister overseas, and they had decided to spend Christmas quietly at home.

"But I had literally just said to Rob, 'I wish we could spend Christmas with friends.'"

And then my text had come in.

Christmas with friends! It seemed like a novel concept, though it had taken such challenging circumstances to make me see how sweet and simple it could be. And what was more natural than to keep this great feast of Giving and Coming in company with

kindred souls? I planned my menu with care, consulting the children over turkey or ham (unequivocally, ham) and filled the freezer with casseroles, cookies, and cakes. I had invited Mama, and our precious friend Monica, to stay over, and I made beds and clipped greenery to my heart's content, though my heart was breaking.

On the 23rd of December, my seventeen year-old neighbor brought over a gift: an arrangement she'd made of crimson roses, with holly and fir and two red candles.

"My mom said that red roses mean a lot to you," she said.

I looked her straight in the eye. "There is not one thing you could have given me that would have meant more."

On Christmas Day seven little Eakers rang the doorbell and I nearly knocked Katie over with a hug on the front walk. Philip and Rob carried Louisa's wheelchair up the front steps while the other children raced to the den to have a look at the tree. Monica was basting the ham; Mama was chatting quite seriously with three year-old Elizabeth Jane; the boys were all telling Philip what they'd gotten for Christmas, all at once. I passed around libations—champagne punch laced with pomegranate and elderflower for the adults, gently warmed cider for the little ones—and proposed a toast.

"To Christmas with friends!"

"The very best of friends," Katie replied, lifting her glass.

Clara wanted to help in the kitchen, so I handed her a pot of newly drained potatoes and a masher. She plopped down on the spot in a sparkly pile of organza and velvet and went to work with such absorption that Monica and I were obliged to take care not to trip over her as we crisscrossed from sink to stove and back again. When everything was ready—the ham glazed to a tart sweetness of red currant and rosemary, the squash casserole bubbling and fragrant beneath a golden crust, the oyster pie a thing of plump succulence, and the potatoes mashed within an inch of their lives—we gathered in the kitchen for the blessing. Philip and Rob each took a turn, and a joy that made me forget there was any such thing as suffering shot through me. Maternal love flowered and flowed from my heart—to my mother, my husband, my daughter-like Monica, our beloved friends—in that moment they were all my children and I exulted over them with a holy affection.

After dinner the children made for the barn in a cacophony of plastic cracker horns, while the ladies lingered at the table for one more pot of tea and a few more logs on the fire. Around dusk we pulled on Wellie boots beneath our festive dresses and went for a ramble to the cemetery, and as we turned back toward the house and emerged from the gloom of the woods, I caught my breath at the sight of the Ruff House, alight and waiting for us, every window a lantern of welcome and warmth. Her heart, it seemed, was as full as mine.

I served the pudding in a glory of ghostly blue flame, and we sang carols around the piano in the parlor while Elizabeth Jane marched about the room tooting her little horn *almost* in time to the music. And at the end of the evening, Monica treated us to a solo rendition of "In the Bleak Midwinter," her rich, rose-red contralto filling the room with a beauty that held even the children transfixed.

Philip and Monica and I washed up after everyone had gone, enjoying the relative quiet of conversation and Christmas jazz. We had dirtied almost every pot, pan, plate, cup, goblet, knife, fork, and spoon I owned, but I was well content. God had answered my prayer, and here was the beautiful mess to prove it. But, with typical munificence, he had gone far beyond what I had asked for, or even thought of. In a year in which sorrow threatened to turn me inward, he had turned my heart and my home inside out with joy. For I knew now, in this fully ripened moment of exhausted satisfaction, what I could never have seen in days of lesser desperation: that every longing has its home in

Jesus. Every desire is an arrow pinning our heart to his. What gifts, then, these thorns of worn-out hope and imminent loss! What treasure is couched within the confines of a broken heart!

The supposed emptiness of my arms and my rooms had been a mirage threatening to obscure the goodness of the life I had and the people with whom I was blessed to share it. The sorrow was real, of course, and the struggle was valid. But how easily might self-consciousness have won this battle. How quickly might self-pity have taken the day. Jesus had intervened, however; he, whose incarnational feast we were celebrating and whose life brought meaning to our own, had bridged the gap between my pain and my peace, tending the arid spaces in my life with the tenderness of a gardener. For grief is always seeded with the germ of fecundity, and at the bowed head and the *be it unto me*, every sort of barrenness bears abundant life.

Over the years, we have had guests around our holiday table from places as far-flung as France, Cameroon, Ghana, Burma, Liberia, Japan, and China, and every time I have loved to hear about the seasonal foods and special traditions in their countries of origin—from the ndomba of West Africa to the sticky rice and banana leaves of Southeast Asia. I have friends who make an event each year of preparing an old family recipe of authentic Italian lasagna with Bolognese sauce, and friends who love nothing better than a Cajun étouffée fortified with crawfish fat.

The first year I hosted Christmas Dinner at the Ruff House, I turned instinctively to the regional standards of my Southern upbringing. For while a holiday meal should be special, it ought to be comfortable at the same time. The very familiarity of certain dishes,

Christmas Music

JOY TO THE WORLD
Pink Martini

SWEET BELLS
Kate Rusby

BRIGHT DAY STAR
The Baltimore Consort

THE JOHN RUTTER
CHRISTMAS ALBUM
The Cambridge Singers,
The City of London Sinfonia

HANDEL'S MESSIAH
The Academy of St. Martin in
the Fields, Sir Neville Marriner

ANGELS ON HIGH:
A ROBERT SHAW CHRISTMAS
Robert Shaw Chamber Singers

THE BIRTH OF JESUS
John Michael Talbot

NOËL
Joan Baez

especially those passed down from people we love, assures us that all that matters most in life is most enduring. My mother's pound cake and my mother-in-law's pork tenderloin are not only good—they are good messengers, reminding me of my place in the story I belong to and bringing me word of a love which is, indeed, stronger than death.

Which is why, though the menu for a Ruff House Christmas Dinner varies slightly from year to year, there are a couple of things you will always find on my table. One is the innocuous-sounding baked squash, which has been a holiday staple for as long as I can remember. Mama made it for both Thanksgiving and Easter, as its sunny disposition compliments both turkey and ham. And we often had it for Sunday dinner. The humble glory of the thing rests in a golden crown of soda cracker crust which has been liberally saturated in butter before baking. The salty crunch is a pleasant foil to the sweetness of the squash, and when those briny juices begin to swim about on your plate they will inspirit every other dish with an extra kiss of flavor.

The other is oyster pie, for even if I were the only one to eat it, I would still make it. I am not, however, the only one who eats it; Philip loves it; my sister Liz loves it, as does anyone at my table who harbors a cordial feeling toward the little mollusks. Most of all, my Daddy loved it, which is really what makes it so indispensable. But adding an oyster pie to the menu also introduces a subtle layer of casual sophistication, of mystery even, and perhaps a touch of profundity. Like the scherzo of a symphony or the subplot of a novel, oysters add depth to a meal, and an element of surprise. I love to delight my guests with the unlooked-for goodness of so uncomely a dish, for the appearance of an oyster pie is not one to inspire ardor. It is plain-featured and grey beneath its bread crumb topping; only to the initiated is it a thing of beauty. To that happy band, however, belongs the culinary felicity of bivalves cradled in Tabasco-laced cream, the brackish, slightly bitter beginning, the nectarous mineral finish. I grew up in a family that prized the seasonal delight of oysters—"Only eat them in months with an 'r'," Mama would remind us—but the lovely thing about this recipe is that there are no gloves or oyster knives required. Pints of fresh oysters are readily available this time of year, shucked and ready for service, and to their palatability one may safely commit this dish. Just be sure to purchase the freshest oysters you can find, from a reputable supplier, or order them in advance from your seafood counter.

Other things dance in and out of my spread from year to year, like the exquisite champagne-and-elderflower punch I often serve before dinner. I love how the warm notes of ginger and spice dance cordially with the crisp, cold bubbly, and how the gold of the champagne is touched with a faint note of coral thanks to infusion of a home-made pomegranate syrup. I also love how the winey bouquet of a poached pear comple-ments the other savory tastes and aromas on a plate. And oftentimes I will prepare, out of sheer love for Philip, the version of fried okra his mother was always able to produce for him at a moment's notice (Janice's secret, she confided, was to shallow-fry the okra until it was nearly done, drain and freeze, then pop it onto a baking sheet to crisp up at serving time). My okra will never be as good as Janice's, but its presence on our table makes *her* present to us in a tangible way. Dainty creamer potatoes tossed with lemon zest and herbs is another favorite, as is the reliable standard of green bean casserole, elevated with fresh mushrooms in a homemade cream sauce and topped, not with greasy shoestring potatoes from a can, but with rich caramelized onions coated in stone-ground meal.

There are a variety of meats to consider (or none at all) for a Christmas Dinner, but a simple spiral-sliced ham will always be a sure foundation for any combination of sides. Many of the hams you buy at the grocery come with their own packet of spices to make a glaze, but I have found that a jar of red or black currant jelly, melted down and steeped with a sprig or two of fresh rosemary, is even easier and much tastier. The only thing that remains is a dessert to round things out, and, after such an array of rich fare, only the most unpretentious will do: in this case, an old fashioned glazed rum cake, which smells almost as good as it tastes. *Almost.*

If my Christmas Dinner is a sit-down meal, my mother's was always more of a pick-up affair. Christmas Day in our house was like a long, laid-back party, with family members arriving at different times and a pervading air of languid festivity. As soon as the breakfast dishes were cleared, Mama would begin to set out an array of treats and tasty bites: freshly sliced vegetables and dip, an assortment of cheeses, homemade cookies, candy-sweet mandarins. There would be a little cut glass bowl of bread-and-butter pickles, made by Daddy's secretary's mother, and the Baxley fruitcake

someone sent to his office as a Christmas gift. There might be devilled eggs, spiced pecans, my Aunt Ellen's sausage balls. Sometimes Mama put out a ham, gently warmed, with soft rolls and little china pots of mayonnaise and mustard, but oftener than not she made her friend Wendy's poppy seed ham rolls, which could be prepared and refrigerated overnight then transferred to the oven for half an hour before serving. Those rolls, dripping with butter and melted Swiss cheese, their tops browned under a basting of Dijon mustard and Worcestershire sauce, were attendant upon so many of our Christmases, it is difficult for me to picture my mother's table without them.

Even at regular parties, people made themselves at home in Mama's kitchen, but never more so than at Christmas. On that day there was always a selection of hot beverages to be ladled, steeped, whisked, or poured at one's whimsy—freshly ground coffee, an arsenal of loose-leaf teas with enchanting names like "Nutcracker Sweet" or "Winter Garden," packets of hot cocoa. But my favorite was always the Russian Tea, a brew of decaffeinated orange pekoe, pineapple juice, and fresh citrus steeped with cinnamon and cloves. Mama would press the oranges and lemons through a chinois with a wooden pestle to extract every last drop of golden juice, and she always said that the extra vitamin C was insurance against the inevitable post-Christmas cold. I loved that tea so much that, after I was married, she sent me home with a jar of it every Christmas night, which I would mete out sparingly over the following days to make it last as long as possible.

One Christmas morning, I walked in the front door and sniffed.

"Where's the Russian Tea?" I asked.

She looked at me and gasped. It was the slightest lapse in a lifetime of remembering everyone's preferences, but she could not allow it. She went straight into the kitchen and started slicing oranges, and, as I joined her, it felt like a sweet, secret bond between my mother and me. She loved that tea for my sake—and I loved it for hers. Years later, when she started coming to my house for Christmas, I would place a mug of steaming, citrusy warmth into her hands the moment she walked in the door with a confiding smile, as much as to say, "I know it's hard for you that things are different. But the more things change, the more they stay the same."

There was continuity in that cup, a wordless transfiguring of simple ingredients into practical affection, sympathy, tenderness, and remembrance. For the only real consideration in planning our holiday menus, or deciding which dish to take to a gathering of family or friends, is love itself. The most elaborate meal without love might as well be hardtack and water. But with that singular seasoning, the humblest offerings become a banquet.

A menu for a *Southern* CHRISTMAS DINNER

RUFF HOUSE
CHRISTMAS PUNCH

RED CURRANT *and* ROSEMARY GLAZED HAM
BAKED SQUASH
OYSTER PIE
NEW POTATOES *in* SAVORY SAUCE
POACHED PEARS
CLASSIC GREEN BEAN CASSEROLE
WENDY'S HAM ROLLS

OLD-FASHIONED RUM CAKE
RUSSIAN TEA

RUFF HOUSE CHRISTMAS PUNCH
SERVES 12

Sparkling pear juice can be hard to come by, which is why I always snatch up a bottle or two whenever I see it—Martinelli's makes a nice one. If you can't find the sparkling version, regular unsweetened pear juice will do, as will a couple of 12-ounce bottles of hard pear cider. Additionally, a non-alcoholic version may be made by substituting plain seltzer for the champagne and elderflower syrup for the liqueur.

1 cup unsweetened pomegranate juice
1 3-inch knob of fresh ginger, peeled and thinly sliced
20 green cardamom pods, crushed with the butt of a knife
1 750 ml bottle extra Brut champagne or Cava, chilled
1 750 ml bottle sparkling pear juice, chilled
½ to ¾ cup St-Germaine elderflower liqueur

In a medium saucepan, combine the pomegranate juice, the ginger, and the cardamom. Bring to a boil, then reduce to a simmer and cook, uncovered, until reduced by half, about 30 minutes. Remove from the heat and cool to room temperature. Strain into a jar through a fine mesh sieve and store in the refrigerator, covered, for at last 2 hours and up to 3 days.

At serving time, place the pomegranate reduction in the bottom of a punch bowl. Pour over the champagne, pear juice, and St-Germaine and serve immediately.

RED CURRANT & ROSEMARY GLAZED HAM

SERVES 8

If you can't find red currant jelly, black currant preserves make a nice substitution.

1 4–5 pound bone-in smoked ham, fat trimmed to
   a ¼-inch thickness
1 10-ounce jar red currant jelly
3 rosemary sprigs
2 teaspoons lemon juice
Pinch of kosher salt
Rosemary sprigs and fresh kumquats
   for garnish

Preheat oven to 325 degrees. Wrap ham with foil and transfer to a large roasting pan. Bake for 1 hour.

In a small saucepan, bring red currant jelly and rosemary to a simmer. Reduce to medium and cook until thick and syrupy, about 3 minutes. Stir in lemon juice and salt.

Remove ham from the oven, unwrap, and transfer to a cutting board. With a sharp knife, score the fat in a cross-hatch pattern, lines about ½ inch apart. Return ham to roasting pan and raise the oven temperature to 375 degrees. Brush ham with currant glaze and bake for 30 minutes. Brush again with glaze and bake for 10 minutes more. Remove from oven and brush again with glaze. Rewarm remaining glaze over low heat until pourable and sauce-like. Remove rosemary.

Remove ham from the oven and transfer to a serving platter. Garnish with fresh rosemary sprigs and kumquats. Slice ham and serve with the sauce.

CHRISTMASTIDE

BAKED SQUASH
SERVES 4–6

I usually make this ahead. You can cover and refrigerate overnight (or freeze, covered with plastic wrap and foil) before adding the cracker topping. If frozen, defrost in the fridge overnight. Let stand 30 minutes at room temperature then bake as directed. It can be easily doubled, but you will need to upsize to a 9 x 13-inch casserole dish.

3 pounds yellow squash

½ cup onions, chopped

¾ cup butter, melted

2 eggs, beaten

½ sleeve saltine crackers

1 teaspoon kosher salt

1 teaspoon sugar

½ teaspoon pepper

Preheat oven to 375 degrees.

Bring a large pot of salted water to a boil. Slice squash ¼ inch thick. Combine with onion and add to the pot, cooking over low-medium heat until squash and onions are tender, about 15–20 minutes. Drain thoroughly in a colander, pressing out excess water with the back of a spoon.

Return squash to pot and add the eggs, sugar, salt, pepper, and ½ of the butter. Mix with a potato masher until well combined. Pour into a greased 8 x 8-inch pan or 2-quart casserole. Crush the saltines with your fingers and sprinkle over the top. Pour the remaining butter over the casserole and bake, uncovered, for 45 minutes or until the top is golden and bubbly.

OYSTER PIE

SERVES 6

Although oysters are in season this time of year, you will need to order them in advance from your local fish dealer or at the seafood counter of your grocery store to ensure the freshest specimens possible. Hilton is a reliable brand. If you've never had oyster pie before, the consistency of the casserole should be thick and the oysters very lightly set. Don't over-cook them!

- ¾ cup unsalted butter
- 3 slices bread, torn by hand into ½-inch pieces
- 2 cups coarsely crushed Ritz crackers
- ½ cup heavy cream
- 1 tablespoon freshly squeezed lemon juice
- 2 teaspoons Worcestershire sauce
- 1½ teaspoons kosher salt
- ¼ teaspoon freshly ground black pepper
- ¼ teaspoon cayenne pepper
- ¼ cup parsley, chopped
- 2 pints fresh oysters, drained
- Paprika, for sprinkling on top

Preheat the oven to 400 degrees. Melt the butter in a small saucepan. Mix half of the melted butter with the torn bread and toss to coat. Mix the remaining melted butter with the cracker crumbs and toss.

Combine the heavy cream, lemon juice, Worcestershire sauce, salt, black pepper, and cayenne pepper in a measuring cup with a pouring spout.

Place half the oysters in a buttered, 2-quart casserole dish. Top with half of the cracker crumbs, half of the bread, and half of the parsley. Pour half of the cream mixture evenly over the top. Repeat the layers, beginning with the oysters, followed by cracker crumbs, parsley, and ending with a layer of breadcrumbs. Pour the remaining cream over the top and sprinkle with a light dusting of paprika.

Bake for 30 minutes until the oysters are plump and gently set and the topping is lightly browned. Serve immediately.

NEW POTATOES IN SAVORY SAUCE
SERVES 4–6

This is an old-fashioned recipe that stands in nicely for mashed or roasted potatoes on the holiday board. You can make the sauce earlier in the day and keep it at room temperature, if you'd like.

2 pounds small new potatoes, unpeeled

¼ cup butter

1 tablespoon olive oil

Grated zest of one lemon

¼ cup chopped fresh parsley or dill

2 tablespoons snipped fresh chives

⅛ teaspoon nutmeg

¼ teaspoon flour

½ teaspoon kosher salt

¼ teaspoon freshly ground black pepper

3 tablespoons freshly squeezed lemon juice

Place potatoes in a medium saucepan with salted water to cover. Bring to a boil over medium heat, then reduce to low, cooking gently until potatoes are fork tender, 15–20 minutes. Drain, then return to the pot, covered, to keep warm.

In a medium skillet, heat the butter and oil over low heat until butter is melted. Stir in the lemon zest, herbs, nutmeg, flour, salt, and pepper, and continue to cook, stirring constantly, until sauce thickens slightly, 3–5 minutes. Do not allow it to boil.

At serving time, gently rewarm the sauce, if necessary, and stir lemon juice into the warm sauce. Pour sauce over the potatoes and toss gently to coat.

POACHED PEARS
SERVES 6

Peel the pears while the sauce is coming to a boil—this will keep them from developing any unsightly brown spots before poaching. And the flavors really pop at room temperature, so be sure to allow at least an hour between removing them from the refrigerator and serving time. I like to include these as a sweet side dish, but they are equally lovely as a dessert with a dollop of vanilla ice cream or crème fraîche.

   2 cups dry red wine

   1 cup port wine

   1½ cups sugar

   4 strips orange peel

   ½ cup freshly squeezed orange juice

   2 teaspoons Madagascar bourbon vanilla extract

   1 cinnamon stick

CHRISTMASTIDE

8 whole cloves

6 Bosc pears, slightly ripe

Combine all ingredients but the pears in a large saucepan and add 1 cup of water. Bring to a boil over medium heat, stirring to combine. Reduce to a simmer and cook until the sugar dissolves, 3–5 minutes. Peel the pears, leaving the stems intact, and add to the syrup as they are peeled. Poach at a bare simmer for 15–20 minutes until just tender, then remove from heat and allow to cool in the liquid. Store, covered, in the refrigerator for up to 2 days. Before serving, let the pears come to room temperature, 1–2 hours. Rewarm the sauce and pour over the pears.

CLASSIC GREEN BEAN CASSEROLE
Serves 4–6

With fresh ingredients and nary a can of cream soup in sight, this dish elevates the rather bland original version to new heights. To freeze before baking, allow casserole to cool, then cover with plastic wrap and aluminum foil. Defrost in the refrigerator overnight, then let stand at room temperature 30 minutes. Bake uncovered on the lowest oven rack at 400 degrees for 25–30 minutes, or until bubbly and heated through, taking care not to let the onion topping burn (cover with aluminum foil if it's getting too dark).

TOPPING:

2 medium onions, thinly sliced

1 tablespoon olive oil

¼ cup all-purpose flour

2 tablespoons panko breadcrumbs

1 teaspoon kosher salt

Nonstick cooking spray

CASEROLE:

2 tablespoons plus 1 teaspoon kosher salt, divided

1 pound frozen French-style beans, thawed and drained in a colander

2 tablespoons unsalted butter

12 ounces white button mushrooms, trimmed and sliced ½-inch thick

½ teaspoon black pepper

2 cloves garlic, minced

¼ teaspoon nutmeg

2 tablespoons all-purpose flour

1 cup chicken broth

1 cup half-and-half

Preheat the oven to 475 degrees.

In a medium-sized bowl, combine the sliced onions and olive oil; toss to coat. In a larger bowl, whisk together ¼ cup flour, bread crumbs, and salt; add the onions and toss to combine. Line a rimmed baking sheet with parchment paper and coat with cooking spray. Spread the onions evenly on the pan and bake on the middle rack of the oven, tossing every 5 minutes, until golden brown, about 30 minutes. Remove from the oven and set aside. Lower oven temperature to 400 degrees.

While the onions are cooking, prepare a large bowl of ice water. In a large saucepan, bring 2 quarts of water and 2 tablespoons of salt to the boil. Add the beans and blanch, 3–5 minutes, then drain immediately and plunge the beans into the ice water. Drain and set aside.

Melt the butter over medium-high heat in a large, cast-iron skillet. Add the mushrooms, 1 teaspoon of salt, and the pepper, and cook, stirring occasionally, until the mushrooms release their liquid, about 5 minutes. Add the garlic and nutmeg and continue to cook for 2 minutes more. Sprinkle the flour evenly over the mixture and stir to combine. Cook for 1 minute, then add the broth and simmer for 1 minute more. Decrease the heat to medium-low and add the half-and-half. Cook, stirring often, until the sauce thickens, about 8–10 minutes.

Remove from the heat and stir in ¼ of the onions and all of the green beans. Spread evenly into a 2-quart casserole dish and top with the remaining onions. Bake until bubbly and heated through, 15–20 minutes.

WENDY'S HAM ROLLS
MAKES 4 DOZEN

Look for rolls packaged in disposable aluminum pans, although any small dinner rolls in the 12-ounce size will do. If you end up going with rolls that come in paper trays, simply transfer them to a greased 9 x 13 or 7 x 11-inch casserole dish and prepare as directed.

4 packages store-bought butter dinner rolls (12 ounces each) in aluminum pans
Cooking spray
1 pound thinly sliced deli ham
16 ounces grated Swiss cheese
1½ sticks unsalted butter, melted
4 tablespoons finely minced onion
4 tablespoons sugar

4 tablespoons poppy seeds

4 tablespoons grainy Dijon mustard

4 teaspoons Worcestershire sauce

Preheat oven to 250 degrees.

Remove the rolls from their pans and slice each package horizontally with a large bread knife without breaking the rolls apart. Grease the original pans (or alternate baking dishes) lightly with cooking spray and return the bottom layers to the pans, topping each one with roughly ¼ of the ham and ¼ of the cheese. Replace the top layers. In a small bowl combine the melted butter, onion, sugar, poppy seeds, mustard, and Worcestershire sauce. Spoon ¼ of the sauce over each pan of rolls, using a spatula to spread it evenly.

Cover with aluminum foil and bake for 20 minutes until warm and the cheese is melted. Uncover and bake for 3–5 minutes more, until the tops of the rolls are browned.

Separate into individual rolls and serve warm.

OLD-FASHIONED RUM CAKE
SᴇRVᴇS 10–12

If you're making this cake ahead of time, reserve half of the glaze to rewarm and pour over the cake at serving time.

Cᴀᴋᴇ:

    2 sticks (1 cup) butter

    2 cups sugar

    6 eggs, room temperature

    2 cups plus 3 tablespoons sifted
       all-purpose flour

    ¼ teaspoon salt

    ¼ cup spiced rum

Gʟᴀᴢᴇ:

    2 sticks (1 cup) butter

    2 cups sugar

    ½ cup water

    ½ cup spiced rum

Grease a 9-inch Bundt pan and dust lightly with flour, shaking off the excess. Preheat oven to 300 degrees.

In a stand mixer fitted with the paddle attachment or with a hand mixer, beat the butter at high speed until light and fluffy, then add the sugar and cream on medium speed. Add the eggs, one at a time, beating well after each addition and scraping down the sides of the bowl with a rubber spatula. Add flour and salt and mix well, scraping again with the spatula to incorporate all the ingredients. Pour in the rum and mix on low speed until thoroughly blended.

Pour the batter into the prepared pan, spreading as evenly as you can with a rubber spatula (the batter will be thick, like a pound cake) and bake for 1 hour and 45 minutes, until a cake tester or toothpick comes out clean. Set the cake on a wire rack and cool in the pan for 10 minutes.

While the cake is cooling, melt the remaining 1 cup butter in a small saucepan, then add 2 cups sugar and ½ cup water. Bring to a boil and cook for 3–4 minutes, stirring constantly, until the sugar dissolves. Remove from heat, stir in the remaining ½ cup rum, and cool slightly.

Turn the cake out onto a serving plate or tray and pierce all over with a toothpick. Using a pastry brush, coat the cake generously with glaze. Drizzle remaining glaze on top of the cake (some of it will pool on the plate), reserving a small amount to spoon over individual pieces at serving time.

Store, covered, at room temperature for up to 2 days.

CHRISTMASTIDE

RUSSIAN TEA

Makes about 2 gallons

Do not be alarmed at the citrus-to-water ratio at the outset of this recipe. The heat will cause the oranges and lemons to break down quickly and release their juices. And, yes, prepare the fruit peel and all—it will add a gorgeous bouquet to your tea.

12 orange pekoe tea bags

6 cups water

8 oranges, sliced

6 lemons, sliced

6 (3-inch) cinnamon sticks

1 tablespoon whole cloves

2 quarts water, divided

1 (46-ounce) can pineapple juice

1½ cups sugar, or to taste

Combine the tea bags and 6 cups water in a small saucepan and bring to a boil. Turn off the heat and allow the tea to steep to room temperature.

In a large non-aluminum saucepan combine the sliced fruit, cinnamon, cloves, and 1 quart water. Bring to a boil and boil steadily for 5 minutes, stirring often. Remove from heat and cool slightly.

Press the fruit mixture through a strainer or chinois, extracting as much juice as possible. Discard the pulp and spices and return the juice to the pot. Strain the tea and add it to the juice, along with the remaining quart of water. Add the pineapple juice and 1 ½ cups sugar (more or less, to taste), stirring well to dissolve the sugar. Serve hot.

Keeping Christmas

After a blessed spate of merrymaking with my loved ones, of coming and goings, of constantly running dishwashers and overflowing rooms and precious people under my roof and around my tables, today is a day of sweet nothing. For weeks, my "to-do" list has shimmered with loved tasks, each days' allotment idealistically exceeding the limits of physical possibility, while my freezers have steadily filled and my rooms have assumed their fairest faces of the year. I've clipped holly and woven ivy and wired pine until it seemed my fingers would keep going through the motions while I slept. I've turned the kitchen inside out over casseroles and cookies and conserve and caramels—and just as soon as everything was tidy once more, I turned it inside out again. We've hauled chairs out of the attic and shuffled furniture and set tables in every conceivable place. And in the very early mornings, I've sat with my Bible and my prayer book, staring at the constellations of stars on my Christmas tree and pondering that astonishing Story, making space for its wonder to re-enchant my heart all over again.

In recent days my hands could hardly "keep pace with my desire."[1] But today is a pajama day, a day of unapologetic indolence. It is a day for leftover Russian Tea and a Miss Read book on the couch and a constant rotation of cats vying for my lap. I'll do a bit of journaling, a bit of napping, a lot of sitting and remembering and enjoying.

[1] Blanche Bane Kuder, "The Blue Bowl"

Tonight, we will load up the Stack-O-Matic with Christmas records and sip from festive cocktails of Philip's devising. We might crack out the backgammon board, or an Elizabeth Goudge story I've been saving to share. And as the last embers of a December day smolder beyond the pines to the west, the winter night will gather out under the walnut trees, creeping up to the windows and moaning about the eaves of the house. But inside, a humble warmth will prevail, accompanied by a festive air of quiet mirth. For dear old Christmas is in her youth, ripened to the lovely possibility of her second day.

I am well aware that a goodly portion of the world has moved on at this point—the Twelve Days of Christmas seem to wear more of the wistfulness of legend than the habit of actuality in many circles. But Christmas is too grand, too dear, too consequential to limit to one day. With Lenten-like solemnity we have walked the Advent way of hope-laced waiting and confident expectation; we have sat with unresolved tension and kept company with imponderability. And now the Light has pierced our darkness—*the darling of the world has come!* Why then cram all of our relief into a single 24-hour period? If Easter is a 50-day feast, why not make room for the staggering implications of the Incarnation?

I am thankful that both the tradition of my faith and the rhythms Philip and I have built into our lives have made these days not just wishful thinking, but an experienced reality. I admit, it felt like pretending at first, back in those early years when we were just beginning to cultivate the culture of our home; to act like Christmas wasn't over when the world deemed otherwise, was a very real challenge. It was like trying to touch a star, or grow into clothes that were too big. But that was just it—we grew into it. Within a few years and with a liberal dose of intention, we seasoned into Christmastide. We gained the confidence—or unconcern—to *keep* Christmas, not just observe it as it flies. And, in many ways, the Ruff House, with its memories and sympathies and secrets, has given us that confidence; she knows what it means to stand still while the current of time swirls madly by.

Keeping Christmas is not just a state of mind. Like the set hours of prayer or the seasonal vestments of the altar, there are things we do which enflesh what is actual. There are certain treats and rituals I save for Christmastide, like a new puzzle, or making Daddy's daddy's eggnog. There is that blessed little stash of comfort food in the freezer downstairs, and a favorite collection of Christmas stories saved for these shielded days. There are records and movies we've held in store, and a gentle succession of friendly visits, now happily unencumbered from the expectations of less expansive days. For expectations have flown out the window, along with lists, schedules, and all but the most basic routines. Even after New Year's, when life starts to pick up speed and things like work and laundry and grocery lists begin to pluck at our sleeves once more, we will seek to guard the precincts of this set-apart time, devoting our evenings to reading by the fire, or daydreaming languidly about the year to come.

It doesn't take much, we have learned, to keep Christmas: just a little forethought and a dash of cultural rebellion. Habits may be formed of the simplest things, and with a touch of tradition to grace each of these days, it is not difficult to prolong an air of laid-back festivity. One bite of shepherd's pie, the Tudor-like lays of Joan Baez's *Noël*, the roll of dice on a felted board, and the sprite of flame atop a taper on the Advent wreath all signal to our senses what our hearts already know: we have come home, once more, to Christmastide.

HOW TO FEED THE *Birds*

At the back of Mama's recipe box, there is a card in my Daddy's bold, almost illegible handwriting: "Bird Butter." I have every reason to think he got it from his cousin, William, who was an ardent backyard birder and lover of all things avian. Mama and Daddy loved the birds, too, and we all enjoyed watching them, especially in the colder months, from the big plate-glass windows on Chestnut Drive. ("If you see a redbird in winter," Mama used to say, "you can make a wish!") There were always a number of birdfeeders ranged throughout the backyard, but Daddy took special ownership of the suet baskets he kept hanging from shepherd's hooks all winter to give the feathered folk an extra measure of protein in a lean season.

Making a special treat for the wildlife in your yard can be a way to show some Christmas-love to God's creation. When my sister and I were little girls, we used to slather pinecones with peanut butter and roll them in birdseed to make edible "ornaments" to hang on the big junipers at each end of the house. The great thing about Daddy's recipe, however, is that while it's easy enough for a child to help make—with adult supervision—the cakes will last for weeks, and they're far more nutritious for the birds.

NOTES: *Daddy adds that these cakes will not melt in summer, and that they are a great source of protein for young birds and their parents. Keep out of reach of dogs and cats as ingesting these cakes whole could pose a danger to their digestive tracts. Additionally, raisins are toxic to dogs.*

RECIPE: *Bird Butter*

1 cup crunchy peanut butter
1 cup lard or other rendered animal fat
2 cups quick-cook oats
2 cups cornmeal
1 cup white flour
1/3 cup sugar
Optional add-ins: Raisins, dried fruit, chopped nuts,
    shelled birdseed

2-4 egg carton tops
Parchment paper

Plastic freezer bags
Hanging metal suet basket,
5 inches square

1. Line egg carton tops with parchment paper and set aside.
2. Melt peanut butter and lard over low heat. Stir in oats, cornmeal,
    white flour, and sugar.
3. Stir in additional ingredients as desired, raisins or other dried
    fruit, chopped nuts, and shelled birdseed. The amount may
    vary, just so long as the peanut butter mixture can coat
    all of the add-ins thoroughly.
4. Spoon the mixture 1 1/2-inch thick into the carton tops and
    freeze until firm.
5. Cut the cakes into 4-inch squares (or to fit your suet basket)
    and store in freezer or refrigerator.

CHRISTMASTIDE

12 WAYS to KEEP the 12 DAYS

DAY 1 — Take a walk after opening presents and before Christmas Dinner. Get outside with your people (and your pets!) and take note together of how "heaven and nature sing."

DAY 2 — Practice generosity in the name of Good King Wenceslas (who was actually a Bohemian duke): give nonperishables to a food bank or pet food to an animal shelter. Or scour your closets for extra coats and blankets and donate them to a local homeless shelter.

DAY 3 — This is the feast day of John the Evangelist. In the lovely Catholic tradition, toast each member of your family at dinnertime "with the love of St. John."

DAY 4 — In Spain, the sadness of the feast of the Holy Innocents is turned adamantly on its head with a day of childish pranks. Defy the darkness on your own with a few harmless practical jokes on the members of your household.

DAY 5 — Invite friends over to drink eggnog and sing carols. Assign each person their own line in "The Twelve Days of Christmas."

DAY 6 Surprise your family with a new, beautifully wrapped package under the tree: a puzzle or board game or read-aloud book.

 DAY 7 Shoot some fireworks if it's legal in your area. Ring bells, blow horns, shout greetings to the neighbors at midnight.

 DAY 8 Start the year off hospitably—host an open house or invite a friend for lunch. Or plan a simple Twelfth Night gathering for January 6th.

 DAY 9 Save a favorite Christmas movie for this night and watch it together as a family, complete with popcorn, hot chocolate, and lots of cozy blankets and throws.

 DAY 10 Feed the birds: fill up your birdfeeders or make Bird Butter (see page 335). Put out some binoculars and a notebook so you can keep track of your feathered visitors.

 DAY 11 Pull down your dead greenery and replace it with a few fresh sprigs and boughs for Twelfth Night. Swap out spent candles for new ones all over the house.

 DAY 12 Bake a Twelfth Night Cake (see page 372). Play Snapdragon or Christmas Candle. Feast and make good cheer!

CHRISTMASTIDE

THE Light Shines

It was the 26th of December, the second day of Christmas by the traditional reckoning, and I'd spent the balance of it on the couch, nursing the cold I'd sustained thanks to late nights and early mornings and running out barefoot onto the frost-touched grass for just one more branch of holly. But I couldn't have been happier—behind me, a glad and golden Christmas Day crowned with laughter and the faces of those I love; before, a long week of indolence punctuated by last-minute gatherings with friends and small flurries of merrymaking.

There was a kingly sunset that night; we watched it over our tea with growing delight as it deepened from a glitter of gold among the pines through every shade of apricot and orange into a fiery splendor of crimson, spanning the pale sky in streaks of wild color. The finest sunset of the season, we said, and a glory that reminded us that this was just the second of twelve glad days. And then, just as the last flame had vanished from the sky and the animals patiently gathering down by the barnyard fence told us it was time to pull on our overalls and get into our coats for the nightly ritual of bedding down, the lights flickered and went out, leaving us in the candlelight of the two tapers on the coffee table and the cheery glow of the Advent wreath in the window.

"This should be interesting," Philip said with a grin. "And kind of neat."

With one of my candle lamps and the two holly-trimmed hurricane lanterns from the front walk, we made our way across the lawn with our dog, Caspian, frisking in the shadows and a waxing gibbous moon sifting a thin dusting of silver over our way. The animals all greeted us at the gate as usual. But they were unnerved by the darkness. And the sheep, at least, were none too sure of the wavering lights we bore to dispel it. We hung the lanterns in the stalls as we worked, and I sang and spoke low to the frightened darlings as they alternately followed me as a body and dispersed in sudden panic. The goats were fine once they realized that grain was still forthcoming and hay was in the offing, and they munched some of their Christmas apples with as unperturbed a satisfaction as ever, their breath showing in fragrant puffs by the light of the lantern. But the sheep were too terrified to enjoy their evening repast, dropping their loved apples down into the straw untasted to be trampled underfoot by the others.

What a parable, I thought. *The Light shineth in the darkness*. And, according to my sturdy old King James, *the darkness comprehended it not*. Other renderings of that verse tease manifold nuance from these mighty words: the NIV tells us that "the darkness has not overcome;"

according to The Message translation, the Light simply couldn't be put out. But "compre-hended it not" lends a poignancy often overlooked in all our joyous affirmations of hope this time of year, foreshadowing the heartbreaking statement with which the passage proceeds: "He was in the world, and though the world was made by him, the world did not recognize him." A Light, in this sense, not only incomprehensible, but *feared*. I've often heard it pointed out that the first words from an angel's mouth when greeting a human being were always, "Fear not!" And watching my poor frightened flock, I caught an image of our terror of the holy.

I knelt down in their midst, calling to them softly by name, soothing and stroking as they drew near, a ring of lovely ovine faces illumined by the glow of the lanterns, their tender eyes and smooth velvet noses blooming out of the murkiness beyond. This is what the barn must have looked like on the night of Jesus' birth, perhaps the light of an oil lamp scattering the shadows of the stable and lighting up the faces of the friendly beasts that gazed with wonder alongside shepherds and mother and father. That sweet tilt of Hermia's head, so gently touched with gold, went to my heart, as did the soft muffle of Benedick's breath in my ear and the rustle and clucking of a hen in the next stall. It all gave me a moment of transport, a flicker of *knowing*.

Let us go then, even unto Bethlehem . . .

The barn was beautiful by candlelight. And even though the animals protested noisily when we took the candles away, we came merrily back across the lawn, lanterns swinging, to the music of utter silence in the world around us, wrapped in a heavenly calm.

I was a little sorry when the lights came on a few hours later.

The Camp Marah Tree

The tree was so small that Philip could carry it in one hand. He set it up for me in the space we had come to refer to as the Common Room. It was an erstwhile guest room that we totally reimagined after the house fire into an open gathering place for guests, with access to a spacious new bath, and stairs leading to a third floor attic bedroom. I laced the tiny tree with twinkle lights, lending a fairy sheen to its darkened corner. The room was directly above the kitchen, where the fire had started, and so it had seen some of the worst damage in the entire house. During the renovation, when we were framing it up, our vision for its new uses gathered force and clarity, so that scarcely were the stairs roughed in that I stood in the alcove beneath them and announced to my contractor, "Next year I'm going to have a Christmas tree right here!"

We hadn't gotten around to putting a tree there that first Christmas back in the Ruff House; we were still too a-whirl, I think, with moving back into our home and finding our rhythms again. So it was that, one year later, I opened the box of ornaments and decorations I had made and collected for Camp Marah, and was caught short by a surge of memory. There were vintage baubles and glittered pinecones, a pair of blown-glass nutcrackers, a small host of dubious-looking hedgehogs fashioned from chestnut burrs and bits of felt with red ribbon hangers and beady glass eyes. I fingered a paper chain in muted stripes and florals, a scarlet cardinal, a kitschy little wooden camper. Two years ago, I had packed a very hard Christmas away in that box, and it wasn't until this moment that I had stopped long enough to give it a good, clear-eyed backward glance.

I remembered the Narnian magic of a rare December snowfall that blanketed all the construction debris with an illusion of calm and swirled in showers of diamonds among the pines the next morning. I remembered the neighbors inviting us to trudge over for dinner and a firelit glass of wine, afterward sending us home to Camp Marah in their own coats and gloves, as all of ours were in storage. I remembered coming back to a collapsed awning—a tangle of canvas and metal, bistro lights and mosquito netting—which we had to clamber over for days until the snow melted.

I remembered the wild relief of a New Year, ushered in with the ringing of the old school bell off the back porch, only to step inside the camper and find that all the pipes had frozen while we were making merry outside by the campfire.

"I think the New Year is laughing at us," I had told Philip dismally.

Most poignantly of all, I remembered crying my eyes out, parked in the empty lot of a Jiffy Lube one Sunday afternoon in mid-December, because I simply could not bear the sadness of my home so empty and desolate at Christmas. I had not allowed myself such a torrent of mourning since the early days after the fire—for one, we were living in the midst of a genuine miracle of restoration, and neither Philip nor I could believe how swiftly and skillfully our contractor was repairing the ravages of the fire. It felt indulgent to lament a lost Christmas when every day brought us closer to our hearts' desire. But we still had such a way to go, and we were tired, and it was December, all of which accumulated into an icy burden of longing and homesickness in my heart.

In that parking lot, however, the dam had burst, and the roiling flood threatened to drown me. I wept, not only for our present circumstances, but for all the grief of the past several years piled up together. I wept for my Daddy, dead these eighteen months.

I cried for dreams unrealized, and children unborn, and for the awful isolation of grief itself. And I whimpered, crumpled and exhausted in my driver's side seat, under the steely silence of God. If he would just pierce this leaden sky with some acknowledgement of his notice I felt I could go on.

As it was, I felt like a hollowed-out shell of Lanier, dark and cheerless as my house itself. Some emotions, and the seasons of life they're associated with, are so overwhelming they seem permanent. Grief had taken up residence in my soul, to the point that both the memory and the hope of a merry Christmas felt like a mockery. I was clinging for life to the flotsam of a wrecked ship; everything safe and familiar had been swept away.

"Lord, save me!" I silently cried, in echo of Peter's desperation upon the Sea of Galilee. "I perish!"

The Camp Marah Christmas was spartan, which was entirely appropriate, and I was too weary to wish it otherwise. But of all the trappings and traditions I was used to, it was my crimson roses I missed the most, that symbol and statement of faith that God is always working to transform the wilderness with beauty and redemption—and never in the way we expect. For even as I was seeing the bones of physical beauty emerge from the ashes of my house this transformational image was hard for me to hold onto. In all honesty, I was muddling through, flinching away from anything that might sharpen the contrast between what was and what had once been, for grief had stripped my landscape so bare I hardly recognized it anymore. Early in the season I'd hung a brave, beribboned wreath on the front door of the Ruff House, only to find it tossed on a pile of debris in the dining room the next day. This, it seemed, wasn't a year for roses.

One afternoon, very close to Christmas, I came home to a quiet construction zone. The contractors had cleared out and Philip was away at work, so I unloaded the groceries, fed the animals, and did the barn chores before going up to the house to see what progress had been made in my absence. It had been a hard and exhausting day, in a hard and exhausting week, and as I wandered through the dark, empty rooms, my dog Bonnie at my heels, the whole place felt haunted with the memory of happier times.

I saw it as soon as I stepped into the front hall: a long box perched on a stack of lumber. And with sudden instinct, I knew what it was, and I knew who it was from. Hastening back to the camper with Bonnie, I tore open the box, and then I sat on the floor, weeping over an armful of long-stemmed crimson roses. I wept for the glorious impracticality of it; the deathless, blood-red symbolism.

April's note said that she'd been praying for weeks about what to send me for Christmas, and that there were so many references to roses in their Advent Lessons and Carols service the weekend before that the Lord had just dropped the idea into her head.

I called her, still crying, and said—without the least exaggeration— that it was one of the most beautiful things that anyone had ever done for me. Her sensitivity to God's prompting made me feel seen, infusing hope and courage into my exhausted heart. But also, in a way my heart understood, Jesus himself had sent me those roses, flinging them out to my flailing hands, and I caught onto their loveliness like a lifeline.

Here, too, they proclaimed, defiant against all appearances and losses and seemings, *here, too, is beauty, and grace, and redemption, and unfailing love.*

Here, in this shell of a house; in this shell of a heart. In this cramped little camper with its leaky roof and miniscule hot water heater—*right here* was where the light invaded my darkness and I glimpsed, through a glass darkly, my great at-homeness in the goodness of God.

Sitting in the tree-lit warmth of my Common Room two years later, I looked back at that memory of myself, crying on the floor of a camper over a box of roses. The distance seemed to expand and then contract sharply as these tangible tissue-wrapped witnesses linked that time to this, and I realized, more lucidly than ever before, that the gloom-cloaked gift of the Camp Marah Christmas was the resounding assurance of how desperately I needed a Savior. For the supposed "wreckage" toward which I'd reached with blind anguish that day in the Jiffy Lube parking lot was not some vague sense of security in a troubled world, or even the physical spaces that meant "home" to me. It was none other than Christ himself. I had been forced to release everything else I was clinging to in order to grasp that lifeline–and it was enough. He had not let me go.

I lifted a glittered pine cone and hooked it onto a sturdy bough, beneath which a clumsily wrought hedgehog twirled dazedly on a branch of its own. I looped tinsel and hung colored glass balls—that tatty little box we'd found in a junk shop—and smiled over gift tags-turned orna-ments. Near the top I clipped the beautiful sequined and befeathered peacock that Lori had given me, always a symbol of renewal, and at the very tip I wired a gold tinsel star. Then I stepped back. The tree filled its little alcove with a gentle luminosity, warm against the darkening of the day outside, and the glitter and tinsel twinkled like fireflies in a dusky wood, or the lights of home on a lonely sea.

Festive Libations

There is an interesting directive tucked in among the Old Testament regulations of Deuteronomy 14. Following a detailed survey of clean and unclean meats, and embedded within the instructions on tithing, God's people are told to present their annual offerings of grain, wine, oil, and the firstborn of their flocks and herds at the sanctuary city and to eat it there together. This feast would comprise basically a tenth of their tenth, the rest being given to the Levites, who, in turn, would distribute an allotment every third year to "the aliens, the fatherless, and the widows." It was a generous system, benefitting both the priests and the less fortunate, not to mention the givers themselves. But with the tender specificity one often encounters in the Pentateuch, a provision is made for the happy circumstance in which a person has been so blessed they are not physically able to carry their tithe. In this case, they are to sell it, take the money to the city, and use it to buy whatever they like—"cattle, sheep, wine or other fermented drink, or anything you wish."

"Then you and your household shall eat there," the text continues, "in the presence of the Lord your God and rejoice" (Deuteronomy 14:24-26).

The implication here is not only that of a holy God who deserves our time and treasure, but of a God who simply wants to be with us, celebrating his outrageous goodness in our lives. Far from a stodgy list of meaningless requirements, the Old Testament feasts are an invitation to intimacy and a hallowing of the ordinary elements of life, prefiguring the great Feast which is central to our faith. From Genesis to Revelation, we can trace the history of our redemption through feasting; the whole of Jesus' earthly ministry, in fact, comprises a call to repentance and an invitation to a feast.[1]

A feast isn't complete without a bit of healthy imbibing, of the alcoholic variety or otherwise. Whatever our preference or persuasion, however, it is imperative that we eat and drink from a place of satisfaction in God himself, the only true source of enjoyment and pleasure, otherwise good food can become an idol and wine an entitlement, rather than a gift. But under his mercy we may eat with gladness and drink with a joyful heart. And since the feast of Christmastide is the time for a touch of innocent indulgence, I find this nowhere easier to manage than in the beverage department.

A pot of aromatic cider or mulled wine, imbued with citrus and spice, will crook a sensory finger of welcome to anyone who passes through the front door, while a nip of cream sherry elevates an ordinary teatime to a bit of an event. When planning my menus for the holidays, I like to give some thought to special drinks and concoctions, hot or cold, that will lend an extra layer of conviviality to the proceedings, be it a decadent dark-chocolate cocoa paired with whipped cream or a frosty bottle of Cava served with fruity kalamata olives. And it's fun to take my anticipated guests' preferences into account: my sister will prize a sophisticated cranberry-infused bourbon shrub, while the young adults in our midst will likely gravitate toward a fruit-forward pomegranate Cosmopolitan.

For myself, no seasonal treat is so potent with Christmas cheer as a small, straight-up martini made with St. George "Terroir" gin. Distilled with Douglas fir, this drink needs no adornment other than the pretty crystal coupe glass in which it is served, and it tastes just like a Christmas tree smells. Which, as far as I am concerned, is delightful.

CHRISTMASTIDE

[1] I am indebted to my priest, Fr. Collin Setterberg, for an enlightening sermon on this passage which solidified many of these ideas for me.

POMEGRANATE COSMOPOLITAN
MAKES 1 DRINK

Serve this drink in a large martini glass as the fruit juices add a lot of volume.

3 ounces vodka

2 ounces unsweetened pomegranate juice

1 ounce freshly squeezed lime juice

1 ounce orange-flavored liqueur, such as Cointreau or Triple sec

Lime slice, for garnish

Fill a cocktail shaker with ice. Add the vodka, pomegranate juice, lime juice, and orange liqueur. Shake until well-chilled, about 30 seconds, and strain into a chilled martini glass. Cut halfway through the lime slice and use it to garnish the edge of the glass.

BOURBON WITH CRANBERRY-GINGER SHRUB
MAKES 1 DRINK

A shrub is a vinegar-based syrup infused with fruit and aromatics that lends a pleasantly intriguing flavor to mixed drinks. For a non-alcoholic version of this cocktail you can substitute an additional 2 ounces ginger beer for the bourbon.

2 ounces bourbon

1 ounce shrub (see recipe below)

1 ounce ginger beer or tonic water

Halved whole cranberries for garnish

Fill a cocktail shaker with ice. Add bourbon and shrub and swirl until combined and condensation begins to form on the outside of the shaker, about 10–12 times. Strain into a rocks glass filled with ice and top with ginger beer or tonic water. Spear the halved cranberries with a cocktail pick and balance on the rim of the glass for garnish.

CRANBERRY-GINGER SHRUB

MAKES 2 CUPS

1½ cups fresh cranberries

2-inch piece fresh ginger, peeled and chopped into 3 or 4 pieces

1 cup sugar

1 cup apple cider vinegar

In a medium saucepan combine the cranberries, ginger, sugar, and vinegar. Bring to a boil, then reduce to low and simmer for 20 minutes, stirring occasionally to dissolve the sugar. Remove from heat and cool completely. Strain into a sterile, quart-sized jar with a tight-fitting lid and allow to sit at room temperature overnight and up to 2 days. Strain out the solids and refrigerate for up to 3 weeks.

DADDY'S DADDY'S SOUTHERN EGGNOG
SERVES 10–12

I never met my father's father, as he died before I was born. But Daddy kept him alive for me in his stories and reminiscences, and I know and love him as a man of warmth, humor, firmness, faith, kindness, and conviction. Grandaddy Adams never went a penny into debt, he talked a would-be robber out of his gun at point-blank range, and he raised two families, marrying my grandmother after being widowed in his late-fifties. He also never missed his Christmas eggnog. An otherwise teetotaler, the story goes that the leftover whiskey from his 'nog one year saved his life when he was having an asthma attack later that spring.

> 6 eggs, room temperature
> 2 egg yolks
> ½ cup plus 2 tablespoons sugar
> ¼ teaspoon salt
> 4 cups whole milk
> 1 tablespoon Madagascar bourbon vanilla extract
> ½ teaspoon freshly grated nutmeg
> 1 cup whiskey or bourbon
> ¾ cup heavy cream

Whisk the eggs, egg yolks, sugar, and salt in a stockpot until well-combined, then whisk in the milk, one cup at a time. Set the pot over low heat and whisk continually for 25–30 minutes, until the mixture reaches 160 degrees and coats the underside of a spoon. (Lots of whisking but keep at it—call in relief pitchers as needed.)

Remove from the heat and strain through a fine sieve into a large bowl. Add the vanilla, nutmeg, and whiskey or bourbon, and whisk to combine. Cover and refrigerate for at least 4 hours until the 'nog is thoroughly chilled.

At serving time, whip the heavy cream and fold into the chilled mixture. Top with more freshly grated nutmeg (this is no time for the tinned stuff), and serve fireside in your most festive lowball glasses, with a stack of nostalgic Christmas records on the turntable.

SPICED CIDER
SERVES 16

Great for a crowd. Mama always served her cider in a 30-cup coffee pot dedicated to that purpose, seeing as the spices will flavor the urn.

1 64-ounce bottle apple cider
1 64-ounce cranberry juice cocktail
2 cinnamon sticks
2 oranges, sliced into wedges
20 whole cloves

Combine apple cider, cranberry juice, and cinnamon sticks in a stockpot. Insert cloves into the wedges of the sliced oranges and carefully add to the pot, clove-side up. Bring to a boil, then reduce heat to low and simmer, covered, for 30 minutes. Remove cinnamon sticks and serve warm in mugs or heat-proof punch cups.

GOOD MEDICINE

MAKES 1 DRINK

This gin cocktail looks absolutely lovely in the glass. The Shrubb in this case (not to be confused with a vinegar-based shrub) is an orange liqueur made of white and aged rhum, sun-dried orange peel, and Créole spices. Blended with the bitter complexity of the Campari it makes for an enlivening drink that tastes like it ought to be good for you.

2 ounces London dry gin

1 ounce Campari

½ ounce Clément Créole Shrubb

Orange peel, for garnish

Combine gin, Campari and Clément in a cocktail shaker filled with ice. Swirl until the outside of the shaker is frosted with condensation (10–12 times) then strain into a coupe glass. Remove a thin strip of orange peel with a vegetable peeler and garnish.

MULLED WINE

Serves 8

*Perfect for an open house or a laid-back evening by the fire.
It can be made ahead, but the flavors will concentrate
over time, so consume within 24 hours. Be sure to
keep it at a simmer after the initial boil or you will
cook all of the alcohol out of it.*

4 cups apple cider

1 (750 ml) bottle red wine (Merlot,
Cabernet Sauvignon, or Malbec)

¼ cup honey

2 cinnamon sticks

1 orange, zested and juiced

4 whole cloves

3 star anise

2 oranges, sliced

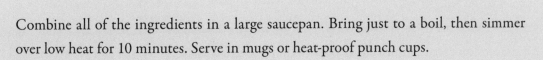

Combine all of the ingredients in a large saucepan. Bring just to a boil, then simmer
over low heat for 10 minutes. Serve in mugs or heat-proof punch cups.

The World at Night

We usually spend New Year's Eve with Luke and Laura, gathered around their fireside for an evening of conviviality and delectable food. But that year I was too sick to go out—the kind of sick that called for soda crackers and painkillers. Philip picked up takeout that I couldn't eat and a bottle of champagne at the grocery store, just in case. We played backgammon by the fire and listened to a stack of Christmas records and reminisced over the highlights of the past twelve months. I kept threatening to go to bed and Philip kept nudging me to stick it out. Nearing midnight he disappeared into the kitchen and came back with toasting glasses: Coke for him and ginger ale for me. The perfect accompaniment to my saltines.

In many ways, such a quiet, reflective evening seemed an appropriate way for this year to go out. It was a wonderful year, rich and heavy with blessings, and we had many treasures to turn over in our talk by the fire that night. But it had also seen the continued deferment of that particular hope long-cherished, the one the very marrow of my soul was worn out with waiting for. January after January I have seen the new year as a fresh chance, a clean slate upon which the Lord just *might* create the desire of our hearts—a miracle, no less, but one which his lovely character has given me courage to keep looking for. But this New Year's I just couldn't seem to find my hope. It was exhausted: buried away like a tired bird in its hidden nest, head tucked under its wing and a thicket of impossibility screening it from view.

I had asked the Lord all that afternoon to show me what faith looked like in this place, what shape hope might take as a symbol for her beleaguered campaign. I wanted to end the year on a positive note, to *know* the radiance and splendor in the darkness, even if I couldn't see it. I didn't want this Christmas season to go out—and thereby be defined—by sadness and disappointment, but by joy, and by a confident expectation in his ultimate goodness. I wanted the statement of faith I had endeavored to make with this holiday, the deep confession it had been of his perfect love and faithfulness, to shine out strong, not in spite of disappointment and deferred hopes, but in the face of them.

But I was so tired.

"If I can't run to you," I told the Lord, "then at least I can lift my head and hold out my arms."

So midnight came, and not a moment too soon for my taste. We listened to the clock in the hall roll out the long chimes and we clinked our soft drinks and laughed about how tame it all was. And then I said I was going to bed in earnest. I hoisted myself up and took a last glance at the Christmas tree, all stars and magic in the gloom.

And then the fireworks began.

It was so long since we'd been home on New Year's, we had no idea what a spectacle our neighbors had cooked up in the interim. I dropped back down beside Philip on the sofa and we sat listening for a while, expecting it to end any moment. But the bangs and reverberations only escalated.

Philip suddenly sat up.

"Those are *big*—I'll bet we could see them!"

So we jumped up and hastened outside into the cold, and there, across the road and all along the winking line of neighboring house lights, we saw blooming explosions of

CHRISTMASTIDE

color and light flaming out above the trees. Red and green, blue and gold: all profusions of falling stars with joyous booms to accompany them. It was glorious, and completely unexpected: fireworks that had undoubtedly crossed the state line from vacations and holidays, flung recklessly out into the night for weary, unknown souls to feast upon. Joy blazed up in both of us—it was as if we had never been tired, as if I had never been sick or sad. Philip ran to gather all the fireworks we had and I ran in the house and came back out on the front porch (in my coat this time) with the bottle of champagne and two glasses.

"I don't care if this makes me sick!" I said, and I laughed as Philip poured and the bubbles foamed up and ran down over the sides of the flute.

It didn't. I sat and watched the show over the trees and the beautiful spectacle my husband was staging for me there on our own front walk, sipping my champagne and looking up at the real stars overhead in the clear, cold sky. Our fireworks were not as impressive as our neighbors', but they were exquisite to me. They were radiance in the darkness and a splendor in my heart, glory flaring out with sudden beauty. They made us laugh, and they also made me want to cry a little bit.

A bird woke in our holly hedge and protested all the noise. I shushed her back to sleep with a smile.

Joy and sorrow—twin eggs of the same nest. They make their home together. Sorrow will wound and ply her merciful steel upon the human heart. But it's joy that breaks it.

It wasn't the New Year's we had planned or expected—even a few moments before. But there we were, sitting out in the cold on our own front steps in coats and pajamas, drinking cheap champagne and watching a New Year bloom in a sudden exultation of falling stars and rising hopes. And although this January was scarcely half an hour old, my mind was filled with the words of The Innocence Mission's song "July":

> *the man I love and I will lift our heads together . . .*
> *the world at night has seen the greatest light: too much light to deny*

New Year's Day

You won't catch a Southerner skipping their collard greens and black-eyed peas on New Year's Day. "Money and luck," Mama used to say, playfully referring to our regional conviction that you'll be wanting for both in the coming year if you neglect so simple (and toothsome) a safeguard. But I have to wonder after all these years if Mama's little joke didn't have a kernel of truth at its core. It was, after all, the only day in the year I can ever remember her cooking collard greens. But she did so, every year without fail, and Daddy relished them so much he would drink the pot liquor right out of the serving bowl when we were done. I didn't much care for the greens when I was a girl, although I always took care to consume a few conscientious mouthfuls—one couldn't take chances with Southern superstition. But I loved the savory black-eyed peas, the hot, buttery cornbread, and the gooey mac and cheese she always served alongside them. It all tasted so wholesome upon the heels of Christmas week with its seemingly endless parade of cookies and sweets. And, like other traditional meals throughout the year, it connected me to this time, this place, these people, with an invisible line that holds to this day.

I have since come to prize the collards as the *pièce de resistance*, going so far as to grow a big bed of them in the garden each winter so that we can enjoy their salubriousness well into early spring. And when it comes to their preparation I don't play around; like my grandmother before me, I braise them with pork, but where she relied upon fatback and Wesson oil, I lean toward butter and thick-sliced bacon. A sweet Vidalia onion cuts the potential bitterness of the greens, as does a splash of Trappey's hot pepper vinegar at serving time. I can promise you that greens prepared in this fashion will, as my Daddy would say, "do you good and help you, too."

A lot of Southerners cook their black-eyed peas with bacon or ham hock, but since I've already given pork pride of place in the greens, I like to simmer mine in chicken broth, with a mixture of butter and herbs stirred in midway through the cooking time. The only requirement here is that peas *must* be served with chowchow relish—atop, alongside, or just swirled with reckless abandon among all the items on your plate. I'm sorry, but it's the law.

It is to this humble king and queen of the New Year's feast that cornbread and mac and cheese pay delectable court, the former making an agreeable sponge for the pot liquor that accrues on the dinner plate and the latter supporting all of the other tastes and aromas with a homely flavor that complements without competing. I like a little tooth to my mac and cheese, which is why I make it with brown rice noodles and a sauce fortified by sour cream and eggs. However you prefer it—chewy or creamy—you can't go wrong with a goodly dollop of gold on your plate. Who knows? It might just lead to the real thing in the year to come.

a MENU for NEW YEAR'S DAY

BACON-BRAISED COLLARD GREENS
BEST-EVER BLACK-EYED PEAS
SOUTHERN MAC AND CHEESE
CORNBREAD

PEPPERMINT HOT FUDGE SUNDAES

ICED TEA
COFFEE

BACON-BRAISED COLLARD GREENS
SERVES 6–8

While not strictly requisite I can't imagine serving greens without a tangy splash of hot pepper vinegar. A bottle of Trappey's, in fact, was one of the only prepared condiments I can remember my mother allowing to appear on her dinner table. When the liquid runs low in the bottle most Southerners top it off with fresh white vinegar, re-using the same peppers two or three times.

2 pounds fresh collard greens

8 ounces thick-sliced bacon, chopped on a ½-inch dice

6 tablespoons unsalted butter

1 medium yellow onion, thinly sliced

2 garlic cloves, minced

2 cups low-sodium chicken broth

Kosher salt and freshly-ground black pepper

Pinch of sugar

Hot pepper vinegar, such as Trappey's brand, for serving

Wash the collard greens thoroughly. Lay each leaf flat on a cutting board and slice along the sides of the stem with a sharp knife to remove the main rib. Tear or roughly chop the leaves into 2-inch pieces and set aside.

In a large saucepan, fry the chopped bacon until crisp, about 5 minutes. Melt the butter in the pan with the bacon and add the onion. Cook over medium heat until onion is soft and slightly translucent, about 5 minutes. Add the minced garlic and toss with a wooden spoon 30 seconds more.

Add the chicken broth and bring to a boil. Reduce to low and simmer, covered, for 15–20 minutes until the onion is thoroughly soft. Add the collard greens one large handful at a time, stirring down to wilt a bit, and cook, uncovered, for 20–30 minutes, until greens are very tender. Season to taste with kosher salt, black pepper, and a pinch of sugar.

Serve hot with pepper vinegar on the side to season as desired.

BEST-EVER BLACK-EYED PEAS
SERVES 6–8

Chowchow is a piquant pickled relish that traditionally made use of the last scraps of the growing season: tomatoes, bell peppers, onions, and cabbage. Recommendations for vinegar, sugar, seasonings, and salt are as varied as the families from which the recipes have sprung, but if you don't have a jar of your grandmother's chowchow on the pantry shelf, a quality store-bought version will do, like Mrs. Campbell's or Braswell's.

1 pound dried black-eyed peas

6–8 cups low-sodium chicken broth (or water)

2 tablespoons unsalted butter

1 large onion, chopped

2 garlic cloves, minced

2 teaspoons fresh thyme leaves (or ½ teaspoon dried)

½ teaspoon chopped fresh sage (or 1 pinch dried)

Kosher salt and freshly ground black pepper

Chowchow relish for serving

CHRISTMASTIDE

Sort peas in a large colander to remove any stones or foreign material, then rinse well with cold water.

In a large saucepan with a lid combine peas and 6 cups chicken broth. Bring to a boil, then reduce to low and simmer, covered, for 1 hour, checking often to make sure the liquid has not boiled down and adding more chicken broth as necessary.

Meanwhile, melt the butter in a skillet and add the onion. Sauté 5–10 minutes until soft and translucent. Add garlic and toss 30 seconds more. Stir in the thyme and sage and turn off the heat. Set aside.

When peas have simmered for 1 hour add the butter and onion mixture and stir to combine. Add 1 teaspoon kosher salt and ½ teaspoon black pepper, and continue to simmer, covered, for 30 minutes more until peas are tender. Taste for seasonings and add more salt and pepper as desired.

Serve with a pretty cut-glass bowl of chowchow relish on the side.

SOUTHERN MAC AND CHEESE

SERVES 6–8

This recipe may be made with regular durum wheat macaroni, if preferred.

- 2 cups (8 ounces) brown rice elbow macaroni
- 4 tablespoons butter, cut into ½-inch pieces
- 2 cups shredded sharp cheddar cheese
- 3 egg yolks
- 1 cup heavy cream
- ½ cup sour cream
- ½ teaspoon kosher salt
- ½ teaspoon dry mustard
- ½ cup shredded Parmesan cheese

Preheat the oven to 350 degrees. Grease a 9 x 13-inch baking dish with butter or cooking spray and set aside.

Bring a large pot of salted water to the boil and cook macaroni according to the package directions. Drain and transfer to a large bowl. Add the butter, tossing until butter is melted and macaroni is thoroughly coated.

In a separate bowl, combine the cheddar cheese, egg yolks, heavy cream, sour cream, salt, and dry mustard and whisk well to combine. Add to the macaroni and stir to thoroughly coat. Pour into the prepared dish and bake for 40 minutes until golden brown on top. Remove from the oven, sprinkle with the Parmesan cheese, and bake 5 minutes more, until the cheese is melted and beginning to brown.

CHRISTMASTIDE

PEPPERMINT HOT FUDGE SUNDAES
SERVES 6–8

A refreshing note of sweetness at the end of the meal—if anyone has room for it!

 1 cup heavy cream
 ⅓ cup light corn syrup
 1 12-ounce bag good quality semi-sweet chocolate chips
 1 teaspoon pure peppermint extract
 Soft peppermint sticks
 ½ gallon vanilla ice cream

Combine heavy cream and corn syrup in a small, heavy bottomed saucepan. Bring to a boil, stirring constantly over medium-high heat.

Remove from the heat and stir in the chocolate chips and the peppermint extract. Whisk until the chocolate is thoroughly melted.

Serve warm over vanilla ice cream, garnished with crushed or whole soft peppermint sticks.

Note: Leftover fudge may be stored in the refrigerator for up to 3 days, but you may need to add a little more corn syrup to adjust the consistency when rewarming.

Twelfth Night

The twelve days of Christmas date back to the sixth century Council of Tours, which decreed, among other things, that the entire interval between Christmas and Epiphany should be observed as the feast of Christmastide. Not only did this fully establish Advent as a season of preparation and penitence, it settled a dispute: the Western Church considered Christmas itself the high, holy day, while its Eastern counterpart gave that honor to Epiphany on January 6th. Under this arrangement, everyone could be right, and liturgical calendars could be reconciled at last. Over time, the Church further dignified these twelve holy days with a succession of saints' days—St. Stephen the Martyr on the 26th, St. John the Beloved on the 27th, Holy Innocents on the 28th, The Holy Family on the 31st—confirming "the holidays" as a time of remembrance as well as celebration. And while Twelfth Night became more of a Christmas Eve to the Eastern Church, the Western regarded it as the official end of the Christmas season, a date that came to be characterized by feasting and frivolity. It was also considered unlucky to leave Christmas greenery up past Epiphany, hence the custom of Twelfth Night bonfires which have arisen in many traditions during which greens are burned with much ceremony.

In the Ruff House tradition, I never take my decorations down before January 6th.

(Once it snowed on the 7th, a holiday in itself for those of us in Georgia, and I left them up until it melted on the 9th!) And, while there will always be some observance of Twelfth Night in our household, I usually wait until somewhere around the Sixth Day of Christmas to determine what it will be, as this midway checkpoint is a reliable indicator of my physical and emotional reserves. Am I up for a big fête, or is this a year for a small clutch of friends? Our Twelfth Night festivities have varied over the years from come-one-come-all bonfires to intimate dinners for two by the fire, complete with a brandy-soaked pudding set ablaze in a witchery of blue flame. More than once, we've had a couple of families for dinner. The Camp Marah Christmas was a cup of tea and a solitary sunset-watching for me while Philip consulted with contractors.

Most years, however, I emerge from this brief barometer-reading with a smile over what I already know: it is time for a Twelfth Night revel! I send out a flurry of emails, bidding old friends and new to an evening of merriment and innocent mischief, doling out food assignments with each RSVP: soup, salad, bread, dessert. One friend promises to bring her divine yeast rolls; another, who owns a Mexican restaurant, pledges a ten-gallon bag of tortilla chips and an assortment of his famous salsas and cheese dip. There will be gluten-free cornbread and spicy cornbread, huge bowls of green salad, and enough hearty stews to feed an army. And army it will be, for it is customary for guests of this party to bring guests of their own. There are dozens of cookies in the freezer earmarked for Twelfth Night, and I will bring out the last of the caramels and peanut butter candies and peppermint sticks. But the real treat will be the Twelfth Night cake, made for us each year by Rachel's daughter Margaret, a delectable brown-butter confection laced with dried fruits and piquant spices. True to tradition, Margaret will hide a bean, a pea, and a clove in the fragrant batter before baking; whoever finds them in their slice of cake will be crowned for the night as our king, queen, and knave, respectively.

Sometimes we set the refreshment tables under the trees in the backyard, festooning the branches above with Japanese lanterns that bloom out like fairy lamps against the winter night; often, however, a dubious forecast urges caution and I stage the party in the house where the tables are ranged along the back porch and Philip runs an intricate network of drop cords over the railing to various plugs in the basement for the forthcoming crock pots. Besides, I genuinely love to dress the Ruff House for Christmas one more time. The holly and roses of Christmas Eve have long gone their way by now, and the ivy is beginning to look a little stiff. But the magnolia in the front hall is salvageable, I decree, even as I pull wisps of cedar from behind the oval picture of Mary, and in the low light of a party no one will notice that the boxwood wreaths in the kitchen are quite dry. This Twelfth Night greening is a more muted affair after the bowery exuberance earlier in the season, but still I repair to the hollies and cedars around the house, snipping odd bits to freshen and adorn. White pine is particularly suited to Twelfth Night, I think, with its long, jade-colored needles and smooth, silvery bark. The goats, however, who think it particularly suited to snacking year-round, have cleared it head-high along the western fence, so I am obliged to jump up and grasp the branches in order to pull down and clip what I need. But it's well worth the effort, as, mounded on the refreshment tables and interspersed with tapers in tall, glass hurricanes, the effect will be positively sylvan.

Though Philip and I look forward to an evening in company with our friends, there is one thing we make quite clear with each invitation: this is a party for the children. There will be wine in sufficience for the adults and plenty of space throughout the house for quiet fireside conversation. But these are only the backdrop of the real attraction. For this night, every child who enters our house is royalty, a small sovereign in party dress, at whose feet are laid our best efforts to enchant, amuse, and otherwise delight in one last display of Christmas magic.

To this end, we have scoured old books for traditional Twelfth Night games that will transform even the shyest of children into a little lord or lady of misrule. The front hall is the setting for "Christmas Candle," in which one child is provided with a fat, lighted pillar, while another is blindfolded, spun about by his peers until adequately disoriented, and instructed to blow out the candle in the direction they think they last saw it. The result is an uproarious spectacle of absurdity as our "it" huffs and puffs into space with a quixotic resolve while the other sprites dance around him shouting, "Over here! Over here!" from the four corners of the room. It may be difficult for the seasoned grown-up, ennuied by the ceaseless onslaught of entertainments with which our society is sated, to see the charms of so simple a game. But to the children it is an endless source of evergreen fun as siblings and friends take turns making themselves ludicrous and the momentary embarrassment of their own misguided efforts gives way to the hilarity of others' attempts.

For the older youths in our midst, most of whom, alas, are no longer children, there is the time-honored game of Snapdragon, in which raisins are plucked from a bowl of burning brandy. Whoever gets the most raisins, of course, wins the game, but while such prizes were traditionally consumed by their possessors, ours are always returned to the bowl for second, third, fourth rounds and beyond. Margaret is our reigning champion—it's a hardy soul that can stand up to her lightning reflexes and unflinching focus—but Eli runs a close second, and Walker is a force to be reckoned with. And always there are those who hold back in the shadows around the dancing blue flames, shooting forth a hesitant hand, only to withdraw it to a safe proximity once more.

"It's just the fumes burning," I used to assure them. "It's not that hot."

I have since learned better, having been challenged by the children themselves to take a round. Rachel and I looked at one another somewhat sheepishly afterward.

"It's hot," she said.

Indeed. But not dangerously so—just risky enough to grant an innocent thrill of excitement, which I can't help but think a good thing in this era of overly cosseted children and undervalued childhood. And so, the game of Snapdragon stands, with all its shaking of hands and blowing at fingers, and as I watch those eager faces clustered around my kitchen table, illumined with ghostly light in the darkened room, I bless the bright alchemy of spirits and fire and youth.

Sometimes there are sparklers on the porch or backyard games of "Kitty Wants a Corner" that deteriorate into shrieking games of tag in the dark. And always, before the littlest ones begin to flag and must needs be carried or ushered off home, there is the Twelfth Night cake. The pedestal table, which has been shoved against the wall for Christmas Candle, is returned to its place in the center of the hall, and a ring of little heads forms a breathless circle in the candlelight. I try to be judicious with my servings, but every time my knife meets a soft obstruction I pass that plate to a child, and the astonishment with which Margaret's prizes are discovered, and the triumph with which they are extracted, is enough to touch the heart of the most hardened cynic. But there are no cynics here; we are all children for this night, under the spell of Christmas itself where even the smallest of things work wonders and an ordinary lima bean confers kingship. We crown our royals with the glittered crowns Rachel made long ago (and which live all the rest of the year under the eaves in my attic) and the sight of those lopsided coronets above their earnest little wearers seems like a vignette of innocence itself.

After every crumb of cake has been consumed and sleeping children have been bundled off into the night to dream, perchance, of sugarplums, those who remain will gather in the parlor. I station myself at the piano, and Joel hands around the old Methodist hymnals from the bottom shelf of the bookcase, and everyone begins to flip through in search of their favorites. For as long as they want to sing, I will play, as one last time we chant out together the old and loved hymns of Christmas: "In the Bleak Midwinter" and "All My Heart This Night Rejoices," "The First Noel," and "Away in a Manger." And when every verse of "We Three Kings" has been done justice to, and hymnals begin to close gently around the room, Rachel and Cathryne and Katie and I will close out the evening, as we have done these twenty years and more, with a rendition of the traditional English carol "The King." Our voices lapse easily into the familiar harmonies as Rachel's birdlike descant soars above the melody and Katie's ripe, mellow alto broadens beneath it. We smile at one another as we sing, for this song feels like friendship itself, holding the memory of kinship and long affection in every verse and chord:

Old Christmas is past, twelve-tide is the last!
And we bid you adieu, great joy to the new!

It's not really "adieu," at least to this cheerful company, for lingerers will remain far into the night, and Monica will not rest until she has helped me wash up. But it is such a fitting farewell to this Christmas, a laying away, as it were, among the treasures of Christmases past and a lilting turn toward the year yet to be.

RECIPE: Melody's White Christmas Chili

We had a tradition in my family that any time we picked someone up from the airport we would stop at the OK Cafe, an Atlanta institution. One of my favorite things on the menu was their white bean chili, slathered in sour cream and grated cheese, paired with a mug of strong black coffee. My mother's friend Melody is an excellent cook, and she developed this recipe that's every bit as good as the original.

8 boneless, skinless chicken breast halves
1 Tbsp. vegetable oil
4 cups chicken broth
1 tsp. kosher salt
1 tsp. ground cumin
3/4 tsp. dried oregano
4 15-oz. cans Great Northern beans, rinsed and drained
1 15-oz. can Great Northern beans, rinsed, drained, and mashed
2 4.5-oz. cans chopped green chilies
Sour cream, shredded Monterey jack cheese, and chopped
    fresh cilantro, for topping

2 medium onions, chopped
2 cloves garlic, minced
1/2 tsp. chili powder
1/2 tsp. black pepper
1/8 tsp. ground cloves
1/8 tsp. red pepper flakes

Cut the chicken into bite-sized pieces. In a large stockpot sauté chicken, onion, and garlic in the oil over medium-high heat for 10 minutes until onion begins to soften and become translucent. Stir in the chicken broth, beans, chilies, salt, and spices and bring to a boil. Reduce heat to low and simmer 30 minutes, stirring occasionally. Serve with sour cream, shredded cheese, and cilantro.

SERVES 6-8

RECIPE: Margaret's Twelfth Night Cake

Be sure and mince the ginger finely so that it doesn't get confused with the bean, pea, and clove. And remember to have a trio of paper crowns on hand with which to invest your king, queen, and knave, respectively.

3 cups all-purpose flour
1 tsp. baking powder
1/2 tsp. salt
2 tsp. cinnamon
1/2 tsp. nutmeg
1/2 tsp. ground cloves
16 Tbsp. (2 sticks) unsalted
    butter, softened
1/2 cup butter-flavored
    shortening
3 cups sugar

5 eggs, room temperature
2 tsp. Madagascar bourbon vanilla extract
1/4 tsp. rum extract
1 cup buttermilk
2 Tbsp. crystallized ginger, minced
2 lemons, zested
1 large dried bean, kidney or lima
small dried pea, black-eyed or black
1 whole clove
Confectioners' sugar,
    for dusting

Preheat oven to 325°. Grease and flour a Bundt pan. Set aside.

In a large bowl whisk the flour, baking soda, salt, cinnamon, nutmeg, and cloves.

In the bowl of a stand mixer, or in a large bowl with a hand mixer, cream the butter and shortening together on low speed until combined. Alternate adding sugar and eggs, mixing well after each addition, until thoroughly combined and batter is fluffy. Mix in the vanilla and rum extracts.

Alternate adding the dry ingredients and the buttermilk to the butter mixture, mixing well after each addition. Stir in the crystallized ginger and the lemon zest.

Spoon batter into the prepared pan and poke the bean, pea, and clove into the batter at regularly spaced intervals. Holding the pan a couple of inches above the counter, drop the pan a few times to release bubbles and level the surface.

Bake for 1 hour and 15-20 minutes on the middle rack until a toothpick inserted into the cake comes out clean or with a few moist crumbs clinging to it. Cool in the pan for 10 minutes, then invert onto a wire rack and cool completely.

At serving time, dust lightly with confectioners' sugar.

SERVES 10-12

CHRISTMAS HATH MADE AN END,
WELL-A-DAY! WELL-A-DAY!
WHICH WAS MY DEAREST
FRIEND,
More's the pity!
FOR WITH A HEAVY heart
MUST I FROM THEE
DEPART,
TO FOLLOW & PLOW & CART
All the Year after.
TRADITIONAL ENGLISH CAROL

Epiphany

On January 6th—or the day after, if it happens to fall on a Sunday—I move through my house with grim resolve, untying ribbons, gathering up balsam-scented candles and bottlebrush trees, pulling down bits of dried holly. I sweep the unfinished Christmas puzzle into its box. I wash out the cookie tins and swap out the holiday mugs in the cupboard for the everyday mugs. In the kitchen, the dining room, the parlor, I mound piles of spent greenery, remembering the merriment these rooms have known and the joyful anticipation with which I adorned them. In the den, I regard the Christmas tree half-guiltily. Then, with a deep breath of determination, I begin removing tin icicles, one at time, counting them in tens and dropping them into slim little aluminum canisters. It feels like a fell deed, an act of betrayal toward this enchanted, but slightly bedraggled, guest in our home.

I take my tea that afternoon in the kitchen, unwilling to confront the darkness of the den with that shadowy form stripped so mercilessly of its glittering store. (I will refuse to watch, later, as Philip pitches the denuded tree from the big, double-hung window at the back of the house; it is undeniably an expedient measure, but it never-theless pierces my heart.) Looking around now, I wonder that I ever could have thought my rooms cozy or warm; bereft of their late trimmings they seem remote and austere,

CHRISTMASTIDE

echoing with unwonted vacuity. I know that in time the simplicity itself will be beautiful to me once more; that the cool, dark hall with its substantial sentinels of Empire furniture will be more soothing than stark, and that my pale blue kitchen will hail me one morning with the sweet prospect of baked apples, homely oatmeal cookies, a rustic gingercake stiffened with black coffee and dark chocolate. Even the den will kindle once more with firelight and gentle cheer, the velvet curtains drawn against a winter's night and the turntable a conduit for Chopin, Tchaikovsky, or Chet Baker. These quiet rooms, now so seemingly bare, will reveal themselves as more of a clean slate for my new year than an empty canvas. For Epiphany is always the New Year's Day of my soul; howsoever tired my body might be, and howsoever sad my post-holiday musings, something will begin to stir amid my inner landscape. I will lift my face to the clean, cool air of the yet-to-be, not with resolutions and lists for personal improvement, but with curiosity and contemplative questions. I will seek to name this year with the word that keeps bubbling to the top of my consciousness and meeting me at every turn, a word like "fidelity," or "fruitfulness," or "ardor," or "abide." I won't choose this word so much as it will choose me. It is mine only to listen for it, and then commit to watch for the ways, usually surprising, in which it will gleam out amid the shadows of the unwritten year.

But first, I must hold space for this sadness, allowing it to trowel out a concavity where seeds of hope might be planted. I hope to know God better in this coming year, to taste his goodness and to see his hand at work in my life and in the lives of those I love. I long to hear news from his far country, and to feel its sunlight and breezes at play in this one. I want to walk through the world with the holy awareness of things beyond my ken, even if they happen to be beyond my sight.

I want to be the kind of person you can confide your dreams in, I pray now.

Looking up and across the kitchen, I see a patch of late-afternoon sunlight wavering in the hallway on the wall above the stairs. I love the winter light in this house, love the way its southward course along the horizon reverses and begins to climb north again after the solstice, baptizing these rooms with a suffusion of gold that is as astonishing as it is familiar. I even love the way that, cleared so ruthlessly of Christmas, my home seems to revel in this simple gilding, relishing it as a woman would the single, perfect adornment of a costly jewel.

Most of all, I love this particular patch of light, for it brought me word one day of God's particular love, and it has been a friend of my heart ever since. It was another late afternoon, this a September one. Philip and I were clambering through the hollowed-out spaces of our post-fire, post-remediation, post-demolition home, which, up until this point had been so depressing a prospect it had kept me out of the house for weeks. Camp Marah was my refuge in those days from air scrubbers and crowbars, power saws and the awful noises of rending. But now the place was quiet. The generator out front was gone, and the lead and asbestos abatement team had stolen away likewise, taking with them a goodly portion of our sheetrock, a heartrending amount of original plaster, and all of our ceilings.

That morning we had attended a much-anticipated meeting with a respected architectural firm in Atlanta. We had been funneling toward this moment all summer, ever since the night of the fire, or, at least, the earliest days after. Somewhere, we knew, was someone who could lift this burden off of our shoulders, restore the Ruff House to "pre-loss condition" and make all these sad things come untrue. To that end, Philip had been vetting contractors right and left for weeks. But no one, it seemed, was able to catch our vision for the project ("Restoration, not remodeling," we kept having to say) or had the historical experience to undertake it.

Until now, we thought, collectively rejoicing that this leg of the journey was nearly over. We had pinned all our hopes on this "contractor of choice" as his portfolio boasted an array of thoughtfully executed projects in some of the older neighborhoods around town. He had already come out to our house with his high-heeled designer and taken a lot of notes on a clipboard, and today was the big reveal: what they could do and when they could start.

When we sat down to the meeting, the firm's owner handed me a slick folder stuffed with high-end appliance spec sheets and asked me what we planned to do about financing.

"Our insurance company is paying for it," I said timidly. They had already completed the Scope of Work and our adjuster had signed off on the estimate.

The owner sneered slightly.

"Insurance companies never get this right," he said. "What you're looking at on this job is roughly two-to-three times what they're giving you."

A cold anxiety began to steal over me, creeping up from the pit of my stomach and spreading out through every vein in my body. I tried to will it back, to pretend that I could actually breathe under the huge weight that was gathering in my chest. But it was painfully obvious. *We were on the wrong track.*

The budget was astronomical. The lead time was dispiriting, and the proposal was unrecognizable from what we had previously discussed. The Ruff House would be further gutted to streamline the rebuild. And we would be effectively banished until the project was completed—which could take anything from a year to eighteen months. I took a sip of ice-cold water and flipped idly through the contents of the folder, seeing nothing. All I wanted was to get out of that office, out in the sunshine and into our hot car where I could find some relief in tears. This meeting was over for me. I could sense by the stiffening of Philip's form beside me, and the uncharacteristic set of his jaw, that it was over for him, too.

"We're right where we started!" I wailed when we were back at Camp Marah, slapping the laminate surface of the dinette with such force that the tealight candles bounced in their votives.

"Turnkey," Philip muttered. "Everyone just wants to give us a new house in an old shell."

"No one seems to understand that we just want what we had."

"No one cares enough to do it right."

As soon as the words were spoken aloud, they seemed to blow open an unseen window between us, admitting a stiffening breeze. We stared at one another, electrified by a sudden shared conviction: we cared enough.

Somehow, in all the trauma of the fire and the disorienting maze of its aftermath, we had lost our sense of agency. For months, loss industry professionals had been telling us what they were going to do, what was going to happen, what would be required of us and which of the loved spaces of our home would just have to go. We had been carried along in a torrent of paperwork, swept under by the tides of grief and exhaustion and chaos, so that helplessness had begun to feel normal.

But we were not helpless. What's more, we were not alone, which was precisely why we weren't helpless. Already God had come alongside us with material provisions, the company of friends, the kindness of strangers. Now, his energy seemed to fill us like an unseen presence. And God is not a god of remodeling or renovation or remediation, but a god of *resurrection*, who calls to life all that was ever hurt or lost or burned away in flame.

"Let's go into the house!" Philip exclaimed with his boyish brand of enthusiasm. I had not seen that light on his face for months, and it leapt across the camper, lighting on me. He was right. The Ruff House needed to be privy to this conversation; it was her future as well as ours.

"We can do this!" we kept saying to one another as we walked through the empty rooms, buoyed by this new awareness. It had been grief upon grief that the fire had done its worst upon the spaces into which we had poured our utmost love and labor: the pretty kitchen which I had papered in pale yellow and Philip had plumbed for gas and together we had painted until the brushes felt almost fused to our hands; the sunroom with its built-in window seat and imperfect upholstery; the den, beloved to us both for

CHRISTMASTIDE

the dark paneled ceiling and walls and wide-plank floor, every inch of which we had installed, sanded, stained and sealed. And the Ruff House had responded to our efforts with a warmth I was only beginning to understand. It was only right that we should be the ones to steward her mending.

With no electricity, no water, no furniture, the Ruff House looked like a shell of herself. Nevertheless, these hewn and battered rooms seemed to prickle with the promise of new life, kindling the very shadows with hope. We would, we knew, need help. And we had only the slightest inkling on that September afternoon of what it would cost us in terms of physical labor and emotional endurance. But the scene had shifted from one of impotent waiting to active, inspirited work, and the joy of it all made us equal to anything.

It was then that I saw it, coming down the stairs, that dancing, tremulous light on the wall where I had never seen light before. I sat down where I was under the power of its suggestion, tracing its course from the yawning aperture that had once been my kitchen windows, through the studded remnants of a wall, to this filigreed pattern fluttering over the plaster surface. It was the first real beauty I had seen in my house since the night of the fire, and I hailed it like a portent of good. It was, I knew, in a way that only God and I could fully understand, a seal of his blessing. It told me that God loved us, was intimately with us on this homeward journey, and that he would most assuredly help us. I looked toward my windowless windows once more, to the space where my kitchen doorway would one day be framed, back to this precious patch of light on the wall. I had to preserve it.

"Philip," I said, eyeing the studs above the theoretical doorway. "I would like a transom." I pointed. *"Right there."*

The commemorations of Epiphany are three-fold: the visit of the Magi, the baptism of Christ in the River Jordan, and the miracle of the wedding at Cana. Although at first glance these events may seem rather randomly associated, for centuries the Church has teased out the critical revelations interwoven between them. In the ardent pilgrimage and adoration of pagan kings, Christ is manifested, not only to the Jews, but to the entire human race. For even as we watch Israel tragically reject her Messiah, as the Apostle Paul has pointed out, "their transgression means riches for the world, and their loss means riches for the Gentiles." Further on, Paul assures us that the mercy we have received as a result of Israel's blindness will ultimately rebound to Israel herself, and the tectonic implication here is of a love so relentless it will even make use of disobedience to further the ultimate cause of mercy.

The very concept of mercy, in fact, was utterly foreign to the ancient world; the Christian God is the only deity to have been characterized by it, which is, in fact, what made first-century honor culture such a tinderbox for the Gospel—both in terms of conversion as well as persecution. But the nature of God's holiness cannot reconcile mercy without justice; there had to be a scapegoat to bear the weight of that disobedience, an idea with which Israel was all too familiar. In order for Christ to fulfill that role he had to enflesh his Godhood in human form, a reality verified in his Baptism and which was, incidentally, one of only two times that God revealed himself as trinitarian (the other being the Transfiguration). And at the Canaan wedding, Jesus performed a miracle with mirth at its core, revealing a God who "makes glad the heart of man," and who transforms the ordinary substance of our lives into messengers of image-bearing grace. This miracle of our merciful, incarnate Lord not only unveiled his public ministry on earth, it foreshadows our destiny at his heavenly table where, with his ransomed Bride all around him, he will joyously taste once more the fruit of the vine. At Epiphany, all three of these wonders align in a single bright star of illumination: we serve a God who is shrouded in a holiness which would consume us at once if it met our humanity unmasked. But we also serve a God who shows his hand from time to time, leaving a trail of lifegiving breadcrumbs for us to follow on our homeward journey. Events so momentous as the Journey of the Kings, the Baptism of Jesus, and the Miracle at Cana can scarcely be relegated to breadcrumbs, of course. But they are the large-scale evidence of the minute and manifold ways in which the veil between the seen and the unseen wavers at times.

We might toss the word "epiphany" around casually enough in our matter-of-fact modern way, but it is far more than a bright idea, or even a sudden revelation. In its highest sense, it is the manifestation of divinity, the flash of the eternal intersecting with our world, which is why our Orthodox brothers and sisters often refer to this feast as a theophany: a visitation, not just of the exceptional or the supernatural, but of God himself. The Feast of Epiphany invites us to pay attention; it asks us to take off our shoes, as it were, to the holiness with which the ordinary is thronged and to acknowledge that, at any moment, our temporal lives might be charged by a lightning crack of lucidity and a sudden knowing which, in the poet Robert Fitzgerald's words, "May come to lift the hair and bless / Even our tired earthliness." We cannot summon such moments, or the piercing—albeit fleeting—sense of certainty that accompanies them. Like the memory of joy, we can cling only to how they have changed us and what they have given us of who God is. For our Lord is a gentle suitor, apportioning only what hints and symbols of his blessedness as he knows we are able to bear in our human frames. And if he cloaks himself otherwise, in mystery, or paradox, or even silence, we may rest assured that he does so in perfect love.

To walk through this world, and all its workaday problems and drudgeries, at ease in the enigmas of God's kingdom is what I think Jesus meant when he entrusted it to the children and the childlike. It brings to mind the Inkling, Charles Williams, who, for all his layered theology and complex structure of spiritual images—physical objects and experiences, in other words, which touched upon something true and otherwise inarticulable about God's nature and ways—was content, delighted, even, to live in an unknowing which was informed by a confident hope. "He built his theology—," writes his commentator Mary McDermott Shideler, "and from the reports, he lived—with the solemn delight of a child balancing along a curbing."

To Williams's sanctified imagination, the world was charged with a spiritual electricity which could not help but break out at times in ordinary, physical ways.

"This, also, is Thou!" he was wont to affirm upon encountering some tangible witness to God's nature, be it a tree in joyous green jocundity, an act of courtesy in city traffic, or the face of a friend, suddenly beatified by a fleeting glimpse of ultimate perfection. Nevertheless, he was always swift to counter this affirmation with the grounding counterpart of "Neither is this Thou." For while everything God has made has the potential to tell us something of who he is, the things God has made are not, in fact, God. The vision is a fleeting one, though no less true for its transience. But this is no matter. The vision has done its work, and like a band of starstruck pagan mystics wandering through a darkened land, we are changed.

The transom was duly effected and Philip fitted it out with a large sheet of reclaimed antique glass. Now the light spills through with a rippling like water, holding firm in its fragile glancings the promise of redemption. I smile, thinking how often I have attempted to capture this living epiphany in a photograph. But it is altogether unnecessary. That light will always be there for me when I need it.

And this is, after all, a very good day to be reminded of that fact. I reach across the kitchen table for my journal and open it to a clean page. After a moment's consideration, I uncap my pen and write the word that has been humming to the top of my mind for days:

Courage.

All the Golden Hours

My holiday is bookended by Robert Herrick. If his lovely poem "What Sweeter Music" launches me forth on my Advent journey with an incarnational perspective, then his "Ceremonies for Candlemas Eve" guides me toward the rest of the year with incarnational intention. Observed in early February, Candlemas marks the midpoint of winter and was traditionally a feast day upon which household candles were brought into the church to be blessed by the parish priest in witness to the return of light. In Herrick's hands, this day becomes a turning point, not only in the natural order of the seasons, but in our very lives, inviting us to pay attention to the ways in which the world around us reflects the realities within. Drawing upon ancient customs of seasonal adornments, Herrick acknowledges the great retelling of the Gospel that rolls out year after year over the course of the Church calendar. From Candlemas, to Easter, to Whitsuntide and beyond, we are urged to integrate the story of our faith into the domestic settings of our lives.

Down with the ROSEMARY and BAYS,
Down with the MISTLETOE;
Instead of HOLLY, now up-raise
The greener BOX (for show).

The HOLLY hitherto did sway;
Let BOX now domineer
Until the dancing EASTER DAY
Or Easter's eve appear.

Then youthful BOX which now hath grace
Your houses to renew,
Grown old, surrender must his place
Unto the crisped YEW.

When YEW is out, then BIRCH comes in,
And many FLOWERS beside;
Both of a fresh and fragrant kin
To honour WHITSUNTIDE.

Green RUSHES, then, and sweetest BENTS
With cooler OAKEN boughs,
Come in for comely ornaments
To re-adorn the house.

THUS TIMES DO SHIFT;
each thing his turn does hold;
NEW things succeed,
as former things grow OLD.

ROBERT HERRICK

I once found myself backstage in Franklin, Tennessee, with Sara Groves, a woman whose music has shaped my perception of God's love in a profound way. We were gathered for an event of stories and songs celebrating the Beauty, Truth and Goodness of God's kingdom, and it was an honor to be included in the lineup. But I confess, when I met the funny, friendly, utterly down-to-earth Sara, I was too star-struck to manage more than a few shy sentences with her. I wanted to tell her how her honesty had soothed frightened places in my heart and how the integrity of her songs had given me hope. I think we talked about clothes.

After my part in the program, I retreated to the balcony to watch the rest of the show. And there, clutching my husband's hand in the darkness, I heard Sara perform "Why It Matters," that exquisitely simple anthem to the sacredness of an intentional life. She explained how, in a season of discouragement, a friend had shared with her the story of the "Cellist of Sarajevo," Vedran Smailović, who played his instrument in the bomb craters of the besieged city as a brave statement on all that endures in the face of chaos and destruction. After hearing that story, Sara made her own statement in a lovely song. And as she delivered it that night in Tennessee, you could feel the packed-out theater hanging on every syllable.

> *Speak to me until I understand*
> *Why our thinking and creating*
> *Why our efforts of narrating*
> *About the beauty, of the beauty*
> *And why it matters*

In writing this book, I haven't exactly been standing up to the lions of injustice in a "war-torn town." But it has been my hope to carry a few cups of cold water to the souls who cross its path. In celebrating all that I love about Christmas—from the bright sadness of Advent through the last shining tapers of Epiphany—the heartbeat behind all this hoopla can be summed up in two simple words: It matters.

It matters to bring as much beauty and presence as we can to our lives, because it enfleshes what we believe about the character of God, the value of life, and the sacred potential of the ordinary. Holidays, and Christmas in particular, are rife with opportunities to incarnate truths thrumming under the surface of life. To spread a lovely meal, to beautify our rooms with seasonal sparkle, to light candles against a deepening darkness—all are ways of saying to God, "Thy kingdom come," and to the world, "Behold your King!" In ways I can't quite understand but wholeheartedly believe, the everyday material of our lives takes on holy significance when received as gift and offered back as sacrifice.

This is precisely why I love Christmas, and why I seek to navigate the waters of "simple and Christ-centered" without jettisoning the crazy labors of love that set it apart from the rest of the year. The beauty of the thing, of course, is that the rest of the year gleams with the same potential. "Heaven and earth are full of God's glory;" *all* the hours are golden hours. If the full radiance beyond the darkness of this world was unmasked at once, I don't think we'd be able to bear it.

One year we had our first forecast of snow on January 6th—*an Epiphany snowstorm!* we rejoiced, and Philip and I were as excited as children. We kept peering out the windows and flipping on the porch light to see if it had started yet. Alas, the morning came with no snow, and I was bitterly disappointed. But not too disappointed to appreciate the beauty of the ice-crusted world. I stepped out on the back porch in the freezing cold to watch the morning sun dance among the prisms of the holly tree. Every time the wind moved through its branches there was a tinkling of tiny bells. The dear old crepe myrtle was made of glass, blinding in each glance of the sun, burning but not consumed. The cedar tree was dusted with glitter, and every needle of every pine was a flashing rapier of green and silver.

In the evening, we walked down to the mailbox in the moonlight, turning often to enjoy that loved prospect of our home still alight with Christmas glow, for I had left all of the candles in the windows, and the wreath was still on the door. As we walked I looked up into the bare branches overhead, glassy in the silver light. It hadn't gotten above freezing all day, and what had melted in the light of the sun had refrozen by nightfall. The whole world was encased in radiance and silence; the only sound was that uncanny fairy chime of wind moving among ice-bound branches.

"Look at this," Philip said as we neared the house once more.

He directed me toward the Autumnalis cherry, that lacy, delicate spray of a tree in our front circle. It blooms twice, in the spring and again in the autumn, just as the man at the nursery told me it would. It's not the showiest bloomer, like one of those confections of a cherry tree that explodes in pink powder puffs, or showers a bridal cascade of pale petals. Years ago I stopped waiting for it to take the prize in springtime, for it doesn't dominate the landscape, it compliments it, like a modest woman not wanting to draw too much attention to herself. It's a pretty tree; it has a pleasing shape, and I love it.

Until that night, however, I had never *seen* it—never glimpsed its true nature. Like every other tree and twig and branch on our property, the Autumnalis was sheathed in ice, and looking at it from the house with the darkness as backdrop there was nothing to see but a rigid black form: spidery, lacy, indistinct. But looking at it in the light of the moon, with the twinkling candle lights in the windows of the house beyond, it was a thing of such beauty I could scarcely tear my eyes away. It was not merely made of silver or crystal, earthly things—but *stars*. The whole tree was a dazzling fretwork of heavenly bodies; a galaxy of light; an immeasurable universe of tiny blazing suns and moons. A few of last year's blossoms clung to the tips of branches here and there, preserved in this spell of glass and fire. It stood like a saint, lifting endless constellations to heaven. And there in the cold under a silver moon, I saw that tree as it *really* is, as it was always meant to be. The glory of the thing was so great I wanted to take off my shoes.

This potential—this essence—had been in and of that tree all along. Had it not been for the dark, the moon, the right amount of rain and the right temperature of the air, I never would have seen it. But I never will forget it.

If God could so unveil his glory in a tree, I thought, *what might not he do with a life?*

And it's just because of such things—ice-bound cherry trees and early daffodils, the daily liturgy of afternoon tea and the thrill of the first frost—that I urge you to look for the Golden Hours. From the solemn aisles of Lent, to the glad garden of Eastertide; from the paper and lace of Valentine's Day, to the sweet in-gathering of Thanksgiving, there is treasure to be mined in the hours of Sacred Time and Ordinary Time alike.

Because it's all sacred time, my friends. Every moment that we are alive on this beautiful old earth of God's begetting is crammed with heaven, as Elizabeth Barrett Browning has said. And as dear old Fra Giovanni wrote back on Christmas Eve of 1513:

THERE IS RADIANCE & GLORY IN THE DARKNESS COULD WE BUT SEE, AND TO SEE We have only to *Look*
— FRA GIOVANNI —

O PRICELESS PEARL, WHOSE CASKET WAS THE WOMB OF GIRL, O ARKENSTONE, WHOSE FORM WAS LOCKED IN CHAMBERED VAULT OF FLESH, COME PIERCE OUR GLOOM. FLASH FORTH THAT GLEAM BY WHICH THE WORLD WAS SHOCKED.

O BUD *that* CRACKS THE CURSE OF WINTER'S HOLD, O GOLDEN BLOSSOM RENDING HEAVEN'S SPHERE, DROP DOWN ON GRIEVING EARTH— O COME! —UNFOLD, IN FRAGRANT MERCIES FRESH, YOUR PETALS HERE.

O SPRING OF DAWN, O DAYSTAR STAINING EAST WITH BRIDAL FLUSH AND LAMP OF JUSTICE BRIGHT, BREAK FORTH UPON THIS PALL OF SHATTERED PEACE, UNSHADOWING THE ORPHANS OF THIS NIGHT.

DISARM ALL SEEMINGS, STAR & GEM & FLOWER; UNVEIL YOUR GLORY IN THAT golden hour.

by Lanier Ivester

THE END.

INDEX OF *Recipes*

VEGETABLES AND SIDE DISHES

DESSERTS & SWEETS

DRINKS

INEDIBLES

ACKNOWLEDGEMENTS

I used to imagine that writing was a solitary affair, a private download of inspiration and a fevered tumble of polished words. Experience has hewed rather bluntly at that myth, however, and I am happy to report that the writing of this book has felled it utterly. A sky-full of paper and an ocean of ink could not convey my gratitude to those who have brought both my book and me to this place, but here is a start:

To Laura Boggs and Rachel Brown, friends of my right hand, as Madeleine L'Engle would say—you divide my sorrows and double my joys and I do not even want to imagine what my life would look like without you. Laura, our early collaboration on the Golden Hours blog was the seed of which this book is the fruit. And Rachel, you have companioned me in every way possible, from penning the text of your Advent Calendar craft to taking my panicked late-night phone calls. *Amicus fidelis protectio fortis.*

To Libba Sevison, Kay Dillard, Amy Lee, and April Pickle—your prayer support has been like the wings of the morning, lifting me over many a rough patch in the writing process.

To the Notions, for making the story of our lives such a rollicking one. And to Katie Eaker, for giving me the only nickname I have ever tolerated, among a thousand other things.

To Louise Lubben and Lori Ramsey, for welcoming me like a sister, and to Ashley Sellers-Smith, whose enthusiasm over this project, as with pretty much everything I've undertaken, has been wine to my soul.

To our family at All Souls Anglican Church, a true home in the wilderness of this world, and to Rhonda Pelfrey and Kristina Guinn, who asked me, every week without fail, how the book was coming.

To my dear "Brownies," Frances, Charlotte, and Margaret—thank you for letting us share you with your parents. Mr. Philip and I love you all.

To my siblings, both Adams and Ivester—Liz, Zach, Irish, Andrew, Heather, Michael, and Edie—I am astonished to have such a steadfast and supportive crowd in my corner.

Testing the recipes for this book was an elaborate and heartwarming scheme involving a lineup of men and women across the country who gave willingly of their time and talents: Jonathan Rogers, Rachel Matar, Sarah Katherine Woodhull, Kara Cline, Jade Payne, Cindy Anderson, Bailey McGee, Megan Jung, Matthew Clark, Rebecca Reynolds, Chris and Jenna Badeker, Christie Bragg, Lindsey Patton, Leanne Bruno, Laura Trout, April Pickle, Pete Peterson, Jennifer Trafton, April Johns, Ray Tabor, Carly Anderson, Caitlin Coats, John Cal, Catherine Illian, Kristen Kopp, Paula Trafton, and Amelia Freidline. Your excitement fueled my own and your feedback was invaluable. I am humbled, indebted, and deeply touched.

To the incredible team at Rabbit Room Press who have shepherded this book with skillful hands and loving attention. Caitlin Coats and Carly Anderson, it is no small thing to make someone else's dream come true. I hail you with esteem and great affection.

Jo Tinker, you are a writer's dream of a proofreader, not to mention a dear friend. Let's saunter through the Oxford Botanic Garden again soon. And Amelia Freidline, your meticulous treatment of these recipes is as much a gift to me as to my readers. Thank you.

To A. S. "Pete" Peterson, peerless editor and publisher par excellence. You've been grimly murdering my darlings for lo, these many years (the sum of them would fill a book of their own, I fear), and, in the process, teaching me to love the revision phase. You believed in this book from the time it was a rough sketch in a Word document, and you have handled my work with respect and the utmost care. My mother taught me to reach for Shakespeare when words fail; in this case I turn, appropriately enough, to Twelfth Night: "I can no other answer make but thanks, and thanks, and ever thanks."

Jennifer Trafton—where on earth do I begin? If ever a book was born out of friendship it's this one. Neither one of us had any idea what we were getting into when we hatched this plan at my kitchen table on that long ago December morning, but it has been a delight, from start to finish. You have pulled things out of me I didn't know were there, and gently nudged me toward the heart of this narrative. You have put me in courage when I felt like a lost ball in high weeds. You have brought this story to life in whimsical, luminous color. Your work has been sacrificial, cheerful, transcendent. I am casting armloads of metaphorical roses at your feet, my friend.

To the memory of my parents, Harris and Claudia Adams, and my in-laws, Harold and Janice Ivester—your faithfulness is an eternal legacy and your love a fire that death cannot quench.

And, of course, to Philip. For giving me a laptop and telling me to write. For building a strong foundation beneath my castles in the air. For your fidelity, faith, and humor, in good times and bad. Wherever you are is home to me, my love.

A NOTE FROM THE ILLUSTRATOR

Nothing Lanier has written about in this book comes naturally to me, not the baking or the hosting or the decorating or even the *noticing*. I tend to live in my head. But at the Ruff House, which has welcomed me for over a decade with the unpretentious dignity of a brooding hen, I have encountered a truly embodied theology. Each time I watch Lanier and Philip move through their daily rhythms of farm life, I am brought home again to the *givenness* of the world and to the grace of ordinary things.

So my goal as illustrator has been to pay tribute to the Ruff House itself and to the beautiful microcosm of hospitality, camaraderie, and sacramental living that the Ivesters have created there. Many illustrations were inspired by the items within its walls—from kitchen sinks to barn stalls, from beloved Christmas ornaments to rose arrangements to chipped china dishes. Lanier's gift for capturing food and homey details with her camera provided me with a gold mine of reference photos. I'm also indebted to the recipe testers for documenting their finished concoctions, and to Kirsten Kopp for her lovely photo of Lanier's feather-adorned package.

As for the illuminated quotations—in the Ivesters' home, words dance. They flame out in wonder and in color, in lively literary discussions and poetry readings, in singing and storytelling and the laughter of old friends. When I think of the Ruff House— burned and reborn, offering healing to so many others—I am reminded of Tolkien's description of the Last Homely House ("homely" in the British sense of cozy and comfortable) in the valley of Rivendell: "the perfect house, whether you liked food or story-telling or singing, or just sitting and thinking best, or a pleasant mixture of them all. Merely to be there was a cure for weariness, fear, and sadness." Illustrating this book has been an artistic sojourn in Rivendell, and my heart is richer for it.

VISIT WWW.GLADANDGOLDEN.COM
FOR RESOURCES, RECIPES, SURPRISES, AND DELIGHTS.

RABBIT ROOM
— PRESS —